ONLINE ARBITRATION

CONTEMPORARY COMMERCIAL LAW

Causation in Insurance Contract Law
by Meixian Song (2014)

Insurance Law in China
by Johanna Hjalmarsson and Dingjing Huang
(2015)

Maritime Law in China: Emerging Issues and Future Developments
by Johanna Hjalmarsson and Jingbo Zhang
(2016)

Illegality in Marine Insurance Law
by Feng Wang (2016)

FIDIC Red Book: A Commentary
by Ben Beaumont (2018)

Online Arbitration
by Faye Fangfei Wang (2018)

ONLINE ARBITRATION

BY
FAYE FANGFEI WANG

LONDON AND NEW YORK

First published 2018
by Informa Law from Routledge

2 Park Square, Milton Park, Abingdon, Oxfordshire OX14 4RN
52 Vanderbilt Avenue, New York, NY 10017

Routledge is an imprint of the Taylor & Francis Group, an informa business

First issued in paperback 2019

Copyright © 2018 Faye Fangfei Wang

The right of Faye Fangfei Wang to be identified as author of this work has been asserted by her in accordance with sections 77 and 78 of the Copyright, Designs and Patents Act 1988.

All rights reserved. No part of this book may be reprinted or reproduced or utilised in any form or by any electronic, mechanical, or other means, now known or hereafter invented, including photocopying and recording, or in any information storage or retrieval system, without permission in writing from the publishers.

Notice:
Product or corporate names may be trademarks or registered trademarks, and are used only for identification and explanation without intent to infringe.

British Library Cataloguing in Publication Data
A catalogue record for this book is available from the British Library

Library of Congress Cataloging in Publication Data
Names: Wang, Faye Fangfei, author.
Title: Online arbitration / By Faye Fangfei Wang.
Description: New York, NY : Routledge, 2017. |
    Series: Contemporary commercial law | Includes index.
Identifiers: LCCN 2017017074| ISBN 9781138888319 (hbk) |
    ISBN 9781315625980 (ebk)
Subjects: LCSH: Online dispute resolution. | Dispute resolution (Law)
Classification: LCC K2390 .W36 2017 | DDC 347/.090285—dc23
LC record available at https://lccn.loc.gov/2017017074

ISBN: 978-1-138-88831-9 (hbk)
ISBN: 978-0-367-87297-7 (pbk)

Typeset in Times New Roman
by Apex CoVantage, LLC

To

James and Oliver

CONTENTS

Abstract xi
Table of cases xiii
Table of legislation xvii

Part I Background

CHAPTER 1 THE CHALLENGES OF THE USE OF ONLINE ARBITRATION IN COMMERCIAL TRANSACTIONS 3
1.1 The concepts of Online Dispute Resolution (ODR) 3
    1.1.1 Traditional means of dispute resolution 3
    1.1.2 The popularity of alternative dispute resolution 4
    1.1.3 The advent of Online Dispute Resolution 5
1.2 Obstacles to the use of online arbitration 8
    1.2.1 Suitability of the types of cases 8
    1.2.2 Technological advancement and constraints 12
    1.2.3 Legislative measures 13
        1.2.3.1 International regulatory development 13
        1.2.3.2 The EU framework 17
        1.2.3.3 The US trend 22
        1.2.3.4 The Chinese approach 23

CHAPTER 2 THE DEVELOPMENT OF BEST PRACTICE FOR ONLINE ARBITRATION 26
2.1 Developing online arbitration best practice 26
    2.1.1 eBay and SquareTrade (past experience) 27
    2.1.2 AAA and Cybersettle 27
    2.1.3 WIPO and ICANN-UDRP 28
    2.1.4 CIETAC and HKIAC 30
    2.1.5 Other established ODR services 33
    2.1.6 The most recent development of ODR services 33
    2.1.7 The growth of ODR best practices 35

	2.1.8	Core principles	37
		2.1.8.1 Efficiency	37
		2.1.8.2 Accountability (transparency) v confidentiality	38
		2.1.8.3 Accessibility	42
		2.1.8.4 Credibility and accreditation	43
		2.1.8.5 Security	46
		2.1.8.6 Enforceability	47
2.2	Purposes and structure of this book		48

Part II   Procedural rules for online arbitration

CHAPTER 3	**ONLINE ARBITRATION PROCEDURES**	**51**
3.1	The further development of general ODR regulations	51
3.2	Choice of service providers	55
3.3	Choice of procedure rules	62
3.4	Selection of online arbitrators	63
3.5	Expert witnesses and electronic evidence	67
3.6	Format of arbitration agreements	70
3.7	Process of hearing/commencement of arbitration proceedings	72
3.8	Format and issuance of online arbitral awards	74

CHAPTER 4	**SYSTEMATIC LEGAL AND TECHNOLOGICAL DEVELOPMENT FOR ONLINE ARBITRATION PROCEDURES**	**78**
4.1	The expansion of general ODR systems	78
4.2	Expertise, authority, reputation and strategic alliance	82
4.3	Appointment of online arbitrators	87
4.4	The admission of electronic evidence	91
4.5	The attendance/testimony of witnesses online in arbitral proceedings	96
4.6	Security, integrity and accessibility of online arbitration platforms	97
4.7	Selection of the seat of online arbitration	100
4.8	Users' awareness and protection in online arbitration	103

Summary	104

Part III   Substantive legal issues of online arbitration

CHAPTER 5	**THE VALIDITY OF AND LAW APPLICABLE TO ONLINE ARBITRATION AGREEMENTS**	**107**
5.1	Validity of online arbitration agreements	107
	5.1.1 The recognition of forming arbitration agreements via electronic communications	107

	5.1.2 The incorporation of an arbitration clause or agreement via electronic means	110
5.2	Online consumer arbitration agreements	117
	5.2.1 Private online consumer arbitration agreements	117
	5.2.2 Public/statutory small claims arbitration	124
5.3	Online commercial arbitration agreements	125

CHAPTER 6   THE ENFORCEMENT OF ONLINE ARBITRAL AWARDS   130

6.1	Legal framework for online arbitral awards	130
6.2	Jurisdiction and applicable law concerning online arbitral awards	133
6.3	Challenge of online arbitral awards	138
6.4	Recognition and enforcement of online arbitral awards	140

Summary   147

Part IV   Conclusions and afterthoughts

CHAPTER 7   THE WAY FORWARD: INTERNATIONAL HARMONISED BEST PRACTICES   151

7.1	Future legislative trends	151
7.2	Solutions to obstacles in online arbitration	154

Appendix I	*Regulation (EU) No 524/2013 of the European Parliament and of the Council of 21 May 2013*	161
Appendix II	*China International Economic and Trade Arbitration Commission (CIETAC) Online Arbitration Rules*	181
Index		195

ABSTRACT

This book seeks to provide innovative initiatives for online arbitration best practices to resolve cross-border commercial and consumer disputes in the EU, UK, US and China. It researches into a comparative study of online dispute resolution (ODR) systems and a model of best practices for online arbitration taking into consideration the features and characteristics of ODR. Firstly, it undertakes a theoretical approach to look into the history/culture of arbitration and analyse the potential adoption of technology-assisted arbitration in resolving certain types of international commercial and consumer disputes. Secondly, it investigates the legal obstacles to adopt online arbitration practice by looking into the compatibility of current technological and legislative development. Finally, it seeks to provide solutions to promote the cooperation and recognition of online arbitration practice for cross-border commercial and consumer disputes and stimulate international harmonisation through standard codes of practice.

After all, this project intends to take initiatives and establish any possible legal theory to promote harmonised practice and procedure in the future due to the limitation of case law and legislation for ODR, in particular online arbitration practice and procedure. Relevant concepts and interpretation in traditional judicial cases will be transplanted and further interpreted in the new technological environment.

TABLE OF CASES

A v Chief Constable of West Yorkshire Police and another [2004] IRLR 573,
 HL; [2003] IRLR 32, CA.. 13.19, 14.7
Aiduoladuo (Mongolia) Co., Ltd. v Zhejiang Zhancheng Construction
 Group Co., Ltd., Supreme People's Court, China, 8 December 2009,
 Min Si Ta Zi No. 46 142
Allen Fabrications Limited v ASD Limited [2012] EWHC 2213 (TCC) 127, 128
Allied-Bruce Terminix Cos. v Dobson, 513 U.S. 265, 273 (1995) 118
Angela Raguz v Rebecca Sullivan [2000] 50 NSWLR 236 101
Astro Nusantara International BV et al. v PT Ayunda Prima Mitra et al.,
 Court of First Instance, High Court of the Hong Kong Special
 Administrative Region, Hong Kong, 21 March 2012, HCCT 45/2010 143
Asturcom Telecomunicaciones SL v Cristina Rodríguez Nogueira Case C-40/08,
 Judgment of the Court (First Chamber) of 6 October 2009 .... 117, 144, 145
AT&T Mobility LLC v Concepcion, 131 S. Ct. 1740 (2011) 119
Avon Products, INC. v Ni Ping, filed with ADNDRC Beijing Office on
 27 April 2007, CN-0600087 31
Barcelona.com, Inc. v Excelentisimo Ayuntamiento de Barcelona, 189 F.
 Supp.2d 367 (E. D. Va. 2002), rev'd and vacated, 330 F. 3d 617 (4th Cir. 2003) . 10
Bayerisches Oberstes Landesgericht [BayObLG], Germany, 16 March 2000,
 4 Z Sch 50/99 142
Beaufort Developments (NI) Ltd. v Gilbert-Ash N.I. Ltd. [1998] 2 WLR 860 135
Bergesen v Joseph Muller Corp., 710 F.2d 928 (1983) 26, 134
Black Clawson International Ltd v Papierwerke Waldhof-Aschaffenburg AG
 [1982] 2 Lloyd's Rep. 446 126
Bremer Handelsgesellschaft GmbH v Westzucker [1981] 2 Lloyd's Rep 130 .... 75, 131
Brower v Gateway 2000, Inc., 676 N.Y.S. 2d 569, 572 (246 A.2d 246
 (N.Y.App. 1998) 119, 120
Buckeye Check Cashing, Inc. v Cardegna, 126 S. Ct. 1204;
 163 L. Ed. 2d 1038; 2006 U.S.LEXIS 1814 (2006) 110, 111
Cable News Network L.P., L.L.L.P. v CNNEWS.COM, No. 00–2022-A,
 E.D. Virginia (21 December 2001) 10
Channel Tunnel Group Ltd v Balfour Beatty Construction Ltd [1993] AC 334 126
China Agribusiness Development Corporation v Balli Trading, High Court of Justice,
 England and Wales, 20 January 1997, XXIV Y.B. Com. Arb. 732 (1999) 145

TABLE OF CASES

China Minmetals Materials Import and Exp. Co. v Chi Mei Corp. 334 F.3d 274
(3d Cir. 2003) 141
China Nanhai Oil Joint Service Corporation Shenzhen Branch v Gee Tai Holdings
Co Ltd., High Court, Supreme Court of Hong Kong, Hong Kong,
13 July 1994, 1992 No. MP 2411 145
Chromalloy Aeroservices v Arab Republic of Egypt, District Court, District of
Columbia, United States of America, 31 July 1996, 94–2339 145
Coleman v Prudential-Bache Securities, Inc., 802 F.2d 1350, 1352 (llth Cir. 1986) 127
Commonwealth Coatings Corp. v Continental Casualty Co. [1968] 393 U.S. 145 66
Compagnie de Navigation et Transports S.A. v MSC Mediterranean Shipping
Company S.A., Federal Tribunal, Switzerland, 16 January 1995 108
Content Services Ltd. v Bundesarbeitskammer ECJ Case C 49/11, EU:C:2012:419;
[2012] EUECJ C-49/11; [2012] WLR(D) 195, 5 July 2012 .... 95, 122, 123
Cosmos Marine Managements S.A. v Tianjin Kaiqiang Trading Ltd., Supreme
People's Court, China, 10 January 2007, Min Si Ta Zi No. 34 142
Danish Buyer v German (F.R.) Seller, Oberlandesgericht [OLG], Köln, Germany,
10 June 1976, IV Y.B. Com. Arb. 258 (1979) 142
Diag Human Se v Czech Republic [2014] EWHC 1639 (Comm) (22 May 2014) 144
Dutch Shipowner v German Cattle and Meat Dealer, Bundesgerichtshof,
Germany, 1 February 2001, XXIX Y.B. Com. Arb. 700 (2004) 141
Egyptian Company for Concrete & Hashem Ali Maher v STC Finance & Ismail
Ibrahim Mahmoud Thabet & Sabishi Trading and Contracting Company,
Court of Cassation, Egypt, 27 March 1996, 2660/59 141
Elisa María Mostaza Claro v Centro Móvil Milenium SL, Case C-168/05,
Judgment of the Court (First Chamber) 26 October 2006 ....117, 144, 145
Encyclopedia Universalis S.A. v Encyclopedia Britannica Inc., Court of
Appeals, Second Circuit, United States of America, 31 March 2005,
04–0288-CV, XXX Y.B. Com. Arb. 1136 (2005) 141, 143, 144
Europcar Italia SpA v Maiellano Tours Inc., Court ofAppeals, Second
Circuit, United States of America, 2 September 1998, 97–7224, XXIV
Y.B. Com. Arb. 860 (1999) 141
Fadal Machining Centers LLC v Compumachine, Inc No.10–55719 (9th
Cir. 15 December 2011) 128
Figueiredo Ferraz e Engenharia de Projeto Ltda. v Republic of Peru, Nos.
09–3925-cv (L), 10–1612-cv (CON), 2011 U.S. App. LEXIS 24748
(2d Cir. 14 December 2011) 146
Fred Freudensprung v Offshore Technical Services, Inc., et al., Court of Appeals,
Fifth Circuit, United States of America, 9 August 2004, 03–20226 108
Fung Sang Trading Ltd. v Kai Sun Sea Products and Food Co. Ltd. [1991]
2 HKC 526 133
Gary Patchett v Swimming Pool and Allied Trades Association Limited (SPATA)
[2009] EWCA Civ 717 ....121, 122
Gas Authority of India Ltd. v SPIE-CAPAG SA and Others, High Court of
Delhi, India, 15 October 1993, Suit No. 1440; IA No. 5206 108
Golden Valley Grape Juice and Wine, LLC v Centrisys Corporation et al,
Case No. CV F09–1424 LJO GSA, 21 January 2010 (US Distr Ct of
Eastern Distr of California) 128, 129
Halsey v Milton Keynes NHS Trust [2004] 1WLR 3002 37

TABLE OF CASES

Heung & Associates, Architects & Engineers v Pacific Enterprises (Holdings) Company Ltd. (May 4, 1995) High Ct of Hong Kong 133, 134
Jivraj v Hashwani [2011] UKSC 40 (27 July 2011), paras. 23, 82; (Rev 2) [2010] EWCA Civ 712 (22 June 2010), para. 13 66
Joined Cases C-317/08, C-318/08, C-319/08 and C-320/08, Rosalba Alassini v Telecom Italia SpA (C-317/08), Filomena Califano v Wind SpA (C-318/08), Lucia Anna Giorgia Iacono v Telecom Italia SpA (C-319/08) and Multiservice Srl v Telecom Italia SpA (C-320/08), Judgment of the Court (Fourth Chamber), 18 March 2010, paras.58, 68 53
Kaverit Steel and Crane v Kone Corp., Alberta Court of Queen's Bench, Canada, 14 May 1991..108
Landgericht Krefeld Case 6 O 186/95. Judgment of 29 April 1996 [1997] ILPr 716 124
Manasher v NECC Telecom, No. 06–10749, 2007 WL 2713845 (E.D. Mich. 2007) 129
Moses H. Cone Memorial Hospital v Mercury Construction Corp, 460 U.S. 1 (1983) 118
Mylcrist Builders Limited v Mrs G Buck [2008] EWHC 2172 (TCC) 118, 124
Nigerian National Petroleum Corporation v IPCO (Nigeria) Ltd., Court of Appeal, England and Wales, 21 October 2008, [2008] EWCA Civ 1157 145
Oil Basins Ltd v BHP Billiton Ltd [2007] VSCA 255 75
Paola Briceño v Sprint Spectrum L.P., 911 So.2d 176, 177–80 (Third District Fla. Ct. App. 2005) 122
Parsons & Whittemore Overseas Co. v Société Générale de l'Industrie du Papier (RAKTA), Court of Appeals, Second Circuit, United States of America, 23 December 1974, 508 F.2d 969, 976 143
PGF II SA v OMFS Company 1 Ltd [2013] EWCA Civ 1288; [2014] 1 WLR 1386   37
Picardi v Cuniberti [2002] EWHC 2923 (QB) 124
Practice Direction for 'pre-action conduct' including the use of ADR to resolve disputes 125
Practice Guideline 17: Guidelines for Arbitrators dealing with cases involving consumers and parties with significant differences of resources, by Charter Institute of Arbitrators (CIArb), 2011 117
Prima Paint Corp. v Flood & Conklin Manufacturing Co., 388 U.S.395 (1967) 111
PT Garuda Indonesia v Birgen Air [2002] 1 SLR 393 .... 101, 139
Ryanair v Billigfluege.de [2010] IEHC 47 123
Sandora (Ukraine) v Euro-Import Group (Russian Federation), Federal Arbitrazh Court, District of Moscow, Russian Federation, 12 November 2010, A40–51459/10–63–440 142
Société Bomar Oil N.V. v Entreprise tunisienne d'activités pétrolières (ETAP), Court of Appeal of Versailles, France, 23 January 1991, upheld by Court of Cassation, France, 9 November 1993 108
Société Nationale d'Opérations Pétrolières de la Côte d'Ivoire – Holding v Keen Lloyd Resources Limited, High Ct of the Hong Kong Special Admin Region, Ct of First Instance, 20 December 2001, 55 of 2011, XXIX Y.B. Com. Arb. (2004) 144
Specht v Netscape Communications Corp, 150 F.Supp.2d 585 (SDNY 2001), aff'd, 306 F.3d 17 (2d Cir. 2002) 115, 120, 121, 123
Sphere Drake Insurance PLC v Marine Towing, Inc., 16 F.3d 666 (5th Cir. 1994) ...109
Spiliada Maritime Corp v Cansulex Ltd [1986] UKHL 10 (19 November 1986) 146

Spurling (J) Ltd v Bradshaw [1956] EWCA Civ 3 115
Star Shipping A.S. v China National Foreign Trade Transportation Corporation
    [1993] 2 Lloyd's Rep. 445 101
Stena RoRo AB v OAO Baltiysky Zavod, Highest Arbitrazh Court, Russian
    Federation, 13 September 2011, A56–60007/2008; Ltd. 'R.L.' v JSC 'Z.
    Factory', Supreme Court, Georgia, 2 April 2004, a-204-sh-43–03 141
Sulamerica CIA Nacional de Seguros SA and others v Enesa Engenharia SA and
    others [2012] EWCA Civ 638 (16 May 2012) 126
Telenor Mobile Communications AS v Storm LLC, District Court, Southern
    District of New York, United States of America, 2 November 2007,
    524 F. Supp. 2d 332 141
Thornton v Shoe Lane Parking Ltd [1971] 2 QB 163 127
Trans World Film SpA v Film Polski Import and Export of Films, Corte di
    Cassazione, Italy, 22 February1992, XVIII Y.B. Com. Arb. 433 (1993) 141
Union Générale de Cinéma SA (France) v XYZ Desarrollos, S.A. (Spain),
    Supreme Court, Spain, 11 April 2000, XXXII Y.B. Com. Arb. 525 (2007) ... 142
XL Insurance v Owens Corning [2000] 2 Lloyd's Rep. 500 126
Yusuf Ahmed Alghanim & Sons, WLL v Toys 'R' Us, Inc., 126 F.3d 15
    (2d Cir. 1997) 134, 135
Zellner v Phillip Alexander Securities and Futures ltd, Landgericht Krefeld
    Case 6 O 186/95, Judgment of 29 April 1996 [1997] ILPr 716; [1997]
    ILPr 730 (QB) 118

TABLE OF LEGISLATION

Additional Procedures for On-line
  Arbitration (On-line Rules), Arbitration
  Court, Czech Republic 2004 52
Alternative Dispute Resolution for
  Consumer Disputes (Amendment)
  Regulations 2015, SI 2015/1392 54
    reg 5 54
Alternative Dispute Resolution for
  Consumer Disputes (Competent
  Authorities and Information)
  Regulations 2015, SI 2015/542 54
Anti-cybersquatting Consumer Protection
  Act (ACPA), USA 10, 11
    sec. 1125 (d)(2)(A),15 USC 10
Appellate Arbitration Rules (AAA),
  (American Arbitration Association
  USA) 72
    rule A-3 72
Arbitration Act 1996
  (UK) 74, 111, 117, 136
    Art 5(2) 111
    Art 7 110
    Art 53 136
    Art 70(4) 75
    Art 91(1) 117
Arbitration Association's Online
  Arbitration Regulation (Russia)
  2015 .... 35, 63
Arbitration Fairness Act of 2009
  (AFA) 119, 120
    s 402 119
Arbitration Law of the People's Republic
  of China (China Arbitration Law) 1
  September 1995 .... 23, 90
    Art 10 23
    Art 11 23
Art 13 .... 23, 63, 64, 90
Art 16 23
Art 49 24
Art 58(3) 64
Bribery Act 2010 (UK) 67
Brussels I Regulation 2009
  (Recast 2012) 17, 18, 138
    Recital 12 18
Charter of Fundamental Rights of the
  European Union 2000 –
    Art 7 166
    Art 8 166
    Art 38 .... 161, 166
    Art 47 .... 164, 166
China Consumer Protection Law 1993
  (Law of the People's Republic of
  China on the Protection of Consumer
  Rights and Interests), 2nd amendment
  25 October 2013 115
    Art 24 115
    Art 26 115
China Contract Law (Contract Law
  of the People's Republic of
  China) 1999 115
    Arts 36-41 115
    Art 39 115
China International Economic and
  Trade Arbitration Commission
  (CIETAC), Online Arbitration
  Rules 2009 (updated 2015) 7, 23, 24,
          32, 35, 51, 52, 59, 63, 69, 92,
             96, 107, 181-87, 191-93
    Art 1 .... 35, 181
    Art 2 181
    Arts 3-5 182
    Art 6 .... 107, 186

xvii

TABLE OF LEGISLATION

Art 7 182
Art 8 183
Art 9 96
Arts 10, 11 183
Arts 12-16 184
Arts 17-20 185
Arts 21-24 186
Arts 25, 26 187
Art 27 .... 190, 191
Art 28 .... 187, 190
Art 29 .... 69, 92, 93, 96, 157, 188
Art 30 188
Art 31 188
Art 32 .... 60, 188
Art 33 .... 60, 189
Arts 34, 35 189
Art 36 .... 69, 92, 96, 189
Art 37 189
Arts 38-43 190
Arts 44-48 191
Arts 49-54 192
Art 55 189
China Internet Network Information Centre (CNNIC) Rules for Domain Name Dispute Resolution Policy –
    Art 37 31
    Art 44 31
Civil Procedure Law (China) 1991 –
    Art 1 24
    Art 51 24
Civil Resolution Tribunal Rules for ODR (Canada), 7 November 2016 .... 33, 35
Commercial Arbitration Rules of the American Arbitration Association (AAA) 128
Consumer Agreements Act 1988 (UK, repealed 31 January 1997) 118
    Art 1(1) 118
Consumer Contracts (Information, Cancellation and Additional Charges) Regulations 2013, SI 2013/3134 (UK) 94, 113
    Practice Note 113
    reg 2 113
    reg 5 123
Consumer Protection (Amendment) Regulations 2014, SI 2014/870 114

Consumer Protection (Distance Selling) Regulations 2000 113
Consumer Rights Act (UK) 2015 114, 125
    Sch 2, para 20(a) 113
Decision 2004/387/EC, 21 April 2004 on Interoperable Delivery of Pan-European eGovernment Services to Public Administrations, Businesses and Citizens (IDABC) 46, 164, 169
    Annex II 164
Dodd–Frank Wall Street Reform and Consumer Protection Act –
    s 1028(a) 119, 124
EC Directive 93/13/EEC, 5 April 1993 on Unfair Terms in Consumer Contracts 123
    Art 3 114
EC Directive 95/46/EC on the Protection of Individuals with regard to the Processing of Personal Data and on the Free Movement of such data ... 165, 174
    Art 2(d) 174
    Art 10 165
    Art 11 165
EC Directive 1997/7/EC on the Protection of Consumers in respect of Distance Contracts - now EC Directive on Consumer Rights (Distance Selling Directive) 1997 .... 112, 123
    Art 7(2) 42
EC Directive 1999/44/EC 123
EC Directive 1999/93/EC 45, 46, 57, 94, 142, 158, 159
EC Directive 2000/31/EC on Electronic Commerce, 8 June 2000 .... 19, 112
    Recital 23 9
    Art 1(4) 9
    Art 2(b) 168
    Art 10 112
    Art 17(1)-(3) 9
EC Directive 2008/52/EC on Certain Aspects of Mediation in Civil and Commercial Matters (Mediation Directive) 2008 .... 18, 47, 163, 168
    Recital 8 18
    Recital 9 18
    Art 4 19
    Art 6(1) 47

Art 6(2) 47
Art 9 19
EC Directive 2009/22/EC on Consumer
Online Dispute Resolution
(ODR) 19, 35, 40, 45, 51,
    89, 94, 103, 117, 151, 161, 177
    Recital 16 45
    Recital 55 45
    Art 1(1) 177
    Art 1(2) 177
    Art 6(2)(b) 177
    Art 7(1) 40
    Annex I 177
EC Directive 2011/83/EU on Consumer
Rights 2011 (implemented in
2014) 95, 112, 113
    Art 2(10) 95, 123
    Art 5 112
    Art 5(1) 123
    Art 6(1)(t) 165
    Art 7 123
    Art 8 .... 123, 165
EC Directive 2013/11/EU of 21 May
2013 on Consumer Alternative
Dispute Resolutions (ADR),
21 May 2013 .... 7, 8, 19, 20, 39,
    40, 45, 47, 89, 90, 94, 117,
    151, 162, 163
    Art 4(1) 168
    Art 4(1)(b)-(d) 168
    Art 4(1)(h) 89, 168
    Art 4(1) 168
    Art 4(1)(i) 168
    Art 4(2) 169
    Art 4(3) 89, 169
    Art 5(4) 173
    Art 5(4)(h) 170
    Art 6(1)(a) 90
    Art 6(6) 103
    Art 7 94
    Art 7(2) 40
    Art 8(e) 173
    Art 10(1) 117
    Art 10(2) 117
    Art 10 165
    Art 10(c) 170
    Art 13 .... 165, 175
    Art 13(1) 179

Art 14(2) 175
Art 18(1) 175
Art 20(2) 39, 89, 162,
    164, 167, 169-71
Art 20(4) 175
Electronic Commerce (EC Directive)
Regulations 2002 113
    reg 1 113
    Sch 2 113
Electronic Signature Law of the
    People's Republic of China 2005 94
Electronic Signatures in Global and
    National Act (E-SIGN) 120
Electronic Signatures in Global and
    National Commerce Act 2000 94
EU Regulation No 2001/45/EC on
    the Protection of Individuals with
    regard to the Processing of Personal
    Data by the Community Institutions
    and Bodies and on the Free
    Movement of such data 165, 170
    Art 2(d) 175
    Art 11 165
    Art 12 165
    Art 22 175
    Art 28(2) 167
EU Regulation No 2006/1896/EC
creating a European order for
payment procedure 36
    Recital 4 124
    Art 2(1) 124
EU Regulation No 2006/2004/EC, 27
October 2004 on Cooperation
between National Authorities
Responsible for the Enforcement
of Consumer Protection Laws 19, 35,
    40, 45, 51, 89, 94, 117, 161, 177
    Annex 177
EU Regulation No 2007/861/EC
establishing a European Small Claims
Procedure 36, 124
EU Regulation No 2008/593/EC (Rome I
Regulation) on the Law Applicable to
Contractual Obligations 138
EU Regulation No 2011/182/EC
Laying Down the Rules and General
Principles Concerning Mechanisms for
Control by Member States of the

xix

TABLE OF LEGISLATION

Commission's Exercise of
Implementing Powers............166, 176
   Art 4..176
   Art 5..176
EU Regulation No 2013/524/EC,
21 May, 18 June 2013 on Consumer
Online Dispute Resolution (ODR)......7,
   19-21, 35, 37, 39, 42, 45-47, 51,
   52, 54, 55, 124, 151, 161-71, 174-78
   Recital 4..20
   Recital 6....................................20, 36
   Recital 8..20
   Recital 13..20
   Recital 20..46
   Recital 27..35
   Recital 29..35
   Art 1.......................................36, 167
   Art 2..............................42, 167, 168
   Art 2(1).................................19, 167
   Art 2(3).................................21, 168
   Art 3..168
   Art 4......................................168, 170
   Art 4(2)..42
   Art 5(1)..178
   Art 5(2)..20
   Art 5(4)............................39, 41, 174
   Art 5(4)(h)....................................170
   Art 5(6)...42
   Art 5(7)..178
   Art 6.............................21, 170, 178
   Art 6(1)..170
   Art 7..170
   Art 7(1)...........................20, 170, 178
   Art 7(2)....................................171, 174
   Art 7(2)(a)..............................172, 173
   Art 7(3)..171
   Art 7(4)..174
   Art 7(5)..178
   Art 7(7)..178
   Art 8..............................20, 169, 171
   Art 8(3)....................................176, 178
   Art 8(4)..178
   Art 9....................21, 169, 173, 174
   Art 9(3).................................21, 173
   Art 9(3)(a).....................................172
   Art 9(3)(b)..............................172, 173
   Art 9(3)(c).....................................172
   Art 9(3)(d)..............................172, 173

Art 9(4)..173
Art 9(4)(b).....................................173
Art 9(4)(c).....................................173
Art 9(5)(e)......................................21
Art 9(8)..20
Art 10......................................21, 174
Art 10(c)................................169, 174
Art 10(c)(iii)..................................174
Art 11......................................174, 178
Art 12..174
Art 12(1)..174
Art 13......................................21, 175
Art 13(2)..174
Art 14......................................175, 177
Art 14(1)..................................175, 176
Art 14(2)..................................175, 176
Art 15..176
Art 16......................................176, 178
Art 16(2)..................................172, 176
Art 16(3)...................170, 171, 176
Art 17.......................171, 176, 178
Art 18......................................21, 177
Art 19..177
Art 20..177
Art 21......................................174, 177
Art 21(1), (2)..................................178
Art 22..177
Annex......................................178, 179
EU Regulation No 2014/910/EC,
23 July 2014 on Electronic
Identification and Trust Services
for Electronic Transactions in the
Internal Market.................45, 46, 56,
          94, 95, 142, 158, 159
   Recital 21..56
   Recital 28..56
   Recital 34..57
   Recital 35..57
   Recital 47..57
   Art 3(6)...56
   Art 3(10)...95
   Art 3(25)...........................95, 142, 158
   Art 3(26)..................................142, 158
   Art 3(27)...95
   Art 3(33)..................................142, 159
   Art 3(34)..................................142, 159
   Art 8...41
   Art 9(3)...42

TABLE OF LEGISLATION

Art 10(d) 54
Art 36 .... 95, 142, 158
Art 42 ....142, 159
EU Regulation No 2015/1051/EC,
1 July 2015 on the modalities for
the exercise of the functions of the
online dispute resolution platform,
on the modalities of the electronic
complaint form and on the modalities
of the cooperation between contact
points provided for in Regulation
(EU) No 524/2013 .... 41, 42, 54
EU Regulation No 2015/2421/EC, 16
December 2015 ....36, 124
Federal Arbitration Act (FAA), 1925
(USA) 118, 119, 134
    s 2 118
International Bar Association (IBA)
Rules on the Taking of Evidence
in International Arbitration
1983 ....69-71, 92, 96
International Bar Association (IBA) Rules
on the Taking of Evidence in
International Arbitration 1999 69-71,
92, 96
International Bar Association (IBA) Rules
on the Taking of Evidence in
International Arbitration
2010 ....69-71, 92, 96
    Art 3(12) 70, 92, 93, 96, 157
    Art 4(3) 96
International Chamber of Commerce
(ICC) Rules of Arbitration (Version 1),
1 March 2017 63
    Art (f) 63
    Appendix IV 63
Law of the People's Republic of China
on Chinese-Foreign Contractual Joint
Ventures, 13 April 1988, (revised 31
October 2000) 25
    Art 25 24
Model Law of Private International Law
of the People's Republic of China
2000 109
New York Convention on the Recognition
and Enforcement of Foreign Arbitral
Awards 1958 .... 4, 7, 14, 25, 26,
37, 62, 64, 102, 108, 109,
125, 134, 135, 140-43, 145,
146, 152, 158
Art I 134
Art I(2) 130
Art I(3) 134
Art II 108, 125, 141
Art II(2) 109
Art II(1) 25, 144
Art III 135, 140
Art IV(a) 32
Art IV(1)(a) 74, 130
Art IV(1)(b) 108
Art V 130, 135, 140, 145, 146
Art V(1) 140, 141
Art V(1)(a) 108, 141, 143
Art V(1)(b) 142
Art V(1)(c) 138, 143
Art V(1)(d) 64, 138, 143
Art V(1)(e) 139, 144
Art V(2) 140, 144
Art V(2)(a) 144
Art V(2)(b) 142
Online Dispute Resolution Protocol
(MSODR) 33
Online Signing Process of Electronic
Contract Regulations (1 December
2013) –
    Art 5.1(5) 116
    Art 8 116
Regulation on Consumer Online Dispute
Resolution (ODR) 2016 34
Rome I Regulation, see EU Regulation
No 2008/593/EC –
Rules for Uniform Domain Name
Dispute Resolution Policy (eUDRP
Rules) 2009 29
Treaty on European Union (TEU) 1992
(Maastricht Treaty) –
    Art 5 166
Treaty on the Functioning of the
European Union (TFEU) 2007 161
    Art 26(2) 161
    Art 114 161
    Art 169(1) 161
    Art 169(2)(a) 161
    Art 290 166
UNCITRAL Arbitration
Rules 1976 .... 14, 28, 64, 68, 92

UNCITRAL Arbitration Rules
  2010............ 14, 28, 64, 68, 92
  Art 1, para 4 14
UNCITRAL Arbitration Rules
  2013................62, 64, 68, 92
  Art 5(1) 64
  Art 6(1) 64
  Art 27(4) 92
  Art 28(4) 69
UNCITRAL Model Law on Electronic
  Commerce 1996................3, 9
  Art 15...............................9
UNCITRAL Model Law on Electronic
  Signatures 2001 94
UNCITRAL Model Law on International
  Commercial Arbitration 1985 (amended
  2006)...... 4, 7, 14, 25, 62, 74, 107, 139
  Art 1 14
  Art 1(3) 14
  Art 1(3)(a).......................133
  Art 1(3)(b).......................133
  Art 1(3)(c).......................133
  Art 7 107
  Art 7(2) 108
  Art 7(4) 25
  Art 20.............................101
  Art 30.......................74, 132
  Art 31(2) 74
  Art 34(2) 139
  Art 34(2)(a)(iii)................138
  Art 34(2)(a)(iv)................138
UNCITRAL Model Law on International
  Commercial Conciliation 2002 4
UNCITRAL Online Dispute Resolution
  (ODR) Rules.....................110
  Track I –
    Article 1(a)....................110
  Track II 110
UNCITRAL (United Nations
  Commission on International TRAde

Law) Arbitration Rules
  (updated 2013)..................101
  Art 18.............................101
Unfair Arbitration Agreements
  (Specified Amounts) Order 1999, SI
  1999/2167 117
Unfair Contract Terms Act (UCTA)
  1977...............................113
Unfair Terms in Consumer Contracts
  Regulations (UTCCR) 1999, SI
  1999/2083 ....113, 114
  reg 5..............................114
  reg 5(1) 114
  reg 6..............................114
UNIDROIT Principles of International
  Commercial Contracts 2010............ 112
Uniform Commercial Code (UCC),
  (USA).......................114, 115
  s 2-207 114
  s 2-302(1).......................114
  s 2-316(2).......................115
Uniform Electronic Transactions Act
  (UETA) 1999 94
United Nations Convention on Contracts
  for the International Sale of Goods
  (CISG)1980 112
  Art 7......................112, 116
  Art 8.............................112
United Nations Convention on the
  Use of Electronic Communications
  in International Contracts
  (New York), 2005..............3, 9, 14, 25,
  ....94, 109
  Article 6....................9, 137
  Article 6(1)-(5) 137
  Article 9(2) 94
  Article 9(4) 94
  Article 10.........................9
United Nations Resolution A/RES/71/138,
  13 December 2016 16

PART I

BACKGROUND

CHAPTER 1

The challenges of the use of online arbitration in commercial transactions

1.1 The concepts of Online Dispute Resolution (ODR)

1.1.1 Traditional means of dispute resolution

Every year, thousands of multinational companies emerge into the world, constantly expanding sales and production internationally through the internet. This is largely seen as the key to growing the economy and stimulating globalisation. Transactions in a global market increase the probability of transnational disputes, and parties situated sometimes in different continents are opposed over small claims.

Traditionally, when people have disputes, they usually go to court to resolve them. However, traditional dispute resolutions become problematic because different countries have different rules for trade and various prohibitive costs of legal action across jurisdictional boundaries. Moreover, for traditional dispute resolutions, the appropriate forum is determined by the place of business or the place of performance.

Traditional litigation is complicated to apply to international business disputes because it is very difficult to determine which court will hear the case and whose law will apply. It will be even more complicated if those international business disputes involve electronic communications or electronic transactions, as the determination of place of business or place of performance over the internet is different from the traditional jurisdiction rules. Currently, there are no specific rules in the model laws and conventions dealing with internet jurisdiction. There are also no jurisdiction provisions in the UNCITRAL Model Law on E-Commerce and the UN Convention on the Use of Electronic Communications in International Contracts.

Although parties may agree in advance a choice of court and choice of law clause, litigation through the court system can still be a time-consuming process because of all of the formalities that must be followed in any court-based process of litigation. Moreover, it is often inflexible as it is based on a formal model that is heavily governed by rules and procedures. It can also be adversarial, which might poison or destroy a more valuable long-term business relationship between the parties over a minor business problem.[1]

---

1. Chow, D. C. K. & Schoenbaum, T. J. (2005), International Business Transactions: Problems, Cases and Materials (New York: Aspen Publishers, 2005), pp. 661–2.

In cyberspace, the localisation factor can be much less obvious as the boundless internet may be accessed from anywhere in the world. Furthermore, when e-disputes only involve a small amount of money, it may not always be cost effective to sue the other party in another country. So how does an e-commerce site resolve disputes? What will be the least costly but more efficient solution?

1.1.2 The popularity of alternative dispute resolution

Alternative dispute resolution (ADR) can be deemed to be a key technique in dispute resolution, a structured process with a third party intervention and an escape from court litigation. In the 1980s, ADR was most commonly used to resolve international commercial transactions disputes other than cross-border litigation. ADR, including arbitration, mediation/conciliation and negotiation, is considered to be more efficient, flexible, confidential and less costly, compared with traditional litigation. ADR can avoid the long court proceedings for international disputes that are affected by the conflicts of jurisdiction and choice of law. International instruments have been developed to promote the harmonisation of international ADR practices, such as the 1958 New York Convention on the Recognition and Enforcement of Foreign Arbitral Awards; the UNCITRAL Model Law on International Commercial Arbitration 1985 and the UNCITRAL Model Law on International Commercial Conciliation 2002.

In the early 1990s, out-of-court dispute resolution mechanisms – ADR involving arbitration, mediation and negotiation – were more frequently employed than courts, taking advantages of their speed, flexibility and cost efficiency. ADR can be chosen by agreement at any time, even after a dispute has arisen. It mainly includes three methods of dispute settlement:

- *Negotiation* Persons seek to resolve a disagreement or plan a transaction through discussion.[2] It can be used in all manner of disputes and transactions.
- *Mediation* is an informal process in which an impartial third party helps others resolve a dispute or plan a transaction but it does not impose a solution.[3]
- *Arbitration* In arbitration, the parties agree to submit their dispute to a neutral party whom they have selected to make a decision.[4]

Furthermore, some mixed processes are also recommended as means of dispute settlement, such as mediation–arbitration. 'med-arb' begins as mediation. If the

---

2. Riskin, L. L. & Westbrook, J. E. (1998), Dispute Resolution and Lawyers (US: West Publishing Co., 2nd edition, 1998), p. 4.
3. Riskin, L. L. & Westbrook, J. E. (1998), Dispute Resolution and Lawyers (US: West Publishing Co., 2nd edition, 1998), p. 4.
4. Riskin, L. L. & Westbrook, J. E. (1998), Dispute Resolution and Lawyers (US: West Publishing Co., 2nd edition, 1998), p. 3.

parties do not reach an agreement, they proceed to arbitration.[5] The differences among them are that 'arbitration' is a form of adjudication with a neutral decision-maker – an arbitrator, rather than a judge – and its award is normally enforceable as a court judgment. 'Mediation' is different from arbitration in that a neutral third party – a mediator – will have no power to adjudicate or impose an award but seeks to help the disputed parties to reach a negotiated agreement. 'Negotiation' is the most informal method of ADR that parties communicate with each other with the aim of making a decision, which is voluntary and non-binding. Sometimes, negotiation can be assisted by a third party chosen by the disputed parties.[6]

From a commercial dispute perspective, as ADR aims to resolve disputes in a more friendly way rather than going to the court, it is used for merchants who make efforts to establish a long-term business relationship with each other. As ADR is also considered to be more efficient, flexible, confidential and less costly, compared with traditional litigation, it is also useful for consumers who seek help for small claims.

However, with the development of digital markets and the growth of globalisation, the traditional ADR system may have lagged behind to some extent due to the complexity and various prohibitive costs of legal action across jurisdictional boundaries; the difficulty of the determination of the place of business or the place of performance in cyberspace; and the need of for experts with the knowledge and practical technique of new technology. So a less costly but more efficient solution to resolve e-disputes needs to match the legal, business and social concerns in the new environment. Modernisation of ADR is required.

1.1.3 The advent of Online Dispute Resolution

In the early 1990s, global computerised transactions or usages increased the probability of cross-border disputes. There were instances where parties situated in different continents were opposed over small claims or cyber-related issues. Such disputes challenged the traditional dispute resolutions because:

- different countries have different rules for trade and various prohibitive costs of legal action across jurisdictional boundaries;
- the much less obvious localisation factor on the Internet causes difficulties in determining the place of business or the place of performance in cyberspace due to the fact that the boundless Internet may be accessed from anywhere in the world;
- cyber-related disputes may require a legal expert who is equipped to adapt to the diverse evolving technological, social nature and commercial practice of cyberspace.[7]

---

5. Riskin, L. L. & Westbrook, J. E. (1998), Dispute Resolution and Lawyers (US: West Publishing Co., 2nd edition, 1998), p. 5.
6. Wang, F. (2010), Internet Jurisdiction and Choice of Law: Legal Practices in the EU, US and China (Cambridge: Cambridge University Press, 2010), p. 143.
7. Wang, F. (2010), Law of Electronic Commercial Transactions: Contemporary Issues in the EU, US and China (Oxford: Routledge, 2nd edition, 2013), p. 271.

In the process of creating the least costly but more efficient solution to resolve Internet-related disputes, the modernisation of ADR – online dispute resolutions (ODR) – was introduced in the mid-1990s by the Virtual Magistrate at Villanova University, the Online Ombuds Office at the University of Massachusetts, the Online Mediation Project at the University of Maryland, and the CyberTribunal Project at the University of Montreal, Canada. The concept of ODR has been further developed by a number of non-profit making public organisations, such as the American Bar Association (ABA), American Arbitration Association (AAA), World Intellectual Property Organisation (WIPO) and China International Economic and Trade Arbitration Commission (CIETAC). It aims to provide more efficient, cost-effective and flexible dispute resolutions in the information society. ODR takes advantage of the Internet, a resource that extends what we can do, where we can do it, and when we can do it. The ABA Task Force on E-Commerce and ADR provides a generic definition of online dispute resolution (ODR):

> ODR is a broad term that encompasses many forms of ADR and court proceedings that incorporate the use of the internet, websites, e-mail communications, streaming media and other information technology as part of the dispute resolution process. Parties may never meet face to face when participating in ODR. Rather, they might communicate solely online.[8]

As defined in the ABA Task Force, ODR is not only an extension of alternative dispute resolutions (ADR) – online arbitration, online mediation and online negotiation – but also an application of cybercourts, although online litigation is not as common as eADR.

The latest definition of ODR was proposed in the UNCITRAL Draft Procedural Rules on Online Dispute resolution for Cross-border Electronic Commerce Transactions 2013 Article 2(1) as follows: "'ODR' means online dispute resolution which is a mechanism for resolving disputes facilitated through the use of electronic communications and other information and communication technology."[9] In the 21st century, with the emergence of new technologies, electronic communications have been increasingly incorporated into methods of litigation and ADR. The phenomenon of ODR has increased with the deployment of advanced dispute resolution technologies. ODR is the equivalent to electronic ADR and the cybercourt, moving traditional offline dispute resolution and litigation online. Its occurrence will boost the confidence of doing business online and certainly be more

---

8. American Bar Association Task Force on E-Commerce and ADR Executive Summary of Final Recommendations, Final Report August 2002, available at https://www.americanbar.org/content/dam/aba/migrated/dispute/documents/FinalReport102802.authcheckdam.pdf (last accessed 30 March 2017).

9. A/CN.9/WG.III/WP.133 – Online dispute resolution for cross-border electronic commerce transactions: draft procedural rules, United Nations Commission on International Trade Law, Working Group III (Online dispute resolution), Thirty-first session, New York, 9–13 February 2015, available at https://documents-dds-ny.un.org/doc/UNDOC/LTD/V14/080/65/PDF/V1408065.pdf?OpenElement (last accessed 30 March 2017), Draft article 2 (Definitions).

efficient than offline methods, for example, in a case that has an international or cross-border factors but which only involves lower financial amounts.

In practice, disputes that use the ODR mechanism are mostly cases involving online shopping (small claims) and domain names disputes. In this book, previous/past experience of international ODR practices will be examined; and new successful experiences will be explored. For example, this book looks into the reasons of the collaboration between SquareTrade and eBay and its eventual termination; and discusses the success of the strategic alliance between AAA and Cybersettle as well as cooperation between the Internet Corporation of Assigned names and Numbers (ICANN) and WIPO, and their limitation to service.

As to the underlying technical principles deployed in the ODR system, this book explores the possibility of employing the intelligent and adaptive system of service-oriented computing to provide intelligence and reasoning capabilities to give automated support to the ODR procedures and help constructing fair outcomes without direct human intervention under defined circumstances. The technical support to online arbitration will be particularly explored, i.e. the theories of decision-based design and automata-based design languages. ODR brings efficiency and convenience to the resolution of conflicts but at the same time faces a number of challenges due to technology, management and legal obstacles, in particular in the area of online arbitration. The book also discusses the possible technical factors in creating an ODR system where the arbitrator is replaced or supplemented by various artificial intelligence techniques. The successful implementation of online arbitration practice depends on parties' confidence and trust in the quality of resolving disputes online in terms of validity, confidentiality and enforceability.

In order to promote the usage of online arbitration in a wider scope of practice (i.e. cross-border commercial and consumer disputes) in the future, both procedural rules and substantive law concerning online arbitration should be harmonised at the international level. The process of harmonisation is slowly moving forward. There are various developments of procedural rules in the EU, US, China and international organisations. In the US ABA adopted the section policy – Recommended Best Practices for E-Commerce and ADR – in early 2000. In China, CIETAC launched a regulation – the Online Arbitration Rules – in 2009. In the EU, the European Commission adopted the EC Directive on Consumer ADR and the EU Regulation on Consumer ODR in 2013, which establishes a single point of entry for consumers and traders seeking the out-of-court resolution of disputes. At the international level, in 2006 the UNCITRAL Model Law on International Commercial Arbitration 1985 adopted amendments, which explicitly recognise the effectiveness of an arbitration agreement concluded by electronic communications if the information contained therein is accessible so as to be useable for subsequent reference. This is to remove the paper-based writing requirement in the New York Convention on the Recognition and Enforcement of Foreign Arbitral Awards (1958). In 2010 the United Nations Commission on International Trade Law (UNCITRAL) formed the working group to draft the procedural rules on online dispute resolution for cross-border electronic commerce transactions. The first draft was published on

17 January 2011. In 2016, the outcome of the group's work had been reduced into Technical Notes on Online Dispute Resolution (2016) for non-binding ODR procedural reference.[10] A well-drafted international regulation should remove the legal uncertainty of using ODR systems by promoting party autonomy and implementing core legal principles with technologically neutral clauses.

In contrast, there is still lack of constructive legislative development on substantive legal matters concerning online arbitration. Currently there is no established single statute or provision regulating the substantive issues in online arbitration. Relevant national, regional and international e-commerce legislation has been used to interpret and determine the validity of online arbitration agreements, the seat of online arbitration and the enforceability of online arbitral awards agreements, which affects the level and scale of the acceptance of online in practice. The establishment of harmonised online arbitration procedure rules and substantive law could contribute to the consistency, fairness and efficiency in the use of online arbitration. This requires recommendation on or amendment to the existing national and regional laws, model laws and international conventions. This book provides in-depth analysis and evaluation of the most up-to-date legislation such as the EU Regulation on Consumer ODR 2013 and the current draft proposal of UNCITRAL ODR procedures; proposes best practices for procedures; provides harmonised interpretation to substantive legal issues; and analyses the feasibility of private enforcement for ODR outcomes.

1.2 Obstacles to the use of online arbitration

1.2.1 Suitability of the types of cases[11]

Businesses, through the use of the Internet, can enter into electronic sale contracts with other businesses located in different countries. Computing technologies make it possible to download intangible/digitised goods onto computers without the need of physical delivery. This has undoubtedly improved economic efficiency, competitiveness and profitability. Resolving cross-border disputes concerning electronic transactions is inevitably more complicated than in a paper-based environment, because connecting factors such as the place of domicile, the place of business and the place of performance are difficult to determine in the online environment. The determination of Internet jurisdiction and applicable law has been greatly challenged when online contracting or transactions are executed in several places and it is difficult to ascertain the principal place of performance.

---

10. Technical Notes on Online Dispute Resolution (2016), available at http://www.uncitral.org/uncitral/uncitral_texts/online_dispute_resolution.html (last accessed 30 March 2017).
11. This session is an update of 10.3.1 Suitable cases for the usage of ODR from Wang, F. (2010), Internet Jurisdiction and Choice of Law: Legal Practices in the EU, US and China (Cambridge: Cambridge University Press, 2010), pp. 145–8.

At the international level, there are no specific rules in the model laws and conventions dealing with Internet jurisdiction and choice of law. The UNCITRAL Model Law on Electronic Commerce and the UN Convention on the Use of Electronic Communications in International Contracts do not contain any jurisdiction or choice of law provisions, but provides the measures of the time and place of dispatch and receipt of data messages or electronic communication[12] and the location of the parties.[13] For example, the connecting factors on parties' business location such as the 'place of business', 'the closest relationship to the relevant contract, the underlying transaction or the principal place of business', or 'habitual residence', may be used to determine Internet jurisdiction and choice of law. In the EU, the EC Directive on Electronic Commerce (Recital 23 and Article 1(4)) also does not establish any additional rules on private international law with regard to jurisdiction and choice of law.[14] Likewise, in China and the US there is no particularised Internet jurisdiction and choice of law legislation. This poses a question as to the suitability of using traditional litigation and ADR for modern commercial and consumer disputes in the information society.

In theory, ODR can be used in most civil and commercial disputes, from contracts to torts; from family to business; and from domestic cases to international cases. However, disputes that involve electronic transactions or Internet-related cases are most suitable for the use of ODR services as documents in such cases are usually formed by electronic means. Electronic documents can be submitted easily via the Internet on the ODR platform and serve as evidence.

In practice, disputes that use the ODR mechanism are mostly cases of online purchase or service (small claims), and domain names disputes. In order to promote the usage of ODR in a wider scope of practice (i.e. international trade disputes) in future, parties choosing ODR must have confidence in the quality of dispute resolutions in terms of expertise, fairness, efficiency and reliability in resolving Internet-featured cases.

The most widely used cases in ODR services are domain names infringement disputes as domain names are non-territorial. They are unique and global in nature. Only one entity in the world can own the right to use a specific domain name that can be accessed globally. In the absence of reliable and accurate contact details of the domain name registrants, it may lead to the situation that plaintiffs would find it hard to sue the defendants in their residence or domicile. In other words, there is no *in personam* jurisdiction under those circumstances on the website. Courts will need a special rule for resolving such cases. A good example can be given

---

12. UNCITRAL Model Law on Electronic Commerce, on the report of the Sixth Committee (A/51/628) 16 DECEMBER 1996, Article 15; and the UN Conventions on the Use of Electronic Communications in International Contracts, 2005, Article 10.

13. The UN Convention on the Use of Electronic Communications in International Contracts 2005, Article 6.

14. Directive 2000/31/EC of the European Parliament and of the Council of 8 June 2000 on certain legal aspects of information society services, in particular electronic commerce, in the Internal Market (thereafter 'the EC Directive on Electronic Commerce'), Recital 23 and Article 1(4).

by the US Anticybersquatting Consumer Protection Act (ACPA), which has set up specific rules – *in rem* jurisdiction – to prevent cybersquatters. *In rem* action can apply where the mark owner cannot establish *in personam* jurisdiction, or is not able to find the registrant's physical location through due diligence (15 USC sec. 1125 (d)(2)(A)). Accordingly, the mark owner can bring a civil action against a disputed domain name itself instead. Take *Barcelona.com, Inc. v Excelentisimo Ayuntamiento de Barcelona*[15] for example; it shows how a foreign losing registrant can obtain standing as plaintiff in a federal court. Barcelona.com was registered by a Spanish couple, providing tourist information about Barcelona, e-mail services, a chat room, advertising and links to other websites. The complainant was the City Council of Barcelona, having approximately 1,000 registrations of the mark 'Barcelona'. The City Council filed a complaint and won the UDRP (Uniform Dispute Resolution Policy) proceeding. The domain name was ordered transferred to the City Council. Before the execution of the transfer, Barcelona.com, Inc. commenced a lawsuit in the District Court for the Eastern District of Virginia, seeking a declaratory judgment and asserting that the registration of the domain name was not unlawful. The Court found that, firstly Barcelona.com, Inc. was registered with the US registrar, NSI; secondly, it had a mailing address in New York but had no office space, no telephone number and no employees. This action meets the ACPA criteria for an *in rem* action. So domain name 'barcelona.com' has been named as a complainant in the lawsuit in the US. The Court's decision validated the transfer according to the ACPA through the *in rem* jurisdiction.

In rem jurisdiction also applies to another case between the US and China – *Cable News Network L.P., L.L.L.P. v CNNEWS.COM*.[16] The plaintiff alleges that cnnews.com violates his rights because cnnews.com is similar to his registered marks 'CNN' in the US. As Ellis, a district judge noted,

> this is an in rem ACPA suit brought by an American company against "cnnews.com" domain name used by a Chinese company in connection with a website that focused chiefly on China and Chinese speakers by providing online services in Chinese language.

This case maintains an *in rem* action because (i) the action is brought in the jurisdiction where the registrar or registry of the infringing domain name is located; and (ii) *in personam* jurisdiction over the registrant does not exist (15 USC sec. 1125 (d)(2)(A)). Under the ACPA, a trademark owner can petition a US court to transfer a foreign national's domain name to the trademark owner despite the fact that the foreign national domain name has never transacted business in any forum within the US.[17]

---

15. *Barcelona.com, Inc. v Excelentisimo Ayuntamiento de Barcelona*, 189 F. Supp.2d 367 (E. D. Va. 2002), rev'd and vacated, 330 F. 3d 617 (4th Cir. 2003).

16. *Cable News Network L.P., L.L.L.P. v CNNEWS.COM*, No. 00–2022-A, E.D. Virginia (21 December 2001).

17. The case examples given above come from the author's journal paper: Faye Fangfei Wang (2006), Domain Names Management and Legal Protection, *International Journal of Information Management*, Volume 26, Issue 2, pp. 116–27.

As shown in the above two cases, there are two features of the domain name disputes. The first feature is that US courts apply the advanced specialised legislation to the subject matter. The second feature is that US courts can enforce the judgement by directly informing the domain name registrars to cancel or transfer the disputed domain names. The withdrawal, cancellation or transfer of domain names will be done by the registrars via the Internet as the disputed objects are in electronic forms.

The growth in the use of domain names appears to have increased the number of bad faith registrations and further raised concerns that trade mark owners' rights are increasingly infringed or diluted by the use of trade marks in domain names.[18] That is, domain names have come into conflict with trade marks. The main reason for such conflict can be attributed to the lack of connection between the system of registering trade marks and the registration of domain names. The former is a system granting territorial rights enforceable only within the designated territory, the latter is a system of granting rights that can be enforced globally.[19] Because trade mark law is territorial, a mark may be protected only in the geographic location where it distinguishes its goods or services. Thus, trade mark law can tolerate identical or similar marks in different territories even within the same classes of goods and services. Domain names, by contrast, are both unique and global in nature.[20] Only one entity in the world can own the right to use a specific domain name that can be accessed globally.[21] According to the specific features of a domain name, in particular, without territory but with a registrar, ODR will be one of the most suitable methods to resolve domain names disputes.

Likewise, consumers are also encouraged to use the ODR system to resolve disputes concerning online purchase or service; and other internet-related issues as those cases involve electronic records, i.e. electronic order form and payment, etc, which can be easily submitted to cyber courts or online arbitration or mediation platforms as supporting evidence. Some online merchants may also offer consumers ODR service for free so as to boost consumer's confidence and trust in shopping at their online marketplaces.

In recent years, ODR has expanded its role across a number of fields, for example, to settle disputes originating in online reputation and feedback systems

---

18. *A Review of the Relationship between Trade Marks and Business Names, Company Names and Domain Names (March 2006)*, Australian Government, Advisory Council on Intellectual Property, p. 5, available at www.acip.gov.au/library/TM,%20business,company,domain%20names-%20Final%20 Report.pdf (last accessed 30 March 2017), thereafter called 'Australian DR Review'.

19. Tunkel, D. and York, S. (2000), E-Commerce: A Guide to the Law of Electronic Business (London: Butterworths, 2nd edition, 2000).

20. Wang, F. (2006), Domain Names Management and Legal Protection, *International Journal of Information Management*, Volume 26, No. 2, pp. 116–27, p. 119.

21. Efroni, Z. (2003), The Anti-cybersquatting Consumer Protection Act and the Uniform Dispute Resolution Policy: New Opportunities for International Forum Shopping? *Columbia Journal of Law and the Arts*, pp. 335–69, p. 343.

(such as customer reviews posted on Yelp.com or TripAdvisor.com).[22] ODR may also become one of the most suitable platforms to resolve disputes relating to digital products using mass data. For example, in 2016, there are a number of exciting global new tech developments that benefit from databases, open data and big data. Google's self-driving cars continue their evolution, racking up over 1.5 million miles in the US. Another competitor – Tesla Motors – has brought up new products including an autopilot function to allow its car to drive semi-autonomously, with little or no driver input on motorways. Whilst the system is undoubtedly advanced, it requires the driver to be ready to take control of the car at a moment's notice, leading to questions of liability in the event of an accident. The volume, variety and velocity of data gathered to be able to employ such technology keeps us curious as to the legal implication of big data. ODR platforms or eCourts may be most suitable to provide case management functions and online hearings, in particular when concerning cross-border disputes. Another new development is a new smartphone game called Pokemon Go, which was released in July 2016, utilising GPS and augmented reality to allow the user to explore a virtual world while walking around the physical world. The game instantly brought up media reports of privacy and safety issues – firstly with the game requiring access to the users' Google account credentials, then with concerns of player's location being reported to others.[23] ODR platforms may provide a cheap and fast initial assessment for resolution for computerised disputes as digital forensics evidence can be submitted to a capable ODR platform for analysis.

1.2.2 Technological advancement and constraints

In the information society, computing storage becomes larger and cheaper over time. This enables datasets to be gathered together from open sources or other databases on a mass scale, which is greater than the traditional significant volume of data in banks or other individual organisations. Smarter statistical and computational analysis of these aggregated datasets from different sources may generate new value, meaning and context.[24] In addition, artificial intelligence enables machines to replicate humans making decisions. Although machines are not as clever as the people that make them, machines have the potential to continuously learn new datasets.[25] Taking advantage of data from various sources, a more sophisticated robot can learn just like a child.[26] When such

---

22. Rule, C. and Singh, H. (2012), ODR and online reputation systems: Maintaining trust and accuracy through online redress. In M.S. Abdel Wahab, E. Katsh and D. Rainey (eds.), ODR: Theory and Practice (The Hague: Eleven International Publishing, 2012).
23. Wang, F. (2010), Introductory Remark, Society of Legal Scholars Annual Conference, University of Oxford, 8 September.
24. Williamson, A. (2014), Big data and the implications for government, *Legal Information Management*, 14(4), 253–7, p. 253.
25. The Life Scientific, Nigel Shadbolt Broadcasts. Tue 14 Apr 2015 09:00. BBC Radio 4. Tue 14 Apr 2015 21:30.
26. The robot which learns like a child, BBC News, 21 October 2015, available at www.bbc.co.uk/news/technology-34446447 (last accessed 30 March 2017).

robot has access to a database of facial expressions, it may have the ability to learn to recognise the expression of other faces and can gradually react to the different humans engaging with it in a different way.[27] Recent research showed that robotics and artificial intelligence could affect almost a third of UK jobs by the 2030s.[28] All of these generate a new phenomenon known as 'open data' and 'big data'. As artificial intelligence continues its advancement making use of big data, a new generation of ODR platforms can potentially employ robots as negotiators, mediators and arbitrators. However, if robots with access to big data become so intelligent and closely connected to human beings, they may potentially cause other social and legal consequences.

In the phenomenon of using big data and cloud services for ODR systems, the traditional way of collecting, processing and storing data has been changing. This new phenomenon challenges traditional legal principles and increases legal uncertainty in the information society. Such challenges have become greater and greater in response to the emerging technologies embedded with machine intelligence. As a result, relevant ODR legislation needs to be updated to factor new technologies.

1.2.3 Legislative measures

1.2.3.1 International regulatory development
The Internet brings together people not only operating under different legal systems, but also people of widely disparate cultural backgrounds. Legal difficulties stem from a basic distrust of the Internet today, because it has grown and is still growing too fast for society to assimilate. Linguistic differences echo cultural differences and therefore translations often fail to bridge the gaps in parties' understandings and expectations. In conjunction with the above difficulties, there are also technical, social and political difficulties. It is challenging to introduce an ODR system taking into consideration all elements across the globe.

Given the divergence of legislation in countries, jurisdictional complexity has been a barrier to creating an international treaty based entity to regular ODR providers.[29] The existing UNCITRAL Model Law on International Commercial

---

27. Cellan-Jones, R., My day with a robot, BBC News, 15 September 2015, available at www.bbc.co.uk/news/technology-34256655 (last accessed 30 March 2017).
28. Robots to affect up to 30% of UK jobs, says PwC, 24 March 2017, available at www.bbc.co.uk/news/business-39377353 (last accessed 30 March 2017).
29. Survey: Addressing Disputes in Electronic Commerce: Final Recommendations and Report, (November 2002) 58 *Business Law*, 415, p. 450, produced by the American Bar Association's Task Force on Electronic Commerce and Alternative Dispute Resolution in Cooperation with the Shidler Center for Law, Commerce and Technology, University of Washington School of Law. (Hereafter 'ODR Survey (2002)'), available at www.abanet.org/dispute/documents/FinalReport102802.pdf (last accessed 30 March 2017).

Arbitration,[30] New York Convention,[31] UNCITRAL Arbitration Rules[32] and UN Convention on the Use of Electronic Communications in International contracts,[33] have provided some useful reference to conduct international online arbitration.

International online arbitration shares one key feature with traditional international arbitration in that they both carry an 'international'/'cross-border' element. Article 1 of the Model Law on International Commercial Arbitration states that arbitration is international if:

> the parties to an arbitration agreement have, at the time of the conclusion of that agreement, their places of business in different states; or one of the following places is situated outside the State in which the parties have their places of business: (i) the place of arbitration if determined in, or pursuant to, the arbitration agreement; (ii) any place where a substantial part of the obligations of the commercial relationship is to be performed or the place with which the subject-matter of the dispute is most closely connected; or (iii) the parties have expressly agreed that the subject-matter of the arbitration agreement relates to more than one country.

It was suggested that international online arbitration cannot truly come into its own as a recognised method of resolving disputes with the existing offline arbitration legislation, unless the international community can resolve nine major legal issues that online arbitration participants will face:

1. What form must an online arbitration agreement take?
2. Who should hear the dispute?
3. Where will arbitration occur?
4. What law will govern the online international arbitration?
5. Who will pay online arbitration costs and what will they consist of?
6. What time limits will govern online arbitration?
7. What evidentiary rules will govern online arbitration?
8. What form will the award take and how will it be enforced?
9. Is confidentiality feasible and advisable in online international arbitration?[34]

These were the nine crucial issues covering both procedural and substantive rules to ensure the success of international online arbitration that were proposed in the

---

30. UNCITRAL Model Law on International Commercial Arbitration, U.N. GAOR, 40th Sess., Supp. No. 53, at 81, UN. Doc. A/CN.9/XVIII/CRP.4 and Add. 1 (1985). It is equivalent to Article 1(3) of the 1985 – UNCITRAL Model Law on International Commercial Arbitration, with amendments as adopted in 2006, available at www.uncitral.org/pdf/english/texts/arbitration/ml-arb/07-86998_Ebook.pdf (last accessed 30 March 2017).

31. Convention on the Recognition and Enforcement of Foreign Arbitral Awards (New York, 1958) (the 'New York Convention').

32. UNCITRAL Arbitration Rules (with new Article 1, para. 4, as adopted in 2013); UNCITRAL Arbitration Rules (as revised in 2010); and UNCITRAL Arbitration Rules (1976).

33. United Nations Convention on the Use of Electronic Communications in International Contracts (New York, 2005).

34. Witt, N. (2001), Online International Arbitration: Nine issues crucial to its success, *American Review of International Arbitration*, Volume 12, pp. 441–64, p. 442.

early 2000s. Scholars have also been calling on international cooperation and agreements on harmonised procedural rules covering process and proceeding of ODR and substantive rules including jurisdiction, choice of law and enforcement issues of ODR settlements.[35] In addition, international ADR organisations have also been urged to work together to develop some basic standards for specialised ODR training and practice.[36] Issues such as confidentiality, impartiality, conflicts of interest, ODR disclosure policies, educational and training requirements, linguistic and cultural skills, and adequate party representation need to be fully addressed and applied to ODR service providers.[37]

In response to the need of an effective order for cross-border dispute resolution, the United Nations (UN) online dispute resolution working group has been working on procedural rules since 2010 (hereafter 'UNCITRAL Draft ODR Procedural Rules'). At its forty-third session (New York, 21 June–9 July 2010), the UN ODR Working Group was established to undertake work in the field of online dispute resolution ('ODR') relating to cross-border electronic commerce transactions, including business-to-business (B2B) and business-to-consumer (B2C) transactions.[38] At its twenty-second session (Vienna, 13–17 December 2010), the Working Group commenced working on draft generic procedural rules for ODR (the 'Rules'), addressing B2B and B2C, cross-border, low-value, high-volume transactions.[39] At its twenty-seventh session (New York, 20–24 May 2013), the Working Group considered a proposal to implement a two-track system – Track I for a binding arbitration phase and Track II for a non-binding outcome phase.[40] At its forty-eighth session (New York, 2015), the Commission decided to work on a non-binding descriptive document reflecting elements and principles of an online dispute resolution process, which includes the principles of impartiality, independence, efficiency, effectiveness, due process, fairness, accountability and transparency.[41]

---

35. Wang, F. (2008), Online Dispute Resolution: Technology, Management and Legal Practice from an International Perspective (Oxford: Chandos Publishing, 2008), p. 43.
36. Wang, F. (2008), Online Dispute Resolution: Technology, Management and Legal Practice from an International Perspective (Oxford: Chandos Publishing, 2008), p. 43.
37. Ponte, L. M. (Spring 2001), Throwing Bad Money After Bad: Can Online Dispute Resolution (ODR) Really Deliver the Goods for the Unhappy Internet Shopper? *Tul. J. Tech. & Intell. Prop.* Volume 3, pp. 55, p. 87.
38. A/CN.9/WG.III/WP.133 – Online dispute resolution for cross-border electronic commerce transactions: draft procedural rules, United Nations Commission on International Trade Law, Working Group III (Online dispute resolution), Thirty-first session, New York, 9–13 February 2015, para. 1.
39. A/CN.9/WG.III/WP.133 – Online dispute resolution for cross-border electronic commerce transactions: draft procedural rules, United Nations Commission on International Trade Law, Working Group III (Online dispute resolution), Thirty-first session, New York, 9–13 February 2015, para. 2.
40. A/CN.9/WG.III/WP.133 – Online dispute resolution for cross-border electronic commerce transactions: draft procedural rules, United Nations Commission on International Trade Law, Working Group III (Online dispute resolution), Thirty-first session, New York, 9–13 February 2015, para. 3.
41. A/RES/71/138 – Resolution adopted by the General Assembly on 13 December 2016, available at www.un.org/en/ga/search/view_doc.asp?symbol=A/RES/71/138 (last accessed 30 March 2017).

The Technical Notes on ODR affirm the technologically neutral definition of ODR provided by the UNCITRAL Draft ODR Procedural Rules.[42] It further explains that 'the process may be implemented differently by different administrators of the process, and may evolve over time'.[43] Compared with traditional ADR, ODR requires a technology-based intermediary that provides a system (known as an 'ODR platform') for generating, sending, receiving, storing, exchanging or otherwise processing communications. It is suggested that an ODR process cannot be conducted on an ad hoc basis that involves only the parties to a dispute and a neutral adjudicator without an administrator.[44]

The Technical Notes on ODR also confirm that the communications that may take place during the course of proceedings have been defined as 'any communication (including a statement, declaration, demand, notice, response, submission, notification or request) made by means of information generated, sent, received or stored by electronic, magnetic, optical or similar means'.[45]

The Technical Notes further clarify the scope of application for the UNCITRAL Draft ODR Procedural Rules that 'an ODR process may be particularly useful for disputes arising out of cross-border, low-value e-commerce transactions. An ODR process may apply to disputes arising out of both a business-to-business as well as business-to-consumer transactions.'[46] They also specify that 'an ODR process may apply to disputes arising out of both sales and service contracts'.[47] The Technical Notes on ODR provide supplementary notes on the ODR process in addition to the clarification of concepts, which sets out as follows:

---

42. A/CN.9/WG.III/WP.133 – Online dispute resolution for cross-border electronic commerce transactions: draft procedural rules, United Nations Commission on International Trade Law, Working Group III (Online dispute resolution), Thirty-first session, New York, 9–13 February 2015, Draft article 2 (Definitions).

43. A/CN.9/WG.III/WP.140 – Online dispute resolution for cross-border electronic commerce transactions: Draft outcome document reflecting elements and principles of an ODR process, United Nations Commission on International Trade Law, Working Group III (Online dispute resolution), Thirty-third session, New York, 29 February–4 March 2016, para. 24.

44. A/CN.9/WG.III/WP.140 – Online dispute resolution for cross-border electronic commerce transactions: Draft outcome document reflecting elements and principles of an ODR process, United Nations Commission on International Trade Law, Working Group III (Online dispute resolution), Thirty-third session, New York, 29 February–4 March 2016, para. 26.

45. A/CN.9/WG.III/WP.140 – Online dispute resolution for cross-border electronic commerce transactions: Draft outcome document reflecting elements and principles of an ODR process, United Nations Commission on International Trade Law, Working Group III (Online dispute resolution), Thirty-third session, New York, 29 February–4 March 2016, para. 29.

46. A/CN.9/WG.III/WP.140 – Online dispute resolution for cross-border electronic commerce transactions: Draft outcome document reflecting elements and principles of an ODR process, United Nations Commission on International Trade Law, Working Group III (Online dispute resolution), Thirty-third session, New York, 29 February–4 March 2016, para. 22. See also UNCITRAL Draft ODR Procedural Rules 2014 (A/CN.9/WG.III/WP.133), Article 1 (Scope of application).

47. A/CN.9/WG.III/WP.140 – Online dispute resolution for cross-border electronic commerce transactions: Draft outcome document reflecting elements and principles of an ODR process, United Nations Commission on International Trade Law, Working Group III (Online dispute resolution), Thirty-third session, New York, 29 February–4 March 2016, para. 23. See also UNCITRAL Draft ODR Procedural Rules 2014 (A/CN.9/WG.III/WP.133), Article 1 (Scope of application).

- Section VI – Commencement of ODR proceedings (Articles 33–36)
- Section VII – Negotiation (Articles 37–39)
- Section VIII – Facilitated settlement (Articles 40–44)
- Section IX – Appointment, powers and functions of the neutral (Articles 45–49)
- Section X – Language
- Section XI – Governance
- Section X – Choice (Arbitration as referred to in draft Article 7 of Track I or The Neutral's recommendation as referred to in Track II)[48]

The Technical Notes on ODR are helpful in a way that they complement the Draft ODR Procedural Rules and provide clear technical procedural guidance. However, there is still need for further explanation on certain areas. For example, Article 44 of the Technical Notes on ODR stipulates that 'If a facilitated settlement cannot be achieved within a reasonable period of time, the process may move to a final stage.' It does not specify the duration of a reasonable period before the process moves to a final stage. In contrast, according to draft Article 6(3) (Facilitated settlement) of the draft ODR Procedural Rules, if the parties have not settled their dispute by facilitated settlement within ten calendar days of being notified of the appointment of the neutral, pursuant to Article 9(1) the ODR proceedings they shall move to the final stage of proceedings pursuant to draft Article 7 (Guidance of ODR Administrator).[49]

1.2.3.2 The EU framework

In the EU, ADR is encouraged to resolve cross-border commercial disputes. Among the methods of ADR, the importance of arbitration in the community is highlighted in the Commission's Report on the Review of the Brussels I Regulation on 21 April 2009 that the Brussels I Regulation has in specific instances been interpreted so as to support arbitration and the recognition/enforcement of arbitral awards.[50] The Green Paper that accompanies this Report further explains 'however, addressing certain specific points relating to arbitration in the Regulation, not for the sake of regulating arbitration, but in the first place to ensure the smooth circulation of judgments in Europe and prevent parallel proceedings'.[51] Subsequently, the Brussels

---

48. A/CN.9/WG.III/WP.140 – Online dispute resolution for cross-border electronic commerce transactions: Draft outcome document reflecting elements and principles of an ODR process, United Nations Commission on International Trade Law, Working Group III (Online dispute resolution), Thirty-third session, New York, 29 February–4 March 2016.
49. See UNCITRAL Draft ODR Procedural Rules 2014 (A/CN.9/WG.III/WP.133), Article 6 (Facilitated settlement).
50. Report from the Commission to the European Parliament, the Council and the European Economic and Social Committee on the application of Council Regulation (EC) No 44/2001 on jurisdiction and the recognition and enforcement of judgments in civil and commercial matters, Brussels, 21.4.2009, COM(2009) 174 final, Commission of the European Communities, p. 9, available at www.ipex.eu/ipex/cms/home/Documents/doc_COM20090174FIN (last accessed 30 March 2016).
51. Green Paper on the Review of Council Regulation (EC) No 44/2001 on Jurisdiction and the Recognition and Enforcement of Judgments in Civil and Commercial Matters, Brussels, 21.4. 2009,

I Regulation (Recast) 2012 excludes 'arbitration' by specifying that 'this Regulation shall not apply to arbitration'.[52] Accordingly, courts of a member state should refer the parties to arbitration if there is a valid arbitration agreement.

Another common method of ADR, mediation, is also encouraged by the community in resolving civil and commercial matters. The EC Directive of the European Parliament of Council on Certain Aspects of Mediation in Civil and Commercial Matters (hereafter 'EC Directive on Mediation') was approved by the European Parliament on 23 April 2008[53] and entered into force in June 2008.[54] The purpose of the EC Directive on Mediation is to facilitate access to dispute resolution, to encourage the use of mediation, and to ensure a sound relationship between mediation and judicial proceedings.[55] It is considered to be an achievement of regulating out-of-court dispute resolutions. It is in favour of electronic communications and, to an extent, online dispute resolution. It encourages the use of mediation in cross-border disputes and the use of modern communication technologies in the mediation process, which is reflected by Recital (8) and (9) of the EC Directive on Mediation:[56]

(8) The provisions of this Directive should apply only to mediation in *cross-border* disputes, but nothing should prevent Member States from applying such provisions also to internal mediation processes.

(9) This Directive should not in any way prevent the use of *modern communication technologies* in the mediation.[57]

Moreover, the provisions of 'ensuring the quality of mediation'[58] and 'information for the general public'[59] also indicate the support of using ODR methods in the EU. For example, Article 4 of the EC Directive on Mediation encourages member states 'by any means which they consider appropriate' to develop voluntary codes of conduct mediation services, as well as other effective quality control mechanisms. In addition, Article 9 of the EC Directive on Mediation also explicitly encourages

---

COM(2009) 175 final, Commission of the European Communities, p. 8, available at www.ipex.eu/ipex/cms/home/Documents/doc_COM20090175FIN (last accessed 30 March 2016).

52. Brussels I Regulation (Recast) 2012, Recital 12.

53. EC Directive of the European Parliament of Council on Certain Aspects of Mediation in Civil and Commercial Matters, Brussels 28 February 2008, 15003/5/07 REV5, available at http://ec.europa.eu/civiljustice/docs/st15003-re05_en07.pdf (last accessed 30 March 2017).

54. Directive 2008/52/EC of the European Parliament and of the Council of 21 May 2008 on certain aspects of mediation in civil and commercial matters, L136/5, Official Journal of the European Union, 24.5.2008, available at http://eur-lex.europa.eu/LexUriServ/LexUriServ.do?uri=OJ:L:2008:136:0003:0008:EN:PDF (last accessed 30 March 2017).

55. EU Press Release Reference: Mediation in civil and commercial matters, MEMO/08/263, Brussels, 23/04/2008, available at http://europa.eu/rapid/pressReleasesAction.do?reference=MEMO/08/263&type=HTML&aged=0&language=EN&guiLanguage=en (last accessed 30 March 2017).

56. Wang, F. (2010), Online Dispute Resolution: Technology, Management and Legal Practice from an International Perspective (Oxford: Chandos Publishing, 2008), p. 44.

57. EC Directive on Mediation 2008, Recitals (8) and (9).

58. EC Directive on Mediation 2008, Article 4.

59. EC Directive on Mediation 2008, Article 9.

member states make service and contact information available to the general public 'by any means which they consider appropriate in particular on the Internet'.

In general, although the EC Directive on Electronic Commerce does not provide substantial ODR rules, it encourages ODR practice by requiring member states to ensure that their legislation 'does not hamper the use of out-of-court schemes, available under national law, for dispute settlement, including appropriate electronic means'.[60] In addition, it requires member states to 'encourage bodies, responsible for the out-of-court settlement of, in particular consumer disputes to operate in a way which provides adequate procedural guarantees for the parties concerned'[61] and to 'encourage bodies responsible for out-of-court dispute settlement to inform the Commission of the significant decision they take regarding Information Society services and to transmit any other information on the practices, usages, or customs relating to electronic commerce'.[62]

On 21 May 2013 the European Parliament and the Council adopted the first regulation concerning ODR,[63] along with the EC Directive on Consumer ADR.[64] The Regulation on Consumer ODR 2013 is considered to be landmark legislation, although it is only applicable to consumer contractual disputes, that is 'the out-of-court resolution of disputes concerning contractual obligations stemming from online sales or service contracts between a *consumer* resident in the Union and a *trader* established in the Union'.[65] This regulation is adopted in response to a growing concern that

> [F]ragmentation of the internal market impedes efforts to boost competitiveness and growth. Furthermore, the uneven availability, quality and awareness of *simple, efficient, fast and low-cost* means of resolving disputes arising from the sale of goods or provision of services across the Union constitutes a barrier within the internal market which undermines consumers' and traders' confidence in shopping and selling across borders.'[66]

Consumers' confidence is so vital for online transactions that 'it is essential to dismantle existing barriers and to boost consumer confidence'.[67] It is possible that 'the availability of reliable and efficient online dispute resolution (ODR) could greatly help achieve this goal'.[68] To boost consumers' confidence, a mechanism should have the merits of being simple, reliable, efficient, fast and low-cost. These

---

60. EC Directive on Electronic Commerce, Article 17(1).
61. EC Directive on Electronic Commerce, Article 17(2).
62. EC Directive on Electronic Commerce, Article 17(3).
63. Regulation (EU) No 524/2013 of the European Parliament and the Council of 21 May 2013 on online dispute resolution for consumer disputes and amending Regulation (EC) No 2006/2004 and Directive 2009/22/EC (Regulation on consumer ODR), OJ L165/1, 18 June 2013.
64. Directive 2013/11/EU of the European Parliament and of the Council of 21 May 2013 on alternative dispute resolution for consumer disputes and amending Regulation (EC) No 2006/2004 and Directive 2009/22/EC (Directive on consumer ADR), OJ L165/63, 18 June 2013.
65. EU Regulation on Consumer ODR 2013, Article 2(1).
66. EU Regulation on Consumer ODR 2013, Recital 4.
67. EU Regulation on Consumer ODR 2013, Recital 6.
68. EU Regulation on Consumer ODR 2013, Recital 6.

credentials are specified by Recital 8 as an addition to Recital 6 and also mirrored by the provision of the standard timeframe of resolving disputes as follows:

> Where the parties fail to agree within *30 calendar days* after submission of the complaint form on an ADR entity, or the ADR entity refuses to deal with the dispute, the complaint shall not be processed further. The complainant party shall be informed of the possibility of contacting an ODR advisor for general information on other means of redress.[69]

There are two key concepts involved in this Regulation: one is 'ODR' and the other is 'consumers'. The concept of 'consumers' is interpreted in Recital 13 that

> the definition of 'consumer' should cover natural persons who are acting outside their trade, business, craft or profession. However, if the contract is concluded for purposes partly within and partly outside the person's trade (dual purpose contracts) and the trade purpose is so limited as not to be predominant in the overall context of the supply, that person should also be considered as a consumer.[70]

As to the concept of ODR, although there is no definition of ODR, the description of an ODR platform is given in this Regulation. The ODR platform is defined in Article 5(2) as:

> a single point of entry for consumers and traders seeking the out-of-court resolution of disputes covered by this Regulation. It shall be an interactive website which can be accessed electronically and free of charge in all the official languages of the institutions of the Union.[71]

According to this definition, the features of the ODR platform should be threefold: 1) a single point of entry at Union level; 2) an interactive website that is free of charge in all the official languages; 3) an out-of-court dispute resolution.[72] In order to create an ODR platform at Union level, each member state is required to designate one ODR contact point.[73] The main ODR procedure includes 'submission of a complaint' (Article 8), 'processing and transmission of a complaint' (Article 9) and 'resolution of the dispute' (Article 10). It requires that parties have to agree on an ADR entity to deal with disputes.[74] Although ADR procedures vary in each ADR entity, the EC Directive on Consumer ADR 2013 has established harmonised quality requirements for ADR entities and ADR procedures.[75] In addition, protective measures are required to protect database processing of personal data, data confidentiality and security. Finally, rules on effective, proportionate and dissuasive penalties are required to be specified by member states.[76]

---

69. EU Regulation on Consumer ODR 2013, Article 9(8).
70. EU Regulation on Consumer ODR 2013, Recital 13
71. EU Regulation on Consumer ODR 2013, Article 5(2).
72. See also the EU Regulation on Consumer ODR 2013, Recital 18.
73. EU Regulation on Consumer ODR 2013, Article 7(1).
74. EU Regulation on Consumer ODR 2013, Article 9(3).
75. EC Directive on Consumer ADR 2013, Article 2(3).
76. EU Regulation on Consumer ODR 2013, Article 18.

It is possible that the outcome of the ADR procedure by electronic means may be binding or non-binding, which depends on the ADR entity that parties agree at the beginning of the process, as a description of the characteristics of each ADR entity includes the binding or non-binding nature of the outcome of the ADR procedure.[77]

The adoption of the EU Regulation on Consumer ODR 2013 shows the recognition of the benefit of using an ODR mechanism for consumers' contractual disputes of online transactions. This significant recognition and pioneer legislative model may be helpful for the future deployment and legal transplantation of an ODR mechanism in other fields such as B2B contractual transactions, financial services or other types of small claim disputes. In November 2015, the Council of Europe's Committee on Legal Affairs and Human Rights further called on Council of Europe member states to:

- make voluntary ODR procedures available to citizens in appropriate cases; raise public awareness of the availability of, and create incentives for the participation in, such procedures, including by promoting the extrajudicial enforcement of ODR decisions and by enhancing the knowledge of legal professionals about ODR;
- ensure that existing and future ODR procedures contain safeguards compliant with Articles 6 and 13 of the European Convention on Human Rights, which may include access to legal advice;
- ensure that parties engaging in ODR procedures retain the right to access a judicial appeal procedure satisfying the requirements of a fair trial pursuant to Article 6 of the Convention;
- undertake to develop common minimum standards that ODR providers will have to comply with, inter alia in order to ensure that their procedures do not unfairly favour regular users over one-time users, and strive to establish a common system of accrediting ODR providers satisfying these standards;
- continue to monitor technological developments in order to promote the use of ICT within courts to improve judicial efficiency, while guaranteeing fair and transparent proceedings, data security, privacy, as well as the adequate and continuous training of court staff and lawyers on the lawful and effective use of ICT in judicial proceedings.'[78]

Moreover, the relationship between the EC Directive on Mediation and EC Directive on Consumer ADR requires some clarification. The admissibility criteria for mandatory mediation procedures in the EU under the two directives also require further clarification. On 14 June 2017, the CJEU handed down a preliminary ruling of *Livio Menini, Maria Antonia Rampanelli v Banco Popolare Società Cooperativa*, clarifying that:

---

77. EU Regulation on Consumer ODR 2013, Article 9(5)(e).
78. Access to justice and the Internet: potential and challenges, Committee on Legal Affairs and Human Rights, Report Doc. 13918, 10 November 2015, available at http://assembly.coe.int/nw/xml/XRef/Xref-XML2HTML-en.asp?fileid=22245&lang=en (last accessed 30 March 2017).

Directive 2013/11/EU of the European Parliament and of the Council of 21 May 2013 on alternative dispute resolution for consumer disputes and amending Regulation (EC) No 2006/2004 and Directive 2009/22/EC (Directive on consumer ADR) must be interpreted as not precluding national legislation, such as that at issue in the main proceedings, which prescribes recourse to a mediation procedure, in disputes referred to in Article 2(1) of that directive, as a condition for the admissibility of legal proceedings relating to those disputes, to the extent that such a requirement does not prevent the parties from exercising their right of access to the judicial system.

On the other hand, that directive must be interpreted as precluding national legislation, such as that at issue in the main proceedings, which provides that, in the context of such mediation, consumers must be assisted by a lawyer and that they may withdraw from a mediation procedure only if they demonstrate the existence of a valid reason in support of that decision.'[79]

Although mandatory mediation is allowed to resolve consumer disputes, conditions for a mandatory mediation procedure should still be met to be compatible with the principle of effective judicial protection in the light of the previous CJEU ruling in Alassini and Others.[80]

1.2.3.3 The US trend

In the US, there is no uniform legislation regulating ODR services. Self-regulation and guidelines of best practices are the approaches recommended by the American Bar Association (ABA).[81] In 2002 the ABA Task Force on 'Electronic Commerce and Alternative Dispute Resolution Final Recommendations and Report on Disputes in Electronic Commerce' emphasised that an ODR transaction is 'an e-commerce transaction in and of itself'. The ABA essentially recommends best practice principles such as ODR providers should adhere to adequate standards and codes of conduct and strive to achieve transparency through information and disclosure as a basis to attain sustainability.[82] A non-profit, educational and informational entity, iADR Centre, is also recommended by the Task Force.

The US self-regulation arbitration and mediation module rules from the American Bar Association (ABA) and American Arbitration Association (AAA) are most widely used in the US ADR practices. In September 2005 the ABA adopted the Model Standards of Conduct for Mediators,[83] which specified nine standard of conduct for mediators, they are: self-determination, impartiality, conflicts of interest, competence, confidentiality, quality of the process, advertising and solicitation, fees and charges, as well as advancement of mediation practice. AAA offers fast, convenient online claim filing through the AAA WebFile® service, an ODR platform that includes functions such as filing claims, making payments, performing

---

79. Case C-75/16, Livio Menini, *Maria Antonia Rampanelli v Banco Popolare Società Cooperativa*, Judgment of the Court (First Chamber), 14 June 2017.
80. Joined Cases C-317/08, C-318/08, C-319/08 and C-320/08, Alassini and Others, Judgment of the Court (Fourth Chamber), 18 March 2010.
81. ABA ODR Survey (2002).
82. ABA ODR Survey (2002), 415, p. 444.
83. Model Standards of Conduct for Mediators, September 2005, available at www.abanet.org/dispute/documents/model_standards_conduct_april2007.pdf (last accessed 30 March 2017).

online case management, accessing rules and procedures, electronically transferring documents, selecting neutrals, using a case-customised message board and checking the status of cases.[84] In 2010 AAA's international division – ICDR (International Centre for Dispute Resolution) – introduced a Manufacturer/Supplier Online Dispute Resolution Protocol for Manufacturer/Supplier Disputes (known as 'the MS-ODR Program').[85] The MS-ODR program is designed to help manufacturers and suppliers to resolve small disputes (where the total amount does not exceed 10,000 USD) quickly, fairly, and inexpensively in order to move on with their business relationship. There are two phases in the process: negotiation and arbitration. At the end a dispute is either settled or decided by an arbitrator. The entire process is designed to take no longer than 66 days.[86] The online negotiation uses the 'double blind bidding' system created by CyberSettle, a strategic alliance with AAA, and if the dispute does not settle within the 12 days of the online negotiation, it then proceeds to the next stage, online arbitration.

In addition, the list of courts providing eFiling services in the US continues to grow. For example, electronic filing has been mandatory in Civil and Probate Trust cases by the Superior Court of California County of San Francisco from 8 December 2014.[87] eFiling service was also employed by the Jackson circuit court in Oregon on 3 June 2013, which was the fourth circuit court that joined the eCourt service since the deployment of the Oregon eCourt in June 2012.[88] Some courts, such as Franklin County, Ohio's Small Claims Court, also offer a pre-trial ODR process where parties can negotiate a settlement before initiating any court proceedings.[89]

1.2.3.4 The Chinese approach

In China, on 31 August 1994, the Arbitration Law was promulgated by the Chinese National People's Congress with the aim of establishing a coherent nationwide arbitral system, entering into force on 1 September 1995.[90] It requires that 'an arbitration agreement shall include the arbitration clauses provided in the contract and *any other written form* of agreement concluded before or after the disputes providing for submission to arbitration'.[91] The form requirement of 'any

---

84. AAA Webfile, available at https://apps.adr.org/webfile/ (last accessed 30 March 2017).
85. The ICDR Manufacturer/Supplier Online Dispute Resolution Protocol: MS-ODR Programme, available at www.adr.org or www.icdr.org (last accessed 30 March 2017).
86. ICDR Manufacturer/Supplier Online Dispute Resolution Program (Frequently Asked Questions), available at www.icdr.org (last accessed 30 March 2017).
87. Electronic Filing, the Superior Court of California County of San Francisco, available at http://sfsuperiorcourt.org/online-services/efiling (last accessed 30 March 2017).
88. Oregon eCourt Implementation News, available at http://courts.oregon.gov/oregonecourt/Pages/index.aspx (last accessed 30 March 2017).
89. Franklin County Municipal Court ODR, available at www.courtinnovations.com/ohfcmc (last accessed 30 March 2017).
90. Arbitration Law of the People's Republic of China (hereafter 'China Arbitration Law'), adopted at the 8th Session of the Standing Committee of the 8th National People's Congress and promulgated on 31 August 1994.
91. China Arbitration Law 1994, Article 16.

other written form' requires further interpretation in that the arbitration clauses concluded by electronic means are equivalent to the 'written form'.

The establishment of online arbitration is subject to the restrictions and requirements due to different local market entries in different provinces in terms of registration,[92] conditions for arbitrators' appointment,[93] and requirements of establishment.[94]

To harmonise the standard of online arbitration practice in China, the China International Economic and Trade Arbitration Commission (CIETAC) promulgated the 'Online Arbitration Rules' on 8 January 2009, which was updated in 2015. These Rules are formulated to arbitrate online contractual and non-contractual economic and trade disputes and other such disputes. The CIETAC Online Arbitration Rules apply to resolution of disputes over electronic commerce transactions, and other economic and trade disputes in which the parties agree to apply these Rules for dispute resolution.[95] The CIETAC has provided successful online arbitration services on .CN domain name disputes since 2002, which offers the first experience of ODR in China. The launch of the CIETAC Online Arbitration Rules can be deemed to be one of the outcomes of the CIETAC ODR experience, which facilitates ODR development in China.

Different from arbitration, mediation is used to resolve commercial dispute resolution to maintain ongoing business relationships.[96] Chinese legislation is in support of mediation in civil and commercial disputes. For example, the Civil Procedure Law (Article 51) permits the parties to 'reach a compromise of their own consent'.[97] The China Arbitration Law (Article 49) stipulates that parties may reach a private settlement even after the commencement of arbitration proceedings.[98] The Law of the People's Republic of China on Chinese–foreign Contractual Joint Ventures (Article 25)[99] also provides that: 'Any dispute between the Chinese and foreign parties arising from the execution of the contract or the articles of the association for a contractual joint venture shall be settled through consultation or mediation.'

With regard to eCourt systems, in recent years the list of national, provincial and local courts providing eCourt services in China has been growing. For example, the Supreme People's Court of People's Republic of China launched China Judicial Process Information Online in 2015.[100] On the China Judicial Process Information

---

92. China Arbitration Law 1994, Article 10.
93. China Arbitration Law 1994, Article 13.
94. China Arbitration Law 1994, Article 11.
95. CIETAC Online Arbitration Rules 2009, Article 1.
96. Tao, J. (2005), Resolving Business Disputes in China, Asia Business Law Series (Netherlands: Kluwer Law International), pp. 1,012–13.
97. China Civil Procedure Law 1991, Article 51.
98. China Arbitration Law 1994, Article 49.
99. The Law of the People's Republic of China on Chinese-foreign Contractual Joint Ventures, adopted by the First Session of the Standing Committee of the Seventh National People's Congress on 13 April 1988, which was promulgated and revised by the Eighteenth Session of the Standing Committee on the Ninth National People's Congress on 31 October 2000.
100. China Judicial Process Information Online, Press Release on 20 January 2015, available at http://www.court.gov.cn/fuwu-xiangqing-13084.html and http://splcgk.court.gov.cn/zgsplcxxgkw/ (last accessed 30 March 2017).

Online Platform, plaintiffs, defendants or their legal representatives are able to file cases, submit documents and track progress. Zhejiang Province eCourt system has been employed for online litigation filings since 2011.[101] Shanghai courts also adopted the eCourt system facilitating litigation procedures online.[102]

As to international harmonisation, China, the US and most of the countries in the EU including the UK have signed and ratified the 1958 Convention on the Recognition and Enforcement of Foreign Arbitral Awards (hereafter 'the New York Convention').[103] The New York Convention is considered to be one of the most successful conventions, which gives the certainty of recognition and enforcement of cross-border arbitral awards. As the New York Convention was adopted far before the birth of the electronic communication society, it did not include a rule to recognise the validity of electronic arbitration agreements and awards. According to Article 2(1) of the New York Convention, each contracting state shall recognise an agreement in writing. Online arbitration has been challenged as to whether electronic arbitration agreements and awards can meet the requirements of the written form under the New York Convention. It is suggested that if the digital arbitral awards can be printed and signed, it would satisfy the written requirement. Electronic arbitration agreements and arbitral awards are considered to be equivalent to the effect of electronic contracts. Subsequently the effectiveness of arbitration clauses/agreements concluded by electronic means will be recognised by the UN Convention on the Use of Electronic Communications in International Contracts 2005 and other relevant national laws concerning electronic commerce. Moreover, the UNCITRAL Model Law on International Commercial Arbitration 1985, with amendments as adopted in 2006, explicitly recognises the effectiveness of an arbitration agreement concluded by electronic communications if the information contained therein is accessible so as to be useable for subsequent reference.[104]

As discussed above, legislative measures for the use of online arbitration in the EU, US and China are still limited. In the phenomenon of using big data, cloud services and artificial intelligence in ODR systems, the traditional way of collecting, processing and storing data has challenged traditional legal principles and increased legal uncertainty in the information society. In other words, the deployment of ODR in particular online mediation and arbitration faces both legal and technological obstacles and challenges. This urges an international-level action on establishing a harmonised legal framework and a set of best practices for ODR systems and services, recommending appropriate legal and technological measures.

---

101. Zhejiang eCourt System, available at www.zjcourt.cn:8088/wsla/login.jsp?fydm=330000 (last accessed 30 March 2017).
102. Shanghai Courts eFiling Service, available at www.hshfy.sh.cn/shfy/gweb/zxfw.jsp (last accessed 30 March 2017).
103. 1958 Convention on the Recognition and Enforcement of Foreign Arbitral Awards, status, available at www.uncitral.org/uncitral/en/uncitral_texts/arbitration/NYConvention_status.html (last accessed 30 March 2017).
104. The UNCITRAL Model Law on International Commercial Arbitration 1985, with amendments as adopted in 2006, Article 7(4).

CHAPTER 2

The development of best practice for online arbitration

2.1 Developing online arbitration best practice

International arbitration is one of the preferred methods for resolving disputes relating to an international commercial contract involving parties from different jurisdictions, partly due to the fact that the New York Convention makes it effective for parties to enforce against multinational companies.[1] It was recognised that:

> "[T]he Convention reflects the efforts of businessmen involved in such trade to provide a workable mechanism for the swift resolution of their day-to-day disputes. International merchants often prefer arbitration over litigation because it is faster, less expensive and more flexible."[2]

Arbitration institutions and tribunals have developed their different arbitration procedural rules in which they share mature best practice for international arbitration. Online arbitration, a fairly new concept within online dispute resolution (ODR), is currently in need of a set of best practices to enhance users' confidence and trust in using it to resolve their disputes. The development of best practice for online arbitration may be based on practical experience of ODR services and traditional arbitration rules. Between 2000 and 2010 some typical examples of successful ODR services across the globe were:

- eBay and SquareTrade (past experience);
- AAA (the American Arbitration Association) and Cybersettle;
- WIPO (World Intellectual Property Organization) and ICANN (the Internet Corporation for Assigned Names and Numbers) – UDRP (Domain Name Dispute Resolution Policy); and
- CIETAC (China International Economic and Trade Arbitration Commission) and HKIAC (Hong Kong International Arbitration Centre).

---

1. Convention on the Recognition and Enforcement of Foreign Arbitral Awards (New York, 1958) (the 'New York Convention').
2. *Bergesen v Joseph Muller Corp.*, 710 F.2d 928 (1983).

2.1.1 eBay and SquareTrade (past experience)

eBay was established in 1995 and has become one of the world's largest online marketplaces providing trading platforms. SquareTrade, set up in 1999, was an industry leader in online merchant verification and dispute resolution. SquareTrade, like eBay, was an independent private company, which shared the common aim with eBay in promoting customers' confidence in doing business or using services online. It is known that the eBay e-trust strategies are designed to make customers comfortable in buying and selling online to maximise the number of sellers and buyers attracted to its online marketplace. The trust-building measures of eBay include: 1) the mutual rating system of trade satisfaction; 2) identity verification; 3) secure online payment services like PayPal or Escrow; 4) insurance policy; and 5) the ODR service provided by SquareTrade until June 2008, which was replaced that year by the eBay dispute resolution centre.

Until June 2008, SquareTrade – eBay's preferred dispute resolution provider – helped eBay users who had disputes in eBay transactions. SquareTrade's position was practically that of an in-house dispute resolution provider as eBay referred its users exclusively to SquareTrade though a link on its website. There were two stages in the general operation of the eBay–SquareTrade system. At the first stage, SquareTrade offered eBay users' a free web-based forum that allowed users to attempt to resolve their differences on their own. It is known as an 'automated negotiation platform'. When settlement could not be reached at the first stage, SquareTrade offered the use of a professional mediator with nominal fees as eBay would subsidise the rest of the cost.[3] This second stage is called 'online mediation'. The usage of SquareTrade by eBay benefited in resolving misunderstandings fairly, providing a neutral go-between for buyers and sellers, reducing premature negative feedback and generating trust in the eBay community.[4] However, due to new development in the eBay feedback system in May 2008, eBay and SquareTrade ceased their collaboration in dispute resolution from June 2008, though SquareTrade continues providing warranty services and trustmark programmes to eBay users. Since then, eBay has continuously reformed its dispute resolution centre and tried to establish other forms of collaboration with other ODR technology providers such as PayPal and Modria.

2.1.2 AAA and Cybersettle

The American Arbitration Association (AAA), established in 1926, is a non-profit making public service organisation and a global leader in conflict management, providing services to individuals and organisations that wish to resolve conflicts out of court. It also serves as a centre for education and training, issues

---

3. Dispute Resolution Overview, available at http://pages.ebay.com/services/buyandsell/disputeres.html (last accessed 30 March 2017).
4. Dispute Resolution Overview, available at http://pages.ebay.com/services/buyandsell/disputeres.html (last accessed 30 March 2017).

specialised publications, and conducts relevant research.[5] Cybersettle, founded in the mid-1990s, is a pioneer in online negotiation and an inventor and patent-holder of the online double-blind bid system. Both AAA and Cybersettle have good reputations and exclusive merits in their fields.

On 2 October 2006, the AAA and Cybersettle announced a strategic alliance that would provide clients of both companies with the opportunity to use the dispute resolution services of both companies exclusively. With the goal of 'ensuring that no one walks away without a resolution', said Cybersettle President and CEO Charles Brofman, AAA clients using the AAA's online case management tools will be able to attempt settlement with Cybersettle before AAA neutrals are selected. Cybersettle clients who have not been able to reach settlement through online negotiation will be able to switch to the AAA's dispute resolution processes, including conciliation, mediation, and arbitration.[6]

This strategic alliance not only makes full use of the reputation and merits of both parties, but also takes advantages of their different successful experiences. For example, AAA offers a broad range of dispute resolution services to business executives, attorneys, individuals, trade associations, unions, management, consumers, families, communities, and all levels of government, while until 2008 Cybersettle had handled almost 200,000 transactions, representing $1,457,299,751 in settlements.[7]

AAA, an experienced public organisation, cooperates with Cybersettle, a young private company, which can be a model or a good strategic plan for the development of the ODR industry. The professional regulations of AAA, such as the Commercial Arbitration Rules and Mediation Procedures, can be integrated into the self-regulation of private ODR services to promote a harmonised standard of ODR practice. AAA's dispute resolutions rules are professional and comprehensive, and contain Procedures for Large, Complex Commercial Disputes; as well as Supplementary Rules for the Resolution of Patent Disputes and a Practical Guide on Drafting Dispute Resolution Clauses, including negotiation, mediation, arbitration and large, complex cases. On the other hand, Cybersettle can also contribute its private practices and work with AAA to promote other services when appropriate and to make joint proposals and business presentations under certain circumstances.

2.1.3 WIPO and ICANN-UDRP

The Internet Corporation of Assigned Names and Numbers (ICANN) and the World Intellectual Property Organisation (WIPO) are both public international organisations but with different functions. ICANN, with responsibility for managing the generic top level domains, was in urgent need of a solution to the dispute resolution

---

5. About us (AAA), available at www.adr.org/about (last accessed 30 March 2017).
6. AAA and Cybersettle Join Forces, (2006) *Dispute Resolution Journal*, available at https://www.highbeam.com/doc/1P3-1193060421.html (last accessed 30 March 2017).
7. Cybersettle makes the case for resolving disputes online, reported on 20 February 2008, available at https://mediationchannel.com/2008/02/20/cybersettle-makes-the-case-for-resolving-disputes-online/ (last accessed 30 March 2017).

problem,[8] while WIPO is responsible for developing a balanced and accessible international intellectual property (IP) system.[9] In 1994, the WIPO Arbitration and Mediation Centre was established to provide ADR services – arbitration and mediation – for the resolution of international commercial disputes between private parties. Its WIPO Electronic Case Facility (WIPO ECAF) has been designed to offer time- and cost-efficient arbitration and mediation in cross-border dispute settlement.[10]

ICANN adopted the Uniform Domain Name Dispute Resolution Policy (UDRP), which went into effect on 1 December 1999, for all ICANN-accredited registrars of Internet domain names. WIPO is accredited by ICANN as a domain name dispute resolution service provider.[11] WIPO Centre has provided ODR services for resolving domain name disputes and has administered over 30,000 proceedings by 2009, of which over 15,000 were under UDRP adopted by ICANN.[12] Statistics show that the Centre has handled around 250 domain names disputes per month on average since 2010.[13]

In December 2008 WIPO submitted a proposal 'eUDRP Initiative'[14] to ICANN. The 'eUDRP Initiative' proposed to remove the requirement to submit and distribute paper copies of pleadings relating to the UDRP process, primarily through the use of email in order to eliminate the use of vast quantities of paper and improve the timeliness of UDRP proceeding without prejudicing either complainants or respondents.[15] eUDRP was adopted by ICANN in 2009.[16] On 1 March 2010, WIPO implemented a paperless filing procedure in light of eUDRP.[17] eUDRP was last updated in 2015.[18]

Scholars have identified the reasons for the success of the WIPO–ICANN UDRP domain name dispute resolution system, such as credibility, transparency,

---

8. The Internet Corporation for Assigned Names and Numbers (ICANN), available at www.icann.org/ (last accessed 30 March 2017).

9. 'What is WIPO?', available at www.wipo.int/about-wipo/en/what_is_wipo.html (last accessed 30 March 2017).

10. The WIPO Arbitration and Mediation Centre, available at www.wipo.int/amc/en/index.html (last accessed 30 March 2017).

11. Frequently Asked Questions: Internet Domain Names, available at www.wipo.int/amc/en/center/faq/domains.html (last accessed 30 March 2017).

12. WIPO Advanced Workshop on Domain Name Dispute Resolution: Update on Practices and Precedents, WIPO, Geneva, Switzerland, Tuesday and Wednesday, 13 and 14 October 2009, available at www.wipo.int/amc/en/events/workshops/2009/domainname/ (last accessed 30 March 2017).

13. WIPO Domain Name Dispute Resolution Statistics, available at http://www.wipo.int/amc/en/domains/statistics/ (last accessed 30 March 2017).

14. WIPO eUDRP Initiative, available at www.wipo.int/export/sites/www/amc/en/docs/icann301208.pdf (last accessed 30 March 2017).

15. Record Number of Cybersquatting Cases in 2008, WIPO Proposes Paperless UDRP, PR/2009/585, Geneva, 16 March 2009, available at www.wipo.int/pressroom/en/articles/2009/article_0005.html (last accessed 30 March 2017).

16. Announcement Regarding Implementation of Modification to Implementation Rules for Uniform Domain Name Dispute Resolution Policy, available at www.icann.org/news/announcement-2009-12-07-en (last accessed 30 March 2017).

17. eUDRP Rules: Implementation Process and Paperless Filing at WIPO: What You Need To Know, available at www.wipo.int/amc/en/domains/rules/eudrp/ (last accessed 30 March 2017).

18. eUDRP Rules, available at www.icann.org/resources/pages/udrp-rules-2015-03-11-en (last accessed 30 March 2017).

self-enforcement, accountability, etc.[19] Firstly, WIPO and ICANN are both public organisations with authority. WIPO's participation in dealing with domain names disputes particularly adds *credibility* to the process due to its professional expertise and resources. Secondly, every dot.com registrant is *compulsorily* governed by the WIPO–ICANN UDRP system, without conflict of rules and procedures, when disputes occur. Thirdly, domain name case decisions are available online immediately in full text,[20] which increases *transparency* of the procedure and imposes a degree of public *accountability*, which protects the rights of lawful domain name holders. Fourthly, the case is usually closed two months after filing and an administrative panel decision is implemented by the registrar ten days after the decision is rendered.[21] No foreign authorities can block the outcome, which promotes the *enforceability* of settlement. Lastly but most importantly, WIPO provides an *efficient* domain name dispute resolutions service, as all complaints and responses can be completed and submitted directly online.[22] The supplementary rule of 'eUDRP' reflects on the efforts of WIPO in promoting efficiency and improving *quality* in online dispute resolution for domain names disputes.

2.1.4 CIETAC and HKIAC

China and Hong Kong enacted the 'One Country, Two Systems' policy. Hong Kong is the only economy with a common law tradition incorporated with English case law (before 1997) in the Greater China Area.[23] Hong Kong law is different from law in mainland China. The business link between China and Hong Kong remains close as it is common that companies have their headquarters in China but branches in Hong Kong, or vice versa. If a company registers a '.com or .net' domain name and has offices in both mainland China and Hong Kong, it can file a case when its rights in domain names are infringed.

To bridge the two systems, in 2002 the Asian Domain Name Dispute Resolution Centre (ADNDRC) was set up as a joint undertaking of the China International Economic and Trade Arbitration Commission (CIETAC) and the Hong Kong International Arbitration Centre (HKIAC) to deal with gTLDs (.com/.org) domain names disputes.[24] There are four offices in the Asian Domain Names Dispute Resolution

---

19. Motion, P. (2005), Article 17 ECD: Encouragement of Alternative Dispute Resolution On-line Dispute Resolution: A View From Scotland, in Edwards, L. (ed.), The New Legal Framework for E-commerce in Europe (Oxford: Hart Publishing, 2005), pp. 137–69, p. 148.
20. UDRP Domain Name Decision (gTLD), available at www.wipo.int/amc/en/domains/decisionsx/index.html (last accessed 30 March 2017).
21. The UDRP Policy 2009, para. 4(k).
22. Case Filing under the UDRP, available at www.wipo.int/amc/en/domains/filing/udrp/index.html (last accessed 30 March 2017).
23. Mo, John (2013), Developing uniform rules for commercial contracts in Greater China, *Uniform Law Review* Vol. 18, 128–53, p. 133–4.
24. Asian Domain Name Dispute Resolutions Centre, available at www.adndrc.org/mten/AboutUs.php?st=2 (last accessed 30 March 2017). Please note that it also includes the Korean Internet Address Dispute Resolution Committee (KIDRC).

Centre, including two offices in China – Beijing in Mainland China and Hong Kong in the Special Economic Zone. Both offices comply with the same policy – UDRP for gTLDs disputes. Complainants can choose one of them to file a case via either email or online system in accordance with the relevant supplemental rules.[25]

In addition, both CIETAC in Beijing and HKIAC in Hong Kong are also appointed by the China Internet Network Information Center (CNNIC) providing dispute resolution services with regard to .CN domain names, known as the 'CIETAC Domain Name Dispute Resolution Centre'[26] and 'HKIAC .cn Domain Name Resolution Centre'.[27] .CN domain name disputes are carried out under the CNNIC Domain Name Dispute Resolution Policy (CNDRP)[28] in both China and Hong Kong centres, while HKIAC uses a different policy Domain Name Dispute Resolution Policy for .hk and .香港 domain names (HKDRP) required by Hong Kong Internet Registration Corporation Limited (HKIRC) for disputes concerning .HK and .香港 domain names.[29]

With these two ODR service providers (CIETAC and HKIAC), the complainant should submit the complaint form in electronic form by email.[30] Generally, a decision should be made on the basis of the statements and documents submitted by the parties. A panel has 14 days to render a decision.[31] With regard to the means of communicating panel's decision, there is no specific requirement in the current HK procedure as it only requires to 'communicate the full text of the decision to each Party' according to Article 16 of Domain Name Dispute Resolution Policy for .hk and .香港 domain names Rules of Procedure (effective 22 February 2011), whilst Article 40 of CNNIC ccTLD Dispute Resolution Policy Rules (effective from 21 Nov 2014) requires that 'The Panel's decision shall be made in electronic form, provide the final decision and the reasons on which it is based, indicate the date on which it was rendered and identify the name(s) of the Panelists'. The decisions will be published on the websites of the service providers except in special circumstances.[32]

---

25. ADNDRC Guidelines for Electronic Submissions, available at https://www.adndrc.org/mten/img/pdf/GuidelinesForElectronicSubmissions.pdf (last accessed 30 March 2017).

26. CIETAC Domain Name Dispute Resolution Centre, available at http://dndrc.cietac.org/static/english/engfrmain.html (last accessed 30 March 2017).

27. HKIAC .cn Domain Name Resolution Centre, available at http://dn.hkiac.org/cn/cne_welcome.html (last accessed 30 March 2017).

28. The China Internet Information Centre (CNNIC) approved and implemented the CNNIC Domain Name Dispute Resolution Policy (CNDRP) on 30 September 2002. The new amended CNDRP came into force on 17 March 2006.

29. Domain Name Dispute Resolution Policy for .hk and. 香港 domain names (HKDRP), available at http://www.hkiac.org/ip-and-domain-name/domain-dispute-resolution/domain-name-dispute-resolutions/hkdrp#policy (last accessed 30 March 2017).

30. Hong Kong International Arbitration Centre (HKIAC), http://dn.hkiac.org/cn/cne_complaint_form.html (last accessed 30 March 2017).

31. Article 37 of the Rules for CNNIC Domain Name Dispute Resolution Policy, available at http://dn.hkiac.org/cn/cne_rules_procedure.html (last accessed 30 March 2017).

32. Article 44 of the Rules for CNNIC Domain Name Dispute Resolution Policy, available at http://dn.hkiac.org/cn/cne_rules_procedure.html (last accessed 30 March 2017).

For example, the case *AVON Products, INC. v Ni Ping*[33] was filed with ADNDRC Beijing Office on 27 April 2007. The complainant is one of the world's most well-known direct sellers of cosmetic products. Since 1886, the claimant claims that it has built up distribution networks covering 145 countries, 8 million customers and 4.8 million independent sales representatives. The claimant has expended extensive amounts of fiscal and temporal capital in preserving the value of its AVON and 'Ya Fang' trademarks in Roman and Chinese characters, including registration of these trademarks throughout the world, including mainland China, Hong Kong, Taiwan and Singapore. It entered into the PRC market in 1990 and now has 77 branches in China, over 6,000 specialty shops, and sales between 2000 and 2004 of products marked with 'Ya Fang' in Chinese characters (or derivative marks) totaled over 681 million USD, thereby providing substantial evidence of a global association of the complainant's 'Ya Fang' marks with its cosmetic products. The claimant asserted that the respondent's use of the domain name 'yafang.net', which was registered on 12 August 2003 in Beijing, would confuse existing and future customers of the claimant, and constitute use and registration in bad faith. When visitors type in www.yafang.net, it will directly connect to www.x-y-f.com. The respondent Ni Ping also registered 'avon.cn', 'yafang.cn' and 'niping.cn' on 17 March 2003, and sold cosmetic products online. Ni Ping transferred the link of 'yafang.net' to 'avon.cn', 'yafang.cn' and 'niping.cn' after the complaint was filed. The panel ordered that the domain name 'yafang.net' be transferred to the complainant, pursuant to Article 4(a) of the UDRP.

The characteristics or advantages of CIETAC and HKIAC ODR services for domain names disputes are similar to the WIPO domain names dispute resolution service in terms of efficiency, accountability, transparency and self-enforceability. The launch of the Asian Domain Name Dispute Resolution Centre successfully combines the two systems in China and Hong Kong, serving as a joint venture providing domain names dispute resolution, which helps enhancing consistency, harmony and certainty.

Meanwhile, in response to the demand for resolving cross-border commercial disputes, CIETAC has also launched a general ODR platform for the resolution of international commercial disputes,[34] which is governed by the CIETAC Online Arbitration Rules. The CIETAC Online Arbitration Rules were adopted by the China Council for the Promotion of International Trade/China Chamber of International Commerce in 2008 and updated on 4 November 2014. The rules are effective as from 1 January 2015.[35]

---

33. *Avon Products, INC. v Ni Ping*, CN-0600087, available at www.adndrc.org/adndrc/bj_statostocs.html (last accessed 30 March 2017).

34. CIETAC ODR Platform, available at www.cietacodr.org/ (last accessed 30 March 2017).

35. CIETAC Online Arbitration Rules 2009 (updated in 2015), available at www.cietac.org/index.php?m=Article&a=show&id=2770&l=en (last accessed 30 March 2017).

2.1.5 Other established ODR services

In Netherlands, in 2007 Rechtwijzer 2.0 was provided by the Netherlands Ministry of Justice and Security for the Dutch Legal Aid Board by the Hague Institute for the Internationalisation of the Law (HiiL). The ODR system is designed to help parties resolve disputes by diagnosing problems, facilitating resolution via asynchronous dialogue and Q&A-based framing. At the negotiation stage, the ODR system provides automated legal guidance, based on the answers in the Q&A session. If negotiation fails, it moves to online mediation or arbitration.[36] In the UK, there are also well-established ADR/ODR services in specific industries, such as the Financial Ombudsman Service (since 2000),[37] Nominet domain names dispute service (since 1996)[38] and the Traffic Penalty Tribunal.[39] In Germany, Online Schlichter has provided online mediation service since 2009,[40] which is considered as one of most successful German ODR platforms. It received around 1,500 cases in 2014, 1,142 cases in 2013 and 859 cases in 2012.[41]

2.1.6 The most recent development of ODR services

Since 2011 some new ODR services have continued emerging with different features and for special market penetration. In the US, Modria was established in 2011 as a private entity, providing a cloud-based ODR platform to eBay and PayPal to resolve their online purchase disputes. Modria technology enables companies to deliver fast and fair resolutions to disputes of any type and volume. It is estimated that its ODR services at eBay and PayPal process 60 million cases per year.[42] In 2011, the International Centre for Dispute Resolution (ICDR) – an international division of AAA – also started to offer the Manufacturer/Supplier Online Dispute Resolution Protocol (MSODR), providing an online negotiation platform for parties.[43] If an agreement cannot be reached by the parties via MSODR, the case

---

36. Rechtwijzer 2.0, available at www.hiil.org/project/rechtwijzer (last accessed 26 March 2017); and see also Online Dispute Resolution for Low Value Civil Claims, Civil Justice Council ODR Advisory Group, February 2015, available at www.judiciary.gov.uk/wp-content/uploads/2015/02/Online-Dispute-Resolution-Final-Web-Version1.pdf (last accessed 30 March 2017), p. 12.
37. Financial Ombudsman Service, available at www.financial-ombudsman.org.uk (last accessed 30 March 2017).
38. Nominet, available at www.Nominet.org.uk (last accessed 30 March 2017).
39. Traffic Penalty Tribunal, available at www.trafficpenaltytribunal.gov.uk (last accessed 30 March 2017).
40. Online Schlichter, available at www.online-schlichter.de (last accessed 30 March 2017).
41. Online Dispute Resolution for Low Value Civil Claims, Civil Justice Council ODR Advisory Group, February 2015, available at www.judiciary.gov.uk/wp-content/uploads/2015/02/Online-Dispute-Resolution-Final-Web-Version1.pdf (last accessed 30 March 2017), p. 15.
42. Modria, available at http://modria.com/product/ (last accessed 30 March 2017).
43. American Arbitration Association (AAA) International Centre for Dispute Resolution (ICDR) Manufacturer/Supplier Online Dispute Resolution Program and ICDR Manufacturer/Supplier Online Dispute Resolution Protocol (MSODR), amended and effective 1 July 2011, available at www.cedr.com/about_us/arbitration_commission/ICDR_Online_Protocol.pdf (last accessed 30 March 2017); and see also ICDR Manufacturer/Supplier Online Dispute Resolution Program, available at www.adr.org/aaa/ShowPDF?doc=ADRSTG_015216 (last accessed 30 March 2017).

will be automatically transferred to online arbitration. In Canada, on 1 June 2017 the Civil Resolution Tribunal began to resolve small claims disputes under 5,000 USD.[44] The online tribunal will operate in several stages: negotiation – to help users explore possible solutions and to provide users with the tribunal's online negotiation platforms; mediation – to assist the parties with a tribunal case manager; and adjudication – to make a final and binding decision by the adjudicator via the online platform and through video conferencing where necessary.[45]

In the EU, in 2014, a private entity, Youstice, established in Slovakia, launched an ODR service, dealing with customer complaints on online shopping,[46] which employs similar ideas (e.g. web-based application and framing arguments) to other private ODR entities on the market. In 2016 a single entry public ODR platform – an EU-wide platform – was established under the ODR Regulation on Consumer ODR to harmonise the ODR practice and build consumers' trust in online marketplaces in the EU. Since 15 February 2016 the ODR platform has been accessible to consumers and traders.[47] The EU ODR platform is the first community-wide web-based dispute resolution platform for consumers and traders to resolve their contractual disputes about online purchases of goods and services. The ODR platform enables online purchase disputes to be resolved out of court in a more affordable, simple and fast way. Online traders are obliged to provide a link to the ODR platform. The single entry ODR platform, safeguarded by legislation, has several unique features compared with commercial ODR platforms on the market. The most distinctive features are that the procedure (i.e. timing) is set to be robust, whilst the standard of available dispute resolution bodies is checked to be consistent. For example, after submitting a complaint form via the ODR platform, consumers have 30 days to agree with traders on the dispute resolution body that will automatically receive the details of the dispute from the ODR platform. The dispute resolution body, which is registered with the national authority and meets the EU standards, is listed on the EU ODR platform.[48] In addition to the trusted dispute resolution bodies registered on the ODR platform, the single entry ODR platform also has two other unique features compared with commercial ODR platforms. They are:

- it allows consumers to use any of the 23 official languages;
- it has a nation contact point to provide assistance to users at all stages.

---

44. Canadian Civil Resolution Tribunal, available at www.civilresolutionbc.ca/ (last accessed 30 March 2017); and see also Rules (effective 7 November 2016), available at www.civilresolutionbc.ca/app/uploads/sites/5/2016/11/CRT-Rules-Revision-Nov-7-16.pdf (last accessed 30 March 2017).

45. Online Dispute Resolution for Low Value Civil Claims, Civil Justice Council ODR Advisory Group, February 2015, available at www.judiciary.gov.uk/wp-content/uploads/2015/02/Online-Dispute-Resolution-Final-Web-Version1.pdf (last accessed 30 March 2017), p. 13.

46. Youstice, available at www.youstice.com/en/ (last accessed 30 March 2017).

47. ADR/ODR, available at http://ec.europa.eu/consumers/solving_consumer_disputes/non-judicial_redress/adr-odr/index_en.htm (last accessed 30 March 2017).

48. EU Online Dispute Resolution Platform, available at https://webgate.ec.europa.eu/odr/main/?event=main.home.show (last accessed 30 March 2017).

These unique features of the ODR platform established under the ODR Regulation provides much greater certainty and confidence to users in the EU.

2.1.7 The growth of ODR best practices

The fact that eBay and SquareTrade ceased their collaboration on online dispute resolution may show that online dispute resolution technologies and services have become well developed and online marketplaces nowadays can build and integrate basic ODR platforms in their own online marketplaces without having to rely solely on ODR specialists' help. Well-designed external ODR services such as Modria in the US and the central public ODR services such as the single EU ODR platform have emerged, being tailored with unique features and special functions to penetrate specific market usage. Other strategic alliances such as ICANN and WIPO; AAA with Cybersettle; and CIETAC and HKIAC, continue their collaboration as they still rely on each other's clients, specific market access, industry-specific dispute resolution services and specialisms.

Currently the majority of arbitration institutions have not offered any specific online arbitration rules but may provide an ODR user guide, roadmap or protocol as a supplementary guideline to their traditional institutional arbitration rules. In China, CIETAC Online Arbitration Rules were the first set of specific institutional rules tackling online arbitration for international commercial disputes. The principles of CIETAC Online Arbitration Rules are to resolve disputes independently, impartially, efficiently and economically.[49] In Russia, in 2015 the Russian Arbitration Association's Online Arbitration Regulation came into force. The Russian Online Arbitration Regulation serves to facilitate the independent, impartial and efficient resolution of commercial disputes.[50] In the US, in 2002 the American Bar Association (ABA) Task Force on E-Commerce and ADR – Recommended Best Practices for Online Dispute Resolution Service Providers – proposed ten important principles/provisions to promote best practices for ODR service providers. They are: transparency; minimum basic disclosures; use of technology; cost and funding; impartiality; confidentiality, privacy and information security; qualifications and responsibilities of neutrals; accountability of ODR providers and neutrals; enforcement; and jurisdiction and choice of law.[51] In 2009 the Advisory Committee of the National Centre for Technology and Dispute Resolution at the University of Massachusetts drafted ODR Standards of Practice, intending to provide 'guidelines for practice across the spectrum of ODR'. The guidelines promote the principles of fairness, transparency and confidentiality of an ODR system, rather than individual

---

49. CIETAC Online Arbitration Rules 2009 (updated in 2015), Article 1.
50. Online Arbitration Rules Come Into Force, 12.10.2015, available at http://arbitrations.ru/en/press-centr/news/the-online-arbitration-regulation-comes-into-force/ (last accessed 30 March 2017).
51. American Bar Association (ABA) Task Force on E-Commerce and ADR – Recommended Best Practices for Online Dispute Resolution Service Providers, available at https://www.americanbar.org/content/dam/aba/migrated/dispute/documents/BestPracticesFinal102802.authcheckdam.pdf (last accessed 30 March 2017).

operation frameworks, in order to be applicable across different subject matters, legal jurisdictions and technological platforms.[52] The ODR Standards of Practice has since been updated and expanded by 'Ethical Principles for Online Dispute Resolution'.[53] In Canada, the Civil Resolution Tribunal Rules for ODR (effective 7 November 2016) promote the principles of confidentiality, fairness, proportionality and being a speedy, efficient, accessible, inexpensive/affordable, informal and flexible process as well as final and binding decisions.[54]

In the EU, the EU Regulation on Consumer ODR[55] provides a single entry EU-wide ODR platform with the principles of data confidentiality and security,[56] as well as being reliable, efficient,[57] independent, impartial, transparent, effective, fast and fair.[58] On 16 December 2015, a regulation was adopted to amend the European small claims regulation (2007), which increases the threshold for the value of a cross-border claim from EUR 2,000 to EUR 5,000 and also the use of distance communication technology for oral hearings and evidence submission in order to enhance the principles of being fair, efficient, cost-effective, transparent and accessible in dispute resolutions.[59] The Regulation is effective from 14 July 2017. In the UK, in 2015 the Civil Justice Council reviewed the shortcomings of the civil justice system and sought for solutions of providing a court-based dispute resolution service for low value claims, that is with the principles such as affordability, accessibility, intelligibility, appropriateness, fast-speed, consistency, trustworthiness, focus, proportionality and fairness.[60] At the

---

52. National Centre for Technology and Dispute Resolution, 2009, Online dispute resolution standards of practice, available at www.icann.org/en/system/files/files/odr-standards-of-practice-en.pdf (last accessed 30 March 2017).

53. Wing, L. 2016. Ethics and ODR: Ethical principles for online dispute resolution. National Center for Technology and Dispute Resolution, available at http://odr.info/ethics-and-odr/#_ftn2 (last accessed 30 March 2017).

54. Canadian Civil Resolution Tribunal Rules for ODR (effective 7 November 2016), available at www.civilresolutionbc.ca/app/uploads/sites/5/2016/11/CRT-Rules-Revision-Nov-7-16.pdf (last accessed 30 March 2017).

55. Regulation (EU) No 524/2013 of the European Parliament and of the Council of 21 May 2013 on online dispute resolution for consumer disputes and amending Regulation (EC) No 2006/2004 and Directive 2009/22/EC (Regulation on consumer ODR), OJ L 165, 18.6.2013, pp. 1–12, available at http://eur-lex.europa.eu/legal-content/EN/TXT/?uri=CELEX:32013R0524 (last accessed 30 March 2017).

56. EU Regulation on Consumer ODR 2013, Recitals (27) and (29), and Article 13.

57. EU Regulation on Consumer ODR 2013, Recital (6).

58. EU Regulation on Consumer ODR 2013, Article 1.

59. Small claims procedure: Council and Parliament agree on new rules, Council of the EU, Press Release 537/15, 29 June 2015, available at http://www.consilium.europa.eu/press-releases-pdf/2015/6/40802200157_en.pdf (last accessed 30 March 2017); and see also Regulation (EU) 2015/2421 of the European Parliament and of the Council of 16 December 2015 amending Regulation (EC) No 861/2007 establishing a European Small Claims Procedure and Regulation (EC) No 1896/2006 creating a European order for payment procedure, OJ L 341, 24.12.2015, pp. 1–13.

60. Online Dispute Resolution for Low Value Civil Claims, Civil Justice Council ODR Advisory Group, February 2015, available at www.judiciary.gov.uk/wp-content/uploads/2015/02/Online-Dispute-Resolution-Final-Web-Version1.pdf (last accessed 30 March 2017), pp. 8–9; and see also UK Courts and Tribunals Judiciary, available at www.judiciary.gov.uk/reviews/online-dispute-resolution/ (last accessed 30 March 2017).

international level, the UNCITRAL Draft ODR Procedural Rules promote the principles of impartiality, independence, efficiency, effectiveness, due process, fairness, accountability, transparency, confidentiality and security.[61]

As shown above, arbitration institutions and public organisations share common principles of establishing an ODR system. The principle of enforceability has not been included by the majority of private ODR entities except for ODR services in specific fields such as domain names disputes. Some public ODR entities such as the Civil Resolution Tribunal may provide final and binding decisions that are enforceable. Since ODR has become more and more popular in resolving cross-border disputes, there is an increasing need of harmonised international rules and procedures for ODR to ensure the quality of ODR services. The quality of ODR services has a high impact on ODR users' trust and confidence. The users' trust and confidence is one of the critical factors that may determine the destiny of ODR and its future trend of development. Thus, core principles for the establishment and maintenance of an ODR system and its platform shall be addressed to enhance the consistent quality standard of ODR services across the globe.

2.1.8 Core principles[62]

2.1.8.1 Efficiency

ADR was introduced to improve efficiency of process and enforcement as opposed to litigation, in particular international litigation. In a leading English case, *Halsey v Milton Keynes NHS Trust*, it was held that no party can be forced to enter into any form of ADR, or to agree an outcome to a non-adjudicative ADR process, but a party should consider ADR. A penalty may be imposed where ADR is unreasonably refused.[63] In *PGF II SA v OMFS Company 1 Ltd*, the court penalised a party in costs that had unreasonably refused to mediate.[64] It was suggested that 'the decision in *PGF II SA* marks a modest, but significant, extension of the principles stated by the Court of Appeal in *Halsey v Milton Keynes General NHS Trust*'.[65]

In response to technological development and the increased number of low-value, high-volume and cross-border Internet-related disputes, ODR was introduced with the intention to provide further improvement in terms of efficiency of resolving disputes through the use of electronic communications, compared with traditional ADR. However, whether ODR can be truly efficient as a means to resolve disputes

---

61. UNCITRAL Draft ODR Procedural Rules 2014 (A/CN.9/WG.III/WP.133).
62. This part is an update from Wang, F. (2008), Online Dispute Resolution: Technology, Management and Legal Practice from an International Perspective (Oxford: Chandos Publishing, 2008).
63. *Halsey v Milton Keynes NHS Trust* [2004] 1 WLR 3002.
64. *PGF II SA v OMFS Company 1 Ltd* [2013] EWCA Civ 1288; [2014] 1 WLR 1386.
65. The Promotion of ADR in the Context of the Recent Civil Justice Reforms, Keynote Speech by Lord Justice Jackson, Chartered Institute of Arbitrators' Centenary Conference on 23 January 2015, available at www.ciarb.org/docs/default-source/ciarbdocuments/speaker-assets/lord-justice-jackson.pdf (last accessed 30 March 2017).

will largely depend on the design of the system. In other words, the ODR system shall be designed in a way that can comply with any pre-defined arbitration procedural rules. Electronic arbitration agreements, evidential documents and arbitral awards should meet the general requirements of durability, authenticity, reliability and integrity of electronic records according to national and international relevant legislation. An Intelligent/Advanced ODR system, which can generate an automated sample of agreements, arguments and decisions for parties' reference and adoption, shall ensure that the content of each auto-generated document covers all mandatory points and provides accurate and reliable suggestion according to the chosen applicable law to the procedure of dispute resolution and the substance of disputes. If there are any procedural irregularities or mistakes, such as the invalidity of arbitration agreements, they may be used as grounds for refusal for recognition and enforcement of arbitral awards under the New York Convention 1958. If this happens, the efficiency of using ADR and ODR to resolve cases may be jeopardised. Both the EU Regulation on Consumer ODR and the UNCITRAL Draft ODR Procedural Rules promote the efficiency of the ODR process. All these issues will be discussed in detail in the following chapters.

2.1.8.2 Accountability (transparency) v confidentiality

Accountability means being answerable to an authority that can mandate desirable conduct and sanction conduct that breaches identified obligations.[66] Transparency means 'the quality of being done in an open way without secrets'.[67] Accountability often goes together with transparency in that accountability mechanisms fall into two categories: one is structure and the other is transparency. Accountability can be internal and external, or both. Internal accountability typically promotes self-evaluation and organisational development and enhances management practices and strategic planning through internal measures and review,[68] while external accountability usually involves evaluation of performance and outcomes by a credible external entity (private or public) in the context of predetermined boundaries.[69]

Transparency is one of the key elements to induce trust in using ODR, because the availability of full information is useful for ODR users to determine whether the ODR provider is trustworthy, whether effective redress mechanisms are available, whether the cost and duration is reasonable and whether it is suitable for their nature of disputes. According to the functions of transparency, the requirement of transparency in ODR systems relates to three categories: disclosure of ODR

---

66. Minow (2003), Public and Private Partnerships: Accounting for the New Religion, *Harvard Law Review*, Volume 116, pp. 1229–70, p. 1260.

67. See Cambridge Dictionary.

68. See generally Panel on Accountability and Governance in the Voluntary Sector, Final Report, Building on Strength: Improving Governance and Accountability in Canada's Voluntary Sector (Feb.1999), cited from Rabinovich-Einy, O. (Spring 2006), Technology's Impact: the Quest for a New Paradigm for Accountability in Mediation, *Harvard Negotiation Law Review*, Volume 11, pp. 253–93, p. 261.

69. Hayllar, M. (2000), The Importance and Attributes of Effective Accountability Relationships, *Asian Review of Public Administration*, Volume 12, pp 60–80, p. 68.

providers, including ownership and location of the provider; disclosure of the ODR process, including duration and costs, the character of the outcome (binding or non-binding), and substantive rules or principles governing the merits;[70] and disclosure of neutrals.[71] If the statistical results of ODR proceedings are published, it may help inducing trust in ODR as users can assess the quality, speed, cost and reliability of using such system.[72]

According to the SquareTrade's past successful experience, SquareTrade generated internal structural accountability by instituting structures for: (1) gathering broad and rich information on neutrals' interventions and party needs as well as ongoing efforts to evaluate the quality of services rendered; (2) monitoring neutrals' performance; (3) developing the standard of confidentiality; (4) internalising incentives for neutrals to perform well and for the system as a whole to identify deficiencies and successes and learn from them.[73] SquareTrade's efforts were mainly internal. In order to enhance the success of providing an accountable ODR system, ODR service providers need to work on external accountability such as oversight by a credible, independent entity. External accountability is important to ODR providers, because it can assist providers in questioning the adequacy of the goals themselves and the means used to achieve them; drawing on the information revealed in the course of monitoring as well as own experience and knowledge from other backgrounds; revealing those instances of poor performance missed in the internal examination and providing an impartial evaluation of potential conflicts of interests between providers.[74] After all, external accountability can be gained by accreditation. The EU Regulation on Consumer ODR, the EC Directive on Consumer ADR and the UNCITRAL Draft ODR Procedural Rules promote the principles of accountability, transparency and confidentiality. According to the EC Directive on Consumer ADR, the requirement of transparency means that Member States shall ensure that ADR entities make publicly available on their websites, on a durable medium upon request, and by any other means they consider appropriate, clear and easily understandable information on:

(a) their contact details, including postal address and e-mail address;
(b) the fact that ADR entities are listed in accordance with Article 20(2);
(c) the natural persons in charge of ADR, the method of their appointment and the length of their mandate;

---

70. American Bar Association Task Force on E-commerce and ADR, 'Recommended best practices for online dispute resolution service providers', available at www.law.washington.edu/ABA-eADR, p. 4.

71. Kaufmann-Kohler & Schultz (2004), p. 110. The term 'neutrals' in this chapter means the third parties, including mediators and arbitrators.

72. Schultz, T., Kaufmann-Kohler, G., Langer, D. and Bonnet, V. (2001), Online Dispute Resolution: The State of the Art and the Issues, E-Com Research Project of the University of Geneva, Geneva, available at https://papers.ssrn.com/sol3/papers.cfm?abstract_id=899079 (last accessed 30 March 2017), p. 39.

73. Rabinovich-Einy, O. (Spring 2006), Technology's Impact: the Quest for a New Paradigm for Accountability in Mediation, *Harvard Negotiation Law Review*, Volume 11, pp. 253–93, p. 282.

74. Rabinovich-Einy, O. (Spring 2006), Technology's Impact: the Quest for a New Paradigm for Accountability in Mediation, *Harvard Negotiation Law Review*, Volume 11, pp. 253–93, pp. 282–283.

(d) the expertise, impartiality and independence of the natural persons in charge of ADR, if they are employed or remunerated exclusively by the trader;
(e) their membership in networks of ADR entities facilitating cross-border dispute resolution, if applicable;
(f) the types of disputes they are competent to deal with, including any threshold if applicable;
(g) the procedural rules governing the resolution of a dispute and the grounds on which the ADR entity may refuse to deal with a given dispute in accordance with Article 5(4);
(h) the languages in which complaints can be submitted to the ADR entity and in which the ADR procedure is conducted;
(i) the types of rules the ADR entity may use as a basis for the dispute resolution (for example legal provisions, considerations of equity, codes of conduct);
(j) any preliminary requirements the parties may have to meet before an ADR procedure can be instituted, including the requirement that an attempt be made by the consumer to resolve the matter directly with the trader;
(k) whether or not the parties can withdraw from the procedure;
(l) the costs, if any, to be borne by the parties, including any rules on awarding costs at the end of the procedure;
(m) the average length of the ADR procedure;
(n) the legal effect of the outcome of the ADR procedure, including the penalties for non-compliance in the case of a decision having binding effect on the parties, if applicable;
(o) the enforceability of the ADR decision, if relevant.[75]

Furthermore, it requires that 'Member States shall ensure that ADR entities make publicly available on their websites, on a durable medium upon request, and by any other means they consider appropriate, annual activity reports.'[76] It appears that the principle of transparency under the EC Directive on Consumer ADR and the underlying principles of availability and durability are interconnected. The principles of transparency, availability and durability are also linked with the principle of accessibility.

While there is a growing demand for transparency in ODR process, confidentiality is still one of most important virtues of mediation and arbitration. Although it is widely recognised that ADR and ODR are strictly confidential, the opposite to court hearings in public, there may still be different legal requirements in terms of mediation and arbitration confidentiality in different countries. In ODR systems,

---

75. Directive 2013/11/EU of the European Parliament and of the Council of 21 May 2013 on alternative dispute resolution for consumer disputes and amending Regulation (EC) No 2006/2004 and Directive 2009/22/EC (Directive on consumer ADR), Article 7(1).
76. EC Directive on Consumer ADR 2013, Article 7(2).

the information of disputants and the information gathered during the proceeding cannot be disclosed, and likewise for the content of the results/outcomes of the cases, unless permission is given by parties to do so. Confidentiality creates a safe and private environment for disputants, allowing them to bring forth disputes that they may not have been willing to pursue through formal and public avenues. However, when process and outcomes of dispute resolution are kept confidential, the general public may be less likely to trust in the process and discourage future first-time users from using it.[77] It was suggested that ODR providers had to strike a balance between the privacy desired by the parties using these techniques, and the transparency, accountability and building of trust, which is engendered by publishing the decisions of the ODR provider.[78] This issue has been tackled by employing a customer rating system on the ODR platform. For example, the European Commission requires that 'the ODR platform shall give the possibility to the parties involved in a dispute to give their feedback pursuant to point (g) of Article 5(4) of Regulation (EU) No 524/2013 upon conclusion of the ADR procedure and for six months thereafter'.[79] Other measures have also been considered.

For example, it is expected that confidentiality is more sensitive in certain types of disputes. In commercial transactions, B2B matters often are more sensitive than B2C, generally because the former ones may involve higher financial stakes as well as a certain level of business techniques and strategies. Therefore, the disclosure of B2B ODR outcomes may affect the reputation of the business and the confidentiality of trade secrets. In principle, information on ODR proceedings and outcomes, which involves high-value claims, and which is deemed to be related to any trade secrets or personal sensitive issues, must be kept confidential, except for where pre-agreements exist. However, in order to increase trust in their ODR services, ODR providers can still allow the disclosure of those outcomes, when agreed by users or which are beyond the conditions of confidential protection. In addition, ODR providers can report some statistics showing the percentage of dispute settlements, as well as the rate of settlement satisfaction. This shall be assessed by authorised bodies, such as accreditation agencies. In addition, effective structural accountability may also be introduced to reconcile confidentiality on the one hand with accountability on the other. Effective structural accountability incorporates both internal and external elements. Internally, goals are defined and targets are set, processes for measuring and monitoring performance are instituted, and improvement is sought. Externally, beyond setting

---

77. Unif. Mediation Act, prefatory note (2001).
78. Motion, P. (2005), Article 17 ECD: Encouragement of Alternative Dispute Resolution On-line Dispute Resolution: A View From Scotland, pp. 137–69, in Edwards, L. (ed.) (2005), The New Legal Framework for E-commerce in Europe (Oxford: Hart Publishing, 2005), pp. 137–69, 154.
79. Commission Implementing Regulation (EU) 2015/1051 of 1 July 2015 on the modalities for the exercise of the functions of the online dispute resolution platform, on the modalities of the electronic complaint form and on the modalities of the cooperation between contact points provided for in Regulation (EU) No 524/2013 of the European Parliament and of the Council on online dispute resolution for consumer disputes, Article 8.

the general framework, particular goals and performance evaluations are audited and questioned in an additional effort to detect and remedy poor performance, misconduct, inefficiencies, and deficient policies.[80]

2.1.8.3 Accessibility

According to the recommendation of the International Chamber of Commerce (ICC), accessibility means 'all relevant correspondence relating to a transaction should be easily accessible and made available to the customer upon request'.[81] It is suggested that ODR systems should be always available to users to the process and to their own cases to access with the exception of scheduled downtime.[82]

Accessibility of ODR systems may be enhanced if ODR service providers are given the responsibility to ensure users have easy access to functions in the systems. In order to enhance accessibility, the design of ODR systems should be user-friendly, being able to be accessed 24/7 and from different computer operating systems, or different web browsers as appropriate. According to the EU Regulation on Consumer ODR, an electronic complaint form also needs to be accessible on the ODR platform. The Commission requires that

> the electronic complaint form to be submitted to the ODR platform shall be accessible to consumers and traders in all the official languages of the institutions of the Union. The complainant party shall be able to save a draft of the electronic complaint form on the ODR platform. The draft shall be accessible and editable by the complainant party prior to submission of the final fully completed electronic complaint form. The draft of the electronic complaint form that is not fully completed and submitted shall be automatically deleted from the ODR platform six months after its creation.'[83]

In addition, a list of all ADR entities also needs to be accessible at any time. The Commission requires that

> the parties shall at any time have access to the list of all ADR entities registered with the ODR platform pursuant to Article 5(6) of Regulation (EU) No 524/2013. A search tool, offered by the ODR platform, shall help the parties to identify the ADR entity competent to deal with their dispute among the ADR entities registered with the ODR platform.[84]

---

80. Rabinovich-Einy, O. (Spring 2006), Technology's Impact: the Quest for a New Paradigm for Accountability in Mediation, *Harvard Negotiation Law Review*, Volume 11, pp. 253–93, p. 269.
81. Resolving Disputes Online: Best Practice for Online Dispute Resolution (ODR) in B2C and C2C transactions, November 2003, International Chamber of Commerce (ICC), Tools for E-business, p. 9.
82. Resolving Disputes Online: Best Practice for Online Dispute Resolution (ODR) in B2C and C2C transactions, November 2003, International Chamber of Commerce (ICC), Tools for E-business, p. 12.
83. Commission Implementing Regulation (EU) 2015/1051 of 1 July 2015 on the modalities for the exercise of the functions of the online dispute resolution platform, on the modalities of the electronic complaint form and on the modalities of the cooperation between contact points provided for in Regulation (EU) No 524/2013 of the European Parliament and of the Council on online dispute resolution for consumer disputes, Article 2.
84. Commission Implementing Regulation (EU) 2015/1051 of 1 July 2015 on the modalities for the exercise of the functions of the online dispute resolution platform, on the modalities of the electronic complaint form and on the modalities of the cooperation between contact points provided for

Furthermore, ODR advisors and other ODR contact points shall also have access to all information necessary. The Commission requires that

> ODR advisors who have access to information concerning a dispute including personal data shall grant access to this information to advisors in other ODR contact points in so far as it is necessary for the purpose of fulfilling the functions referred to in Article 7(2) of Regulation (EU) No 524/2013.[85]

2.1.8.4 Credibility and accreditation

The principles of credibility and accreditation apply to ADR entities, arbitration institutions and practitioners such as mediators and arbitrators. Accreditation is deemed to be a precondition for practitioners to practise, involving a practitioner meeting certain levels of education, training or performance.[86] In the US, the Association for Conflict Resolution (ACR) and the American Bar Association (ABA) have each developed task forces on promoting a mediation certification to overcome the lack of uniformity in the various mediation practice codes since 2002.[87] The Final Report Alternative Dispute Resolution Section of the ABA Task Force on Mediator Credentialing was concluded in August 2012 recommending an effective credentialing programme.[88] The final report of the ABA Section of Dispute Resolution Task Force on Improving Mediation Quality also provides a set of general recommendations by which mediation can be improved,[89] which includes the creation of comprehensive mediation user guides together with a video for parties and their attorneys.[90]

Similar to the US, Australia was one of the first countries that has strongly recommended and developed an accreditation system for ADR practitioners. In August 2004, the Australian National Alternative Dispute Resolution Advisory

---

in Regulation (EU) No 524/2013 of the European Parliament and of the Council on online dispute resolution for consumer disputes, Article 4(2).

85. Commission Implementing Regulation (EU) 2015/1051 of 1 July 2015 on the modalities for the exercise of the functions of the online dispute resolution platform, on the modalities of the electronic complaint form and on the modalities of the cooperation between contact points provided for in Regulation (EU) No 524/2013 of the European Parliament and of the Council on online dispute resolution for consumer disputes, Article 9(3).

86. Tyler, M. C. and Bornstein, J. (Spring 2006), Accreditation of On-line Dispute Resolution Practitioners, *Conflict Resolution Quarterly*, Volume 23, Number 3, pp. 383–404, p. 383.

87. ACR Task Force on Mediator Certification, Report and Recommendation to the Board of Directors, 2004 ACR. Rep. 1, available at www.mediate.com/articles/acrCert1.cfm (last accessed 30 March 2017). ABA Section of Dispute Resolution Task Force on Credentialing, Discussion Draft: Report on Mediator Credentialing and Quality Assurance, 2002 A.B.A Sec. Dispute Resolution Rep. 1–2, available at www.americanbar.org/content/dam/aba/directories/dispute_resolution/0116_report_mediator_credentialing.authcheckdam.pdf (last accessed 30 March 2017).

88. Final Report Alternative Dispute Resolution Section of the American Bar Association Task Force on Mediator Credentialing, August 2012, available at www.americanbar.org/content/dam/aba/images/dispute_resolution/CredentialingTaskForce.pdf (last accessed 30 March 2017).

89. ABA Section of Dispute Resolution Task Force on Improving Mediation Quality, Final Report, April 2006 – February 2008, available at www.americanbar.org/content/dam/aba/migrated/dispute/documents/FinalTaskForceMediation.authcheckdam.pdf (last accessed 30 March 2017).

90. ABA Section of Dispute Resolution Task Force on Improving Mediation Quality, Final Report, April 2006 – February 2008, p. 3.

Council (NADRAC) took an initiative on mediator accreditation released in two working papers: one is called 'Who says you're a mediator? Towards a national system for accrediting mediators';[91] and the other is called 'Who can refer to, or conduct, mediation? A compendium of Australian legislative provisions covering referral to mediation and accreditation of mediators'.[92] In 2006, at the 8th National Mediation Conference in Hobart, the Draft National Mediation Accreditation System was approved. The Committee strongly recommended moving the scheme to an implementation phase reported in 'Mediation Accreditation in Australia'.[93] On 1 January 2008 the new National Mediator Accreditation System was introduced to implement harmonised standards of accrediting mediators. The current version of the National Mediator Accreditation System (NMAS) was effective from 1 July 2015 including practice standards, recognised mediator accreditation bodies and register of nationally accredited mediators.[94] The NADRAC previously highlighted that 'a major difficulty for policy-makers in relation to accreditation has been the absence of a nationally co-ordinated approach to the accreditation of ADR practitioners'.[95] It was suggested that establishing minimum standards for ADR practitioners and mechanisms for selecting those practitioners are important for an ADR system.[96]

Likewise, in ODR systems, mediators and arbitrators that provide online mediation and arbitration services shall also be accredited to meet certain levels of education, training and performance[97] and ethical requirements. Accreditation will bring credibility to ODR by ensuring that the practice of ODR is built on a foundation of quality assurance.[98] Accreditation can be imposed or monitored by approved ODR service providers or by governments and international organisations. Although NADRAC concluded in 2013, its recommendations on principles of good practice concerning dispute resolution and information technology remain

---

91. Who says you're a mediator? Towards a national system for accrediting mediators, prepared for a national workshop on mediation standards, facilitated by NADRAC, at the 7th National Mediation Conference in Darwin on 2 July 2004, available at www.ag.gov.au/LegalSystem/AlternateDisputeResolution/Documents/NADRAC%20Publications/who-says-youre-a-mediator.pdf (last accessed 30 March 2017).

92. Who can refer to, or conduct, mediation? A compendium of Australian legislative provisions covering referral to mediation and accreditation of mediators, prepared by the NADRAC Secretariat as at August 2004, available at www.ag.gov.au/LegalSystem/AlternateDisputeResolution/Documents/NADRAC%20Publications/who-can-refer-to-or-conduct-mediation-august2004.doc (last accessed 30 March 2017).

93. National Mediator Accreditation System (NMAS) – A History of the Development of the Standards, available at www.msb.org.au/sites/default/files/documents/A%20History%20of%20the%20Development%20of%20the%20Standards.pdf (last accessed 30 March 2017).

94. National Mediator Accreditation System: the Standards, Effective July 2015, available at www.msb.org.au/sites/default/files/documents/NMAS%201%20July%202015.pdf (last accessed 30 March 2017).

95. Legislating for alternative dispute resolution: A guide for government policy-makers and legal drafters (November 2006), NADRAC working paper, pp. 9–10.

96. The System and the Standard are included as Appendix 3 in the Guide 2006, p.114

97. Tyler, M. C. and Bornstein, J. (Spring 2006), Accreditation of On-line Dispute Resolution Practitioners, *Conflict Resolution Quarterly*, Volume 23, Number 3, pp. 383–404, p. 383.

98. Tyler, M. C. and Bornstein, J. (Spring 2006), Accreditation of On-line Dispute Resolution Practitioners, *Conflict Resolution Quarterly*, Volume 23, Number 3, pp. 383–404, p. 384.

useful. It was suggested that online practitioners shall have specific knowledge including online cultures, online technology, online communication, online negotiation processes, online context, online procedures and online decision-making.[99] Online practitioners shall also have specific skills that enable them to access a dispute for ODR, gather and use information online, define the dispute online, manage the online process and interaction between parties, and conclude the ODR process.[100] It is suggested that the standard of accreditation of ODR practitioners can be achieved in four ways: 1) incorporation of ODR practitioner accreditation into traditional practitioner accreditation systems; 2) independent accreditation of ODR practitioners; 3) accreditation of specialist ODR skills; 4) accrediting agencies to provide ODR service.[101] The recent UNCITRAL Draft ODR Procedural Rules have not established an accreditation system for neutrals, but have required that the neutral shall devote the time necessary to conduct the ODR proceedings diligently, efficiently and in accordance with the time limits in the Rules;[102] and the neutral shall also, at the time of accepting his or her appointment and throughout the ODR proceedings, ensure his or her impartiality and independence.[103]

Furthermore, it would also be helpful if there were accreditation schemes for ODR technological systems and ODR service providers. In recent years, there has been a general practice of introducing trust mark schemes for online service. Customer rating systems have also been developed for online service. However, there is no specific regulatory development in the field of ODR accreditation across the globe. In the EU, in 2014 the Regulation on Electronic Identification and Trust Services for Electronic Transactions was adopted, which generally promotes users' confidence of online service.[104] With regard to ODR services, in order to ensure that ADR entities function properly and effectively, the EC Directive on Consumer ODR requires that each member states should designate a competent authority or competent authorities which closely monitor the quality of ADR entities.[105] As the EU Regulation on Consumer ODR is considered in conjunction with the EC Directive on Consumer ODR,[106] competent ADR entities are considered as competent ODR entities.

---

99. Dispute Resolution and Information Technology: Principles of Good Practice, March 2002, National Alternative Dispute Resolution Advisory Council.

100. Dispute Resolution and Information Technology: Principles of Good Practice, March 2002, National Alternative Dispute Resolution Advisory Council.

101. Tyler, M. C. and Bornstein, J. (Spring 2006), Accreditation of On-line Dispute Resolution Practitioners, *Conflict Resolution Quarterly*, Volume 23, Number 3, pp. 383–404, p. 390.

102. UNCITRAL Draft ODR Procedural Rules 2014 (A/CN.9/WG.III/WP.133), Article 9(2).

103. UNCITRAL Draft ODR Procedural Rules 2014 (A/CN.9/WG.III/WP.133), Article 9(3).

104. Regulation (EU) No 910/2014 of the European Parliament and of the Council of 23 July 2014 on electronic identification and trust services for electronic transactions in the internal market and repealing Directive 1999/93/EC, OJ L 257, 28.8.2014, pp. 73–114.

105. Directive 2013/11/EU of the European Parliament and of the Council of 21 May 2013 on alternative dispute resolution for consumer disputes and amending Regulation (EC) No 2006/2004 and Directive 2009/22/EC (Directive on consumer ADR), OJ L 165, 18.6.2013, pp. 63–79, Recital (55).

106. Regulation (EU) No 524/2013 of the European Parliament and of the Council of 21 May 2013 on online dispute resolution for consumer disputes and amending Regulation (EC) No 2006/2004 and Directive 2009/22/EC (Regulation on consumer ODR), OJ L 165, 18.6.2013, pp. 1–12, Recital (16).

2.1.8.5 Security

Security is another core issue for the use of ODR systems or services, because it reflects not only the safety and reliability of users' identity but also the protection for confidential information. In the online environment, it is important to ensure that the person one is dealing with is who he/she claims to be, and that all electronic records are kept safe with integrity. Legal and technological measures have been continuously developed, including qualified advanced electronic signatures, electronic seals, electronic authentication certificates, time stamps and other trust services.[107] In ODR systems, qualified advanced/digital signatures shall be required to sign legal and evidential documents, verify the owner of documents and protect confidential electronic communications. The ODR systems shall ensure the confidentiality and integrity of information submitted on the ODR platforms, by employing appropriate technological measures. For example, the Secure Multipurpose Internet Mail Exchange Protocol (S/MIME) and the Pretty Good Privacy (PGP) may be used to secure email communications, whilst Transport Layer Security (TLS) and other cryptographic tools may be deployed to provide secure communications and data transmissions on the ODR platforms. When video conferencing is used for online hearings, it is possible that sensitive information and data communicated across internal and external networks is susceptible to hackers. Thus, security protocols shall be in place for data storage and data transmissions. It may be safer to encrypt and store data in an offsite network separate from internal networks. In the EU, the Regulation on Consumer ODR requires that

> the ODR platform should enable the secure interchange of data with ADR entities and respect the underlying principles of the European Interoperability Framework adopted pursuant to Decision 2004/387/EC of the European Parliament and of the Council of 21 April 2004 on interoperable delivery of pan-European eGovernment services to public administrations, businesses and citizens (IDABC).[108]

2.1.8.6 Enforceability

Enforceability of ODR refers to the enforcement of arbitral awards or mediation settlement agreements. It was suggested that 'the enforcement in court of mediation and negotiation outcomes, on the one hand, and of arbitral awards, on the other hand, follows different procedures. In a nutshell, one may say that the enforcement of the former requires an ordinary court action, whilst the enforcement of the latter can be granted in summary proceedings without a review of the merits of the award.'[109]

---

107. See for example, Regulation (EU) No 910/2014 of the European Parliament and of the Council of 23 July 2014 on electronic identification and trust services for electronic transactions in the internal market and repealing Directive 1999/93/EC, OJ L 257, 28.8.2014, pp. 73–114.
108. EU Regulation on Consumer ODR 2013, Recital (20).
109. Kaufmann-Kohler, G. & Schultz, T. (2004), Online Dispute Resolution: Challenges for Contemporary Justice (Netherlands: Kluwer Law International, 2004), p. 211.

With regard to enforceability of agreements resulting from mediation (often known as 'settlement agreements'), it is understood that a settlement agreement is a contract that does not have the binding force of a judgment.[110] Parties may enforce a settlement agreement by bringing a contract action in court, obtaining a judgment, and possibly starting enforcement of judgment proceedings.[111] The EC Directive on Mediation provides that

> Member States shall ensure that it is possible for the parties, or for one of them with the explicit consent of the others, to request that the content of a written agreement resulting from mediation be made enforceable. The content of such an agreement shall be made enforceable unless, in the case in question, either the content of that agreement is contrary to the law of the Member State where the request is made or the law of that Member State does not provide for its enforceability.[112]

It further stipulates that 'the content of the agreement may be made enforceable by a court or other competent authority in a judgment or decision or in an authentic instrument in accordance with the law of the Member State where the request is made.'[113] The EC Directive on Mediation is silent on the validity of an electronic mediation agreement and an electronic settlement agreement. In the light of relevant legislation concerning electronic records, both electronic mediation agreements and settlement agreements shall be valid, if parties have given their consent to them by electronic signatures and that those agreements are kept on a durable medium. A valid electronic mediation agreement shall be enforced if the parties show their strong intention to form that mediation agreement.[114] An electronic mediation settlement agreement can be recognised and enforced by a court or other competent authority in a judgment or decision or in an authentic instrument.[115]

With regard to arbitration, an arbitration agreement concluded by any electronic means shall have the same effect as a traditional arbitration agreement in writing if it meets form requirements. An electronic arbitration agreement shall be signed by parties (e.g. using qualified digital signatures) and kept in a durable medium for future reference. Likewise, an arbitral award concluded by electronic means shall also be recognised and enforced as a traditional arbitral award, unless there are procedural irregularities and mistakes during the arbitral proceedings. This will be discussed in detail in Chapter 6.

---

110. Kaufmann-Kohler, G. & Schultz, T. (2004), Online Dispute Resolution: Challenges for Contemporary Justice (Netherlands: Kluwer Law International, 2004), p. 211.
111. American Bar Association Task Force on E-Commerce and ADR, 'Addressing Disputes in Electronic Commerce', pp. 35–38.
112. Directive 2008/52/EC of the European Parliament and of the Council of 21 May 2008 on certain aspects of mediation in civil and commercial matters, OJ L 136, 24.5.2008, pp. 3–8, Article 6(1).
113. EC Directive on Mediation 2008, Article 6(2).
114. Wang, F. (2010), Internet Jurisdiction and Choice of Law: Legal Practices in the EU, US and China (Cambridge: Cambridge University Press, 2010), p. 170.
115. Wang, F. (2010), Internet Jurisdiction and Choice of Law: Legal Practices in the EU, US and China (Cambridge: Cambridge University Press, 2010), p. 170.

2.2 Purposes and structure of this book

This book discusses legislative movement and practice in online arbitration with the main focus on the laws in the EU, UK, US and China. It critically evaluates the most recent legislation and legislative development, such as the EC Directive on Consumer ADR; the EU Regulation on Consumer ODR; and the UNCITRAL Draft ODR Procedural Rules. It seeks for the establishment of a harmonised legal framework and best practices for online arbitration procedures, taking into consideration the development of arbitration institutional rules and their online dispute resolution services across the globe. It provides interdisciplinary research based at the cutting edge of technology, management and law, which offers insights into legislative reform and ODR technological development in the future. The systematic legal and technological measures proposed in this book can be used as a framework for the design of both basic and intelligent/ advanced ODR systems. The intertwined understanding of law and technology would aid the working practices of a professional working within this discipline as it may help professionals to better engage in the online arbitration procedures and enhance the validity of outcomes according to specific legal requirements. Overall, the book provides a methodical theory and constructive advice on best practices of online arbitration and bridges the gap of understanding between law and technology; and of knowledge between theoretical research and industrial practice. It seeks to provide solutions to promote the cooperation and recognition of online arbitration practice for cross-border commercial and consumer disputes.

PART II

PROCEDURAL RULES FOR ONLINE ARBITRATION

CHAPTER 3

Online arbitration procedures

3.1 The further development of general ODR regulations

Online dispute resolution (ODR) – a concept building upon alternative dispute resolution (ADR) and with the deployment of electronic communications – largely relies on traditional ADR regulations, especially in the early stage of its development. However, it is argued that ADR itself is a low governance field because in most countries ADR practitioners are often unlicensed and the ADR field is mostly unregulated.[1] In order to induce trust and promote the use of ADR, ADR is often embedded in courts where ADR divisions are monitored and regulated by courts. It is also a common practice that ADR is implanted in other wider frameworks (organisations, communities, professional organisations) that seek to hold their members to certain standards.[2] In the US the joint promulgation of Model Standards of Conduct for Mediators by the American Arbitration Association (AAA), American Bar Association (ABA) and Association for Conflict Resolution (ACR) in 2005 is a good example.[3]

Since 2010 there have been two major developments of general ODR procedures by international and regional organisations across the globe: one is the United Nations Commission on International Trade Law (UNCITRAL) Draft ODR Procedural Rules and the other is the EU Regulation on Consumer ODR (known as the 'ODR Regulation').[4] There are also online arbitration rules provided by public national arbitration organisations or institutes such as the China International Economic and Trade Arbitration Commission (CIETAC) Online

---

1. Ebner, N. and Zeleznikow, J. (2016), No sheriff in town: Governance for the ODR field, *Negotiation Journal* 32(4), p. 17.
2. Ebner, N. and Zeleznikow, J. (2016), No sheriff in town: Governance for the ODR field, *Negotiation Journal* 32(4), p. 17.
3. Model standards of Conduct for Mediators, by the American Arbitration Association (AAA), American Bar Association (ABA) and Association for Conflict Resolution (ACR), September 2005, www.americanbar.org/content/dam/aba/migrated/dispute/documents/model_standards_conduct_april2007.authcheckdam.pdf (last accessed 30 March 2017).
4. Regulation (EU) No 524/2013 of the European Parliament and of the Council of 21 May 2013 on online dispute resolution for consumer disputes and amending Regulation (EC) No 2006/2004 and Directive 2009/22/EC (Regulation on consumer ODR), OJ L 165, 18.6.2013, p. 1–12.

Arbitration Rules.[5] The UNCITRAL Draft ODR Procedural Rules, the EU Regulation on Consumer ODR and the CIETAC Online Arbitration Rules share the same virtues in that they regulate the process of ODR proceedings in general from the commencement of ODR proceedings to the settlement of disputes. They are different in that UNCITRAL draft ODR Procedural Rules provide legal and technical process guidance to resolve cross-border B2B and B2C disputes by any dispute resolution bodies on any ODR platforms, whilst EU Regulation on Consumer ODR provides specific process rules to resolve B2C disputes across Europe on a single ODR platform by ADR entities supervised and monitored by national competent authorities. The CIETAC Online Arbitration Rules provide an internal organisational ODR process to resolve disputes arising from economic and trade transactions of a contractual or non-contractual nature by CIETAC. Since 2004 the Arbitration Court in the Czech Republic has enacted 'additional procedures for on-line arbitration (on-line Rules)' including definition, principles, calculation of time period, statement of claim, notification and place of arbitral award referring to online arbitration.[6]

While all of these rules are helpful in that they promote the confidence of using ODR to resolve disputes by providing a certain level of standards in the ODR process, there is still scope for improvement in terms of harmonised codes of conduct of ODR service providers and neutrals. For example, e-commerce service providers may integrate an ODR system into their online marketplaces to offer their customers out-of-court dispute resolution service. If online redress processes were imposed inappropriately, it would impede consumers' right of access to justice.[7] In the Court of Justice of the European Union (CJEU) the joint cases of *Rosalba Alassini v Telecom Italia SpA (C-317/08)*, *Filomena Califano v Wind SpA (C-318/08)*, *Lucia Anna Giorgia Iacono v Telecom Italia SpA (C-319/08)* and *Multiservice Srl v Telecom Italia SpA (C-320/08)*, the Court interpreted the 'principles of equivalence and effectiveness or the principle of effective judicial protection' as national legislation can impose an out-of-court settlement procedure to electronic communications disputes as long as that procedure does not result in a decision that is binding on the parties and cause a substantial delay for parties to bring legal proceedings.[8] A mandatory out-of-

---

5. China International Economic and Trade Arbitration Commission (CIETAC) Online Arbitration Rules, the first version was adopted in 2009 and the second version was adopted in 2014 (effective as from 1 January 2015), available at www.cietac.org/index.php?m=Article&a=show&id=2770&l=en (last accessed 30 March 2017). See also www.cietacodr.org/defaultonlinearbi.html (last accessed 30 March 2017).

6. Additional Procedures for On-line Arbitration (On-line Rules), the Arbitration Court, Czech Republic, available at https://arbitrationlaw.com/sites/default/files/free_pdfs/Czech%20On-line%20Arbitration%20Rules.pdf (last accessed 30 March 2017).

7. Cortes, P. and Lodder, A. R. (2014), Consumer Dispute Resolution Goes Online: Reflections on the Evolution of European Law for Out-of-Court Redress, *Maastricht Journal of European and Comparative Law*, Volume 1, p. 21.

8. Joined Cases C-317/08, C-318/08, C-319/08 and C-320/08, *Rosalba Alassini v Telecom Italia SpA* (C-317/08), *Filomena Califano v Wind SpA* (C-318/08), *Lucia Anna Giorgia Iacono v Telecom*

court settlement procedure may suspend a period for the time-barring of claims but should not give rise to costs – or only give rise to very low costs – for the parties.[9] Imposing the settlement procedure to be carried out only by electronic means may impede end-users from exercising their rights.[10] Thus, a mandatory out-of-court procedure is allowed provided that it does not force consumers to use electronic means as the only means to resolve the disputes and prevent the parties from accessing the courts after unsuccessful conciliation.

In Europe, in the light of the European Parliament Resolution of 25 October 2011 on Alternative Dispute Resolution in Civil, Commercial and Family Matters (2011/2117(INI)), the e-Justice portal has provided a simple online filing system for the European Small Claims Procedure, which include four standard web-based small claim forms for users. They are Form A – Claim form, Form B – Request by the court or tribunal to complete and/or rectify the claim form, Form C – Answer form and Form D – Certificate concerning a judgment in the European small claims procedure.[11] Users can complete these forms online by clicking one of the links to those forms. Users will be able to fill in a form, save a draft and upload it in the system.[12]

With the deployment of the EU single ODR portal, it is arguable that the quality of ODR service providers (that is so-called 'ADR entities' or 'dispute resolution bodies' in the Regulation) is harmonised as they are supervised and monitored by national competent authorities among member states. Subsequently, the quality of ODR neutrals are harmonised as they are qualified by approved ADR entities on the list on the ODR portal. However, without a harmonised code of conduct of ODR service providers and neutrals across Europe, national competent authorities may have different standards for interpreting the abstract requirements of the standard of dispute resolution bodies under EU Law. Under EU Law, dispute resolution bodies must be transparent, independent, impartial, fair and effective. The EU ODR portal only lists dispute resolution bodies on its site once they have been approved by their own EU country.[13] It is worth noting that on the single ODR platform, both consumers and traders can manage

---

Italia SpA (C-319/08) and *Multiservice Srl v Telecom Italia SpA* (C-320/08), Judgment of the Court (Fourth Chamber), 18 March 2010, para. 68.

9. Joined Cases C-317/08, C-318/08, C-319/08 and C-320/08, *Rosalba Alassini v Telecom Italia SpA* (C-317/08), *Filomena Califano v Wind SpA* (C-318/08), *Lucia Anna Giorgia Iacono v Telecom Italia SpA* (C-319/08) and *Multiservice Srl v Telecom Italia SpA* (C-320/08), Judgment of the Court (Fourth Chamber), 18 March 2010, para. 68.

10. Joined Cases C-317/08, C-318/08, C-319/08 and C-320/08, *Rosalba Alassini v Telecom Italia SpA* (C-317/08), *Filomena Califano v Wind SpA* (C-318/08), *Lucia Anna Giorgia Iacono v Telecom Italia SpA* (C-319/08) and *Multiservice Srl v Telecom Italia SpA* (C-320/08), Judgment of the Court (Fourth Chamber), 18 March 2010, para. 58.

11. EU e-Justice Portal, available at https://e-justice.europa.eu/content_small_claims_forms-177-en.do (last accessed 30 March 2017).

12. EU e-Justice Portal, available at https://e-justice.europa.eu/content_small_claims_forms-177-en.do (last accessed 30 March 2017).

13. General Questions on the EU ODR Portal, available at https://webgate.ec.europa.eu/odr/main/?event=main.help.faq (last accessed 30 March 2017).

a complaint, agree on a dispute resolution body and exchange information,[14] but have no control over whether the chosen dispute resolution body will conduct the procedure through the ODR platform. This is because according to Article 10(d) of the EU Regulation on Consumer ODR, an ADR entity that has agreed to deal with a dispute shall not be required to conduct the ADR procedure through the ODR platform.[15] However, this seems to contradict the factsheet issued by the Commission that 'the ADR entity handles the case entirely online and reaches an outcome in 90 days'[16] if the wording of 'entirely online' includes the ADR procedure. According to the EU Regulation on Consumer ODR, an ADR entity shall at least confirm the date of receipt of the complete complaint file and the subject matter of the dispute or transmit the refusal to the ODR platform; and, upon the conclusion of the dispute, transmit to the ODR platform the date of conclusion of the ADR procedure as well as its result.[17] It appears that on the EU ODR platform, the ADR procedure (in particular the online hearing) conducted by the chosen ADR entity is blind to both consumers and traders. Both consumers and traders may not be able to choose a specific type of ODR such as negotiation, mediation or arbitration. In practice, for example, in the UK, ADR entities such as Financial Ombudsman Service employ ADR officials (similar to neutrals) to deal with disputes. This is in line with the UK Alternative Dispute Resolution for Consumer Disputes (Competent Authorities and Information) Regulations 2015 and the Alternative Dispute Resolution for Consumer Disputes (Amendment) Regulations 2015,[18] which implement the EU Regulation on Consumer ODR. According to the UK legislation, 'ADR official' means 'an individual who (solely or with other persons) is involved in the provision of alternative dispute resolution procedures offered by an ADR entity, or ADR applicant, whether as a case handler or in a management capacity'.[19] It appears that from the UK experience, consumers and traders do not seem to have an option to choose their own ADR officials (neutrals) as they are offered by an ADR entity on the EU ODR portal. The design of the EU ODR portal is for

---

14. ODR User Guide (Version 2016/11/21), available at https://webgate.ec.europa.eu/odr/userguide/pdf/MA/userguide-en.pdf (last accessed 30 March 2017).

15. EU Regulation on Consumer ODR 2013, Article 10(d).

16. Settling consumer disputes online, European Commission, Factsheet, January 2016, available at http://ec.europa.eu/consumers/solving_consumer_disputes/docs/adr-odr.factsheet_web.pdf (last accessed 30 March 2017).

17. Commission Implementing Regulation (EU) 2015/1051 of 1 July 2015 on the modalities for the exercise of the functions of the online dispute resolution platform, on the modalities of the electronic complaint form and on the modalities of the cooperation between contact points provided for in Regulation (EU) No 524/2013 of the European Parliament and of the Council on online dispute resolution for consumer disputes, OJ. L 171/1, 2 July 2015, available at http://eur-lex.europa.eu/legal-content/EN/TXT/PDF/?uri=CELEX:32015R1051&from=EN (last accessed 30 March 2017).

18. The Alternative Dispute Resolution for Consumer Disputes (Amendment) Regulations 2015, 2015 No. 1392, available at www.legislation.gov.uk/uksi/2015/1392/pdfs/uksi_20151392_en.pdf (last accessed 30 March 2017).

19. The Alternative Dispute Resolution for Consumer Disputes (Amendment) Regulations 2015, 2015 No. 1392, reg 5.

simplified ODR processes – that is, when consumers and traders use the ODR portal, it means that they are bound by the EU Regulation on Consumer ODR and other relevant legislation. They only need to agree on a dispute resolution body instead of agreeing on a whole range of dispute resolution issues such as procedural rules, applicable law, types of dispute resolution, assisted online negotiators, online mediators and online arbitrators in a complete ODR environment. If the EU ODR portal offers a complete ODR environment in the future, the Regulation on Consumer ODR needs to be revised to take into consideration all new legal and technical elements.

Moreover, in response to the fast development of automated technology, there is need to foresee legal challenges to robotic ODR service. Taking advantage of technologies including cloud computing, big data and automated computing, robotic negotiators, mediators and arbitrators may become a reality. It is possible that robotic negotiators, mediators and arbitrators may become more advanced than human negotiators, mediators and arbitrators. This has happened in the gaming industry. Dong Kim was one of the four professional poker players defeated by the AI program in poker game but won the prize for the best human player.[20] Thus, it is vital that regulations and law adopt technologically neutral concepts in order to keep steady pace alongside technological developments in the fast-moving global society.

3.2 Choice of service providers

ODR service providers are established in different ways across the globe. Some can be just private companies, which either build ODR systems or buy ODR systems to provide customer dispute resolution services. Others may be state-owned organisations, such as the EU ODR portal. There are no harmonised international standards as to the minimum technological and legal requirements as to the establishment of ODR service providers.

It is noted that most of the early ODR service providers, and many of the current ones, are private companies whose management team behind the company are not personally identified or even named at all. The majority of ODR service providers provide only online negotiation and online mediation and have no substantive information of the identity, qualifications, or training of their neutrals (assisted negotiators and mediators). These private companies often do not publish their codes of practice and disclose the technology that is used in the process. There is no precise explanation of what service is provided, by whom, and how.[21] A lack of transparency – of actors, standards, technology, and process – may diminish users' confidence in ODR services being accountable

---

20. AI program beats humans in poker game, BBC News on 31 January 2017, available at www.bbc.co.uk/news/technology-38812530 (last accessed 30 March 2017).
21. Ebner, N. and Zeleznikow, J. (2016), No sheriff in town: Governance for the ODR field, *Negotiation Journal* 32(4), p. 14.

and trustworthy, and consequently weaken clients' sense that the process is fair and secure, which are critical issues in ODR.[22]

Because of a lack of standardisation, there are a number of key factors that may help clients to make decisions about which ODR service providers may be more trustworthy than others. For example, the first possibility is that if private ODR service providers are established for a long time, some of them may gain good market reputation through their long-time practice.

The second possibility is that if private ODR service providers are newly established, they can also gain trust by embedding their service with trustmarks. ODR trustmark schemes can be used as one of the benchmarks to choose competent ODR service providers. The trustmark service centres certify that ODR service providers meet agreed-upon ODR standards. A trustmark scheme may endorse the quality of service areas such as the practitioner's character, knowledge, skills, education, professional training and experience. When there was no EU legislation directly regulating trustmarks, trustmarks were addressed by a comprehensive set of rules protecting consumers in e-commerce.[23] In 2014 the EU Regulation on Electronic Identification and Trust Services for Electronic Transactions in the Internal Market was adopted, establishing a set of general legal frameworks including a framework for the use of trust services to the public that have effects on third parties.[24] The Regulation defines 'trust service' as

> an electronic service normally provided for remuneration which consists of: (a) the creation, verification, and validation of electronic signatures, electronic seals or electronic time stamps, electronic registered delivery services and certificates related to those services, or (b) the creation, verification and validation of certificates for website authentication; or (c) the preservation of electronic signatures, seals or certificates related to those services.[25]

There are different types of trust services, namely qualified and non-qualified. The purpose of the establishment of qualified trust services and qualified trust service provider is to ensure a high level of security of trust services and products[26] following common essential supervision requirements in member

---

22. Ebner, N. and Zeleznikow, J. (2015), Fairness, Trust, and Security in Online Dispute Resolution, *Hamline Journal of Public Law and Policy*, Vol. 36, No. 2, pp. 143–60.

23. Possibilities and opportunities of creating a pan-European trustmark for e-commerce, 28 June 2012, by Civic Consulting, available at www.europarl.europa.eu/document/activities/cont/201206/20 120628ATT47908/20120628ATT47908EN.pdf (last accessed 30 March 2017).

24. Regulation (EU) No 910/2014 of the European Parliament and of the Council of 23 July 2014 on electronic identification and trust services for electronic transactions in the internal market and repealing Directive 1999/93/EC, OJ L 257, 28.8.2014, pp. 73–114, Recital (21).

25. Regulation (EU) No 910/2014 of the European Parliament and of the Council of 23 July 2014 on electronic identification and trust services for electronic transactions in the internal market and repealing Directive 1999/93/EC, Article 3(6).

26. Regulation (EU) No 910/2014 of the European Parliament and of the Council of 23 July 2014 on electronic identification and trust services for electronic transactions in the internal market and repealing Directive 1999/93/EC, Recital (28).

states;[27] and to ensure due diligence, transparency and accountability of their operations and services.[28] Accordingly, an EU trust mark can be created to identify the qualified trust services provided by qualified trust service providers,[29] though the use of an EU trust mark by qualified trust service providers should be voluntary.[30] In the EU, there are trust marks provided by private companies such as EMOTA[31] and Ecommerce Europe.[32] Ecommerce Europe has liaised with its 19 national associations in compliance with its self-regulation – the Ecommerce Europe Code of Conduct.[33] It is noteworthy that when trust services are accredited and supervised by competent authorities, they may be better monitored and self-regulated. For instance, as discussed before, in Europe on 15 February 2016, the European Commission established an Online Dispute Resolution (ODR) portal for use by consumers located in the European Union to settle their domestic or cross-border online purchase disputes out of court.[34] ADR entities can gain approval on the EU ODR portal. Once approved, qualified ADR entities are listed on the EU ODR portal. There are obligations for online traders to provide a link to the ODR platform.[35] The EU ODR portal can be considered as a qualified trusted service approved by the European Commission.

The third possibility is that ODR service providers may form a partnership with a well-reputed traditional dispute resolution bodies; for example, in the US Cybersettle, established in 1996, has formed an alliance with the American Arbitration Association (AAA) for online mediation services.

The fourth possibility is that ODR service providers may collaborate with successful e-commerce marketplaces to provide their customers exclusive services. For example, before eBay's Resolution Centre was established, SquareTrade

---

27. Regulation (EU) No 910/2014 of the European Parliament and of the Council of 23 July 2014 on electronic identification and trust services for electronic transactions in the internal market and repealing Directive 1999/93/EC, Recital (34).

28. Regulation (EU) No 910/2014 of the European Parliament and of the Council of 23 July 2014 on electronic identification and trust services for electronic transactions in the internal market and repealing Directive 1999/93/EC, Recital (35).

29. Regulation (EU) No 910/2014 of the European Parliament and of the Council of 23 July 2014 on electronic identification and trust services for electronic transactions in the internal market and repealing Directive 1999/93/EC, Recital (47).

30. Regulation (EU) No 910/2014 of the European Parliament and of the Council of 23 July 2014 on electronic identification and trust services for electronic transactions in the internal market and repealing Directive 1999/93/EC, Recital (47).

31. EMOTA trustmarks launched on1 July 2015, available at http://europeantrustmark.eu/fileadmin/emota_content/documents/EMOTA_Press_Release_Trust_Mark_Launch_010715.pdf (last accessed 30 March 2017).

32. Ecommerce Europe, available at www.ecommerce-europe.eu/ (last accessed 30 March 2017).

33. Ecommerce Europe, available at www.ecommerce-europe.eu/ (last accessed 30 March 2017). UK is not one of the 19 national associations.

34. European Commission – Press release, Solving disputes online: New platform for consumers and traders, Brussels, 15 February 2016, available at http://europa.eu/rapid/press-release_IP-16-297_en.htm (last accessed 30 March 2017).

35. Alternative and Online Dispute Resolution (ADR/ODR), available at http://ec.europa.eu/consumers/solving_consumer_disputes/non-judicial_redress/adr-odr/index_en.htm (last accessed 30 March 2017).

collaborated with eBay offering eBay users dispute resolution with a fast process that generally took ten days.[36]

The fifth possibility is to choose ODR service providers offered by international organisations or approved by dispute resolution organisations specialising in certain dispute resolution services. For example, the World Intellectual Property Organisation (WIPO) Arbitration and Mediation Centre is widely recognised as particularly appropriate for technology, entertainment and other disputes involving intellectual property; and approved by the Internet Cooperation for Assigned Names and Numbers (ICANN) as one of the leading dispute resolution service providers for disputes arising out of the abusive registration and use of Internet domain names.[37] WIPO offers a case administration facility called the WIPO Electronic Case Facility (WIPO ECAF), which allows for secure filing, storing and retrieval of case-related submissions in a web-based electronic docket, by parties, neutral(s) and the Centre from anywhere in the world; and facilitates case management by providing, in addition to the online docket, a case overview, time tracking and finance information.[38]

With regard to choice of online arbitration service providers, there are a number of additional factors that need to be taken into consideration in addition to the above general points. There are not many online arbitration service providers in a private/commercial model (that is private companies) across the globe as online arbitration involves more formal and complicated procedures compared with negotiation and mediation. It is hard for private companies to survive even if they employ experienced arbitrators. For example, eQuibbly, established in 2012, was one of only a few ODR services in North America focused exclusively on online arbitration where former trial judges and experienced arbitration attorneys arbitrated cases entirely online. eQuibbly ceased operation in 2016 as there was not enough demand for online arbitration.[39] As binding arbitration means giving up going to a court, dispute parties may be more reluctant to use private online arbitration sites in particular for disputes between traders. Thus, when users chose an online arbitration service, it is preferable to choose established public and not-for-profit ADR organisations. The majority of traditional ADR organisations such as AAA offer arbitration service partially via electronic communications. That is, ADR organisations usually accept communications via emails, cross-platform instant messaging application and their video conferencing. Some ADR organisations even offer users filing a

---

36. Dispute Resolution Overview, available at http://pages.ebay.com/services/buyandsell/disputeres.html (last accessed 30 March 2017).
37. WIPO Arbitration and Mediation Centre, available at www.wipo.int/amc/en/center/background.html (last accessed 30 March 2017).
38. WIPO Arbitration and Mediation Centre, available at www.wipo.int/amc/en/center/background.html (last accessed 30 March 2017).
39. Online Dispute Resolution Site eQuibbly Shuts Down, 23 March 2016, available at www.lawsitesblog.com/2016/03/online-dispute-resolution-site-equibbly-shuts-down.html (last accessed 30 March 2017).

case online on their online filing platform and online administration tools. For example, AAA offers an online claim filing system called AAA WebFile service where clients can file claims, make payments, perform online case management, access rules and procedures, electronically transfer documents, select neutrals, use a case-customised message board and check the status of their case. The functions of AAA WebFile are similar to the EU ODR portal in that they are both case filing and management systems, though the European Commission considers the file management system as an ODR platform. On 5 July 2016, AAA also introduced online À La Carte Services that permit parties to use various services as stand-alone procedures.[40] Currently, À La Carte Services include Arbitrator Select: List Only or List and Appointment Services; Arbitrator Challenge Review Procedures for Non-Administered Arbitrations; CaseXplorer® Arbitration™; Judicial Settlement Conference; Optional Appellate Arbitration Rules and Hearing Room Rentals.[41] CaseXplorer® Arbitration™ is an online case analysis tool developed in conjunction with DecisionQuest, a leading jury and trial consulting firm where experienced arbitrators not associated with cases offer their opinions/insights to attorneys and businesses with objective evaluation and feedback on the strengths and weaknesses of their arbitration cases.[42] This tool intends to help shaping clients' case strategies and leading to settlement. On the online CaseXplorer Arbitration platform, users need to select a panel of three or five arbitrators by keyword, expertise and locale; and provide in writing a set of facts, legal arguments, and questions. Then users should receive a consolidated written report of each arbitrator's views within three to four days.[43] Since 2011 AAA has also introduced special ODR service for manufacturers and suppliers, which is called the ICDR Manufacturer/Supplier Online Dispute Resolution Protocol (MSODR).[44]

Parties may prefer to choose an ODR service provider that provides the online arbitration process entirely online. Currently there are only a few public and not-for-profit ADR organisations offering online arbitration platforms that conduct the arbitration procedure entirely online such as the CIETAC Online Arbitration Platform; however, there is no disclosure as to how their systems actually function and work in terms of legal measures, appropriate technologies and competent neutrals. According to the CIETAC Online Arbitration Rules, unless the parties agree to hold oral hearings, or the arbitral tribunal decides it is necessary to do

---

40. News Alert American Arbitration Association launches À La Carte services Resources, available at www.adr.org/aaa/ShowPDF?doc=ADRSTAGE2041699 (last accessed 30 March 2017).
41. À La Carte Services, 'available at http://info.adr.org/a-la-carte-services/ (last accessed 30 March 2017).
42. CaseXplorer® Arbitration™, available at http://info.adr.org/cxa/ (last accessed 30 March 2017).
43. CaseXplorer® Arbitration™ online process, available at http://info.adr.org/cxa/ (last accessed 30 March 2017).
44. American Arbitration Association (AAA) International Centre for Dispute Resolution (ICDR) Manufacturer/Supplier Online Dispute Resolution Program and ICDR Manufacturer/Supplier Online Dispute Resolution Protocol (MSODR), amended and effective 1 July 2011.

so, the arbitral tribunal shall hear the case on a documents-only basis in accordance with the written materials and evidence submitted by the parties.[45] It also indicates 'where an oral hearing is to be held, it shall be conducted by means of online oral hearings such as video conferencing or other electronic or computer communication forms. The arbitral tribunal may also decide to hold traditional oral hearings in person based on the specific circumstances of each case.'[46] In light of these rules, it is possible that the CIETAC Online Arbitration Platform may not provide an integrated online hearing system either. It has been argued that conducting an online arbitration procedure exclusively online as opposed to using information technology facilities partially is usually feasible in consumer and domain names disputes. Arbitration procedures for other complex disputes such as investment arbitration are more likely to use information technology facilities for communications between the arbitrators and the parties, as well as the dispute resolution provider if any.[47] There is significant scope for improvement for future integrated ODR platforms for all disputes that conduct the process entirely online including online hearing. Appropriate legal and technological measures need to be built in to ensure due process in the ODR environment.

Nevertheless, from a technical perspective, before users choose an ODR service provider, they should always enquire as to their technological measures to check whether their standards are acceptable. The UK Bar Council provides a good example of guidelines concerning IT issues within professional practice and ethics that can be learned from ODR service providers or ADR entities, though the Council provides a unique legal profession of specialist advocates and advisers service rather than ADR service.[48] The Bar Council IT issues guidelines include matters such as back-up work on users; bring your own device (BYOD) policy; cloud computing; data protection: notification – the obligation to register; email guidelines; hard drive disposal; information security; Internet security; mobile device security; online arbitration and mediation and secure email.[49]

In the web-based ODR environment, it is anticipated that users entering data into an ODR system will not require offline access. An appropriate deployment of an ODR system might be to use a SaaS (software as a service) model in which the system is hosted in a central location and accessed via a thin client. Such systems allow clients to utilise cheap hardware, whilst central servers can be provisioned according to need. Providers will typically offer a subscription service rather than permanent licences. The crucial issue here is how to store a backup

---

45. CIETAC Online Arbitration Rules 2015, Article 32. Available at www.cietac.org/index.php?m=Article&a=show&id=2770&l=en (last accessed 30 March 2017).
46. CIETAC Online Arbitration Rules 2015, Article 33.
47. Mirèze Philippe, ODR Redress System for Consumer Disputes: Clarifications, UNCITRAL Works & EU Regulation on ODR, *International Journal of Online Dispute Resolution* 2014 (1) 1, pp. 57–69, p. 59.
48. The Bar Council Professional Practice and Ethics, available at www.barcouncil.org.uk/practice-ethics/professional-practice-and-ethics/it-issues/ (last accessed 30 March 2017).
49. The Bar Council IT Issues, available at www.barcouncil.org.uk/practice-ethics/professional-practice-and-ethics/it-issues/ (last accessed 30 March 2017).

of ODR work. In recent years, cloud technology allows 'access to computing resources (storage, processing and software), on demand, via a network'.[50] That is, the cloud service is available and accessible anywhere for remote storage and processing of data. This type of technologic innovation and optimisation may change the way an organisation or individual works, communicates with each other and shares information, because access to computing resources has shifted from an internal network to a public network in particular in the public cloud environment.[51] If ODR service providers use the cloud service for storage, the backup may be made automatically at specified intervals of time. If so, files may need to be encrypted for security because if ODR case files are stored on a server overseas, it is possible that those files containing personal data may be disclosed by law enforcement or by accident. For example, if the ODR service providers are registered in the EU, storing case files in a server based in any country outside the protection of the EU data protection regime may not be legal unless it can be satisfied that the protection put in place meets the standards of protection in their home countries where ODR services are registered.[52]

In addition, ODR service providers may permit their employees such as ADR officials or neutrals to use their personal IT equipment for work purposes. This may be an attractive proposition for companies, but requires robust security policies to mitigate against data loss. Moreover, disposal of IT equipment can lead to the possibility of data loss, even in a cloud computing environment where data is hosted centrally. ISO/IEC 27001:2013 provides asset management and disposal standards, to ensure that personal information is wiped clean from unwanted equipment. With regard to Internet security for ODR services, it is standard practice for devices to connect to a private network, behind a firewall that can block or accept traffic depending on a set of rules. This can reduce the possibility of loss of personal data arising from both targeted and widespread random attacks from outside the company. Use of anti-virus software can further mitigate operating system and third-party software vulnerabilities from within the private network. Depending on the nature of personal data, security policies can be implemented to prevent use of USB memory sticks and prevent installation of unapproved software. If dispute parties conduct their ODR process using their mobile devices, questions may be raised concerning mobile device security. ODR service providers' company policy should specify which personal data, if any, is accessible from mobile devices. Modern smartphones and tablet PCs commonly encrypt user data, making access difficult if the device is lost or stolen. A suitable length password or PIN should be set to prevent unauthorised access.

---

50. Guidance on the Use of Cloud Computing, UK Information Commissioner's Office, 20121002 Version 1.1, October 2012, available at https://ico.org.uk/media/for-organisations/documents/1540/cloud_computing_guidance_for_organisations.pdf (last accessed 30 March 2017), at 1.

51. Wang, F. (2013), Jurisdiction and Cloud Computing: Further Challenges to Internet Jurisdiction, *European Business Law Review*, Volume 24, Issue 5, pp. 589–616, p. 590.

52. The Bar Council Back up Work on your PC, available at www.barcouncil.org.uk/media/486487/back_up_work_on_your_pc.pdf (last accessed 30 March 2017).

With regard to secure email communications for ODR processes, depending on the nature of the personal data, a standard email account hosted internally or externally in the cloud may be appropriate. For highly sensitive data, there are dedicated providers of secure email, such as NHSmail in the UK.[53] Last, but not least, with regard to software maintenance, ODR service providers have to assess the risks and associated costs in updating the operating system. Proprietary software may require modifications to remain fully functional. Third-party software may need updating. Information technology governance also involves the products themselves. The computing industry has developed codes of testability and of quality control to ensure software engineering standards.[54]

3.3 Choice of procedure rules

There are different types of procedural rules that parties may choose for their dispute resolution process. The first options are international procedural rules that include legal sources (binding law) and supernational sources (non-binding rules).[55] For example, as discussed before, UNCITRAL had been working on draft ODR Procedural Rules between 2010 and 2016, which were subsequently concluded as Technical Notes on Online Dispute Resolution (2016). There are also the UNCITRAL Model Law on International Commercial Arbitration (1985), the UNCITRAL Arbitration Rules (last updated in 2013) and the UNCITRAL Notes on Organizing Arbitral Proceedings (2016) upon which 'parties may agree for the conduct of arbitral proceedings arising out of their commercial relationship and are widely used in ad hoc arbitrations as well as administered arbitrations'.[56] There is no legal requirement binding on the arbitrators or the parties and imposed by the Notes,[57] which is different from the effect of the Convention on the Recognition and Enforcement of Foreign Arbitral Awards (New York, 1958) (the 'New York Convention'). Once countries have signed and ratified the Convention, it is enforced among those countries.

The second option is institutional arbitration rules. There are a wide range of specialised arbitration institutions across the globe, such as the American Arbitration Association (AAA), the International Chamber of Commerce (ICC) International Court of Arbitration and the China International Economic and Trade Arbitration Commission (CIETAC), which provide specialised arbitration procedural rules depending on the types of disputes, such as commercial disputes

---

53. See https://digital.nhs.uk/nhsmail (last accessed 30 March 2017).

54. Verhoef, C. (2007), Quantifying the effects of IT-governance rules. Science of Computer Programming, 67 (2–3): pp. 247–77.

55. Greenberg, S., Kee, C. and Weeramantry, J.R. (2011), International Commercial Arbitration (New York: Cambridge University Press, 2011), pp. 30–3.

56. UNCITRAL Arbitration Rules (last updated in 2013), available at www.uncitral.org/uncitral/en/uncitral_texts/arbitration/2010Arbitration_rules.html (last accessed 30 March 2017).

57. UNCITRAL Notes on Organizing Arbitral Proceedings (2016), available at www.uncitral.org/pdf/english/texts/arbitration/arb-notes/arb-notes-e.pdf (last accessed 30 March 2017).

or investment disputes. The majority of arbitration institutions are encouraging electronic communications and reinforcing this essence in their updated procedural rules; for example, on 4 November 2016 the ICC announced its amendments to the ICC Rules of Arbitration, which comes in force as from 1 March 2017. According to Appendix IV – Case Management Techniques – of ICC Arbitration Rules (Version 1 March 2017), online communication is considered as a good case management technique. Its Article (f) provides that 'Using telephone or video conferencing for procedural and other hearings where attendance in person is not essential and use of IT that enables online communication among the parties, the arbitral tribunal and the Secretariat of the Court.'[58] Some of the arbitration institutions have even launched supplementary online arbitration rules such as the CIETAC Online Arbitration Rules and the Russian Arbitration Association's Online Arbitration Regulation (known as 'Work of Order' in Russian) 2015.[59]

The third option is self-regulated rules. Arbitration procedural rules are often regulated by parties in an ad hoc arbitration that is not administered by an arbitration institution. Parties need to determine all aspects of the arbitration procedure by themselves including but not limited to the number of arbitrators, appointing arbitrators, process for conducting the hearing and applicable law – and agree on them. Whichever option that parties may choose, they are subject to international, regional and national arbitration procedure law. For example, in the EU parties are subject to the Regulation of Consumer ODR for consumer online purchases disputes.

3.4 Selection of online arbitrators

Traditionally, the quality of arbitration proceeding depends to a large extent on the quality, experience and skills of the arbitrators chosen. Similar to the selection of arbitrators in the traditional world, parties can also nominate or appoint online arbitrators of their choice. Parties may agree on the appointment procedure as to the number of arbitrators and how they would be appointed in their arbitration agreement. Such agreements can be generated or submitted and then signed by parties in the ODR system. In general, there are no formal qualifications required in order to act as an arbitrator. Sometimes, parties choose an engineer or other technical person whose expertise relates to the issues of the case.[60] Arbitrators appointed by arbitration institutions/commission are often subject to their appointment criteria set out by their national law. For example, according to China Arbitration Law 1995, Article 13 an arbitration commission shall appoint

---

58. Rules of Arbitration of the International Chamber of Commerce 2017, available at www.iccwbo.org/News/Articles/2016/ICC-Court-amends-its-Rules-to-enhance-transparency-and-efficiency/ (last accessed 30 March 2017).

59. The Russian Arbitration Association's Online Arbitration Regulation, available at http://arbitrations.ru/upload/medialibrary/a95/final_2016.pdf (last accessed 30 March 2017).

60. Greenberg, S., Kee, C. and Weeramantry, J.R. (2011), International Commercial Arbitration (New York: Cambridge University Press, 2011), p. 22.

its arbitrators from among righteous and upright persons. An arbitrator shall meet one of the conditions set forth below: (1) to have been engaged in arbitration work for at least eight years; (2) to have worked as a lawyer for at least eight years; (3) to have served as a judge for at least eight years; (4) to have been engaged in legal research or legal education, possessing a senior professional title; or (5) to have acquired the knowledge of law, engaged in the professional work in the field of economy and trade, etc, possessing a senior professional title or having an equivalent professional level.[61] It is important to appoint arbitrators according to the agreed procedure, otherwise the arbitral awards may be set aside according to the New York Convention and national arbitration law.[62]

In the ODR environment, in order to ensure the quality of arbitration proceeding in the online world, online arbitrators should also be familiar with the ODR system and environment that they are using. Moreover, there are various technical issues that may affect the quality of online arbitrators. The first issue is about identity theft of online arbitrators – a sole arbitrator, a panel of arbitrators, party-appointed arbitrators and chairman. All parties should be assigned unique, private usernames and should be required to choose their own personal password upon logging into the ODR system for the first time. Optionally, further validation of registration can be carried out by sending the user an email with a link that completes the registration process. It may also be advisable to log IP addresses of users to build confidence that one party is not attempting to log in to the account of another for the purpose of accessing or modifying privileged information.

The second issue is about technical obstacles on allowing multiple parties joining in the online process with only access to relevant materials by each party. For example, during the process of appointing arbitrators, the parties may nominate a third party or the arbitration institution to make the appointment of arbitrators for and on their behalf. According to the UNCITRAL Arbitration Rules, each party may be represented or assisted by persons chosen by it.[63] The parties may also nominate an appointing authority to make the necessary appointments. According to the UNCITRAL Arbitration Rules, unless the parties have already agreed on the choice of an appointing authority, a party may at any time propose the name or names of one or more institutions or persons, including the Secretary-General of the Permanent Court of Arbitration at The Hague (hereinafter called the 'PCA'), one of whom would serve as appointing authority.[64] Some ODR service software may not have such built-in functions, which make it technically impossible to have a third party play a role in the online environment. Or, if possible, confidential information may not be well kept

---

61. China Arbitration Law 1995, Article 13, available at www.wipo.int/edocs/lexdocs/laws/en/cn/cn138en.pdf (last accessed 30 March 2017).
62. New York Convention 1958, Article V. 1 (d) and China Arbitration Law 1995, Article 58(3).
63. UNCITRAL Arbitration Rules, Article 5(1).
64. UNCITRAL Arbitration Rules, Article 6(1).

in the system. A system should be designed with fine-grained access control and versioning in mind. Documents uploaded by one party will only be accessible by permitted users such as their representative or arbitrator. It should be clear by means of explicit consent for a document to be accessible to all parties. Once a document has uploaded, it should be tagged with a time stamp and version. At this point, parties with access can be given a notification that a document has become available. If subsequent revisions of the document are uploaded, the tagging will ensure that modifications cannot go unnoticed. Once all materials are available for the arbitrator to make a decision, it should be clear that the decision is formed from documents with a certain timestamp. It may be beneficial to prevent further uploads once the decision-making process starts, unless the arbitrator invites further information.

In addition, in practice, the parties may change the institution named in the arbitration agreement before the institution is notified of its nomination and accepts the appointment. This raises technical challenges as to when the initial institution is notified of its nomination in the online environment. As opposed to the real world, notification can be made in a split second, which makes it impossible to change the institution according to the traditional practice. In order to make it feasible, the technical environment should have the time period option for parties to notify the nominated institution. Once the time period ends, parties would no longer be able to change the institution. The nominated institution should have the option to access or reject the offer at any time until the time period expires. Upon expiry, the offer will automatically be considered rejected.

The third issue is about the ethics of online arbitrators. There is a Code of Ethics for Arbitrators in Commercial Disputes by AAA effective on 1 March 2004,[65] which can be applied to online arbitrators if parties choose AAA to resolve their disputes. There are a number of common key rules concerning ethical requirements for arbitration in the AAA Code of Ethics for Arbitrations. They require an arbitration should a) uphold the integrity and fairness of the arbitration process; b) disclose any interest or relationship likely to affect impartiality or which might create an appearance of partiality; c) avoid impropriety or the appearance of impropriety in communicating with parties; d) conduct the proceedings fairly and diligently; e) make decisions in a just, independent and deliberate manner; and f) be faithful to the relationship of trust and confidentiality inherent in that office.[66] There are also International Bar Association (IBA) Rules of Ethics for International Arbitrators that require a prospective arbitrator

---

65. The Code of Ethics for Arbitrators in Commercial Disputes AAA Effective 1 March 2004, available at www.adr.org/aaa/ShowProperty?nodeId=%2FUCM%2FADRSTG_003867&revision=la testreleased (last accessed 30 March 2017).

66. The Code of Ethics for Arbitrators in Commercial Disputes AAA Effective 1 March 2004, Conon I – VI.

to make 'sufficient enquiries' to inform regarding his impartiality, independence, disclosure, competence and availability.[67]

It is suggested that parties' agreements on the appointment of arbitrators are sometimes difficult to accomplish due to the understanding of the ethical requirements of arbitrators.[68] For example, in *Jivraj v Hashwani*, the English Court of Appeal struck down an arbitration agreement requiring the three arbitrators to be of a particular religious group, in this case the Ismaili community, as it constituted unfair employment.[69] However, the Supreme Court of the United Kingdom reversed the judgment in 2011, holding that it was legitimate to select a person of a particular religion to be an arbitrator because the role of an arbitrator is not naturally described as employment under a contract personally to do work.[70] It concluded that

> a religious or faith-based community's or organisation's power first to select and then to direct its own employed lawyers would be a secure means of ensuring that its employed lawyers valued, understood and prioritised the handling of English law work so far as possible on a non-confrontational basis, using alternative dispute resolution procedures wherever possible. A refusal to employ anyone other than a member of the particular religion or faith would in that context seem unlikely to be justified or proportionate.[71]

With regard to the interpretation of impartiality, in the US case of *Commonwealth Coatings Corp. v Continental Casualty Co.* an arbitral award was set aside even though the award was unanimous. It concluded that, regardless of the agreement between the parties, if an arbitrator has any prior business relationship with one of the parties of which he fails to inform the other party, however innocently, the arbitration award is always subject to being set aside.[72] A national court may have the authority to appoint arbitrators for international arbitration in a situation where parties fail to select arbitrators under law, according to their arbitration agreement or via their appointed arbitration institutions. However, it is noted that 'judicial appointment of arbitrators is limited to cases where parties have not agreed upon means of selecting arbitrators or where their agreed means have failed to function'.[73] Likewise, in the online arbitration system, national courts can exercise power for selection of online arbitration when parties can-

---

67. International Bar Association Rules of Ethics for International Arbitrators, Released on 9 July 2008, Rule 5, available at www.ibanet.org/ (last accessed 30 March 2017).
68. The Role of Ethics in International Arbitration, International Council for Commercial Arbitration (ICCA 2013), available at www.arbitration-icca.org/media/2/13826154612930/yicca_report_6oct2013.pdf (last accessed 30 March 2017).
69. *Jivraj v Hashwani* (Rev 2) [2010] EWCA Civ 712 (22 June 2010), para. 13, available at www.bailii.org/ew/cases/EWCA/Civ/2010/712.html (last accessed 30 March 2017).
70. *Jivraj v Hashwani* [2011] UKSC 40 (27 July 2011), para. 23, available at www.bailii.org/uk/cases/UKSC/2011/40.html (last accessed 30 March 2017).
71. *Jivraj v Hashwani* [2011] UKSC 40 (27 July 2011), para. 82.
72. *Commonwealth Coatings Corp. v Continental Casualty Co.* [1968] 393 U.S. 145.
73. Born, G. (2011), International Arbitration: Cases and Materials (New York: Aspen Publishers, 2011), p. 639

not agree on means of selecting arbitrators. Accordingly, an online arbitration platform should have a function for parties or appointing authority to connect and communicate with courts on their decision on appointing arbitrators. In other words, due to national courts having the power to appoint and remove arbitrators under certain circumstances, ODR systems should have appropriate technological functions for national courts to recommend appointment or removal of arbitrators where necessary.

In the ODR system, it may be possible to build in an automated ethical checking system to check against submitted disclosure information from parties and nominated arbitrators. Nonetheless, online arbitrators may require more credentials on certain areas due to the features of online conduct. It was suggested that online negotiators, mediators and arbitrators should also complete professional ethics courses and follow the code of conduct of the professional computing societies.[74] The job of an online arbitrator will require vocational training specific to the requirements of the ODR platform environment. Basic IT skills will be required, of which a business involved in ODR software may wish their employee to complete a digital skills training course such as that provided by the BCS (British Computer Society). Ethics are highly important in the role of arbitrators. The UK Bribery Act 2010 makes bribery a specific offence. Businesses involved in ODR software may wish to enrol their employees in appropriate ethical and anti-bribery compliance training courses.

Although there may be technological challenges to the appointment of online arbitrators, there are benefits of using online arbitrators selected from the ODR platforms as opposed to traditional arbitrators. In the ODR environment, service providers can adopt an online arbitrator rating system that enables clients to review and rate the service of online arbitrators. However, arbitrators are usually registered with specific arbitration institutions. Arbitrators may be listed under specific arbitration institutions chosen by the parties. Different ODR service providers may employ different rating systems to rate the individual work of arbitrators. In other words, the same arbitrators may have different rating scores under different ODR service platforms. Moreover, it is likely the winning party rates the arbitrator favourably and the losing party rates the arbitrator unfavourably. Nevertheless, review and rating of online arbitrators on an ODR system, as long as realisable rating systems are employed, may provide helpful reference to parties during the process of the selection and appointment of arbitrators.

3.5 Expert witnesses and electronic evidence

Expert determination means 'a process where a dispute is referred to an expert for determination, not usually involving an opportunity to present formal arguments

---

74. Ebner, N. & Zeleznikow, J. (2016). No sheriff in town: Governance for the ODR field. *Negotiation Journal* 32(4), p. 11.

or make formal submissions'.[75] When disputes require specialised knowledge, such as engineering or science in which arbitrators have a lack of expertise, expert evidence is required. Expert witnesses can be appointed by both parties and tribunals. Party-appointed experts are freely appointed by parties, whereas tribunal-appointed experts are appointed by tribunals independently. There is no guarantee that expert evidence will be admitted by the arbitral tribunal. There has been debate over whether testimony of party-appointed experts may be biased as they are appointed by parties.[76] However, arbitral tribunals have control over the admissibility of evidence in any case by giving due consideration as to the merits, reliability and weight of witnesses evidence.[77]

Arbitration institutions usually provide general guidelines on the format of evidence. For example, according to CIETAC Guidelines on Evidence 2015 concerning expert opinions,

> a party may submit an expert opinion on specific issues to support its claims. An expert opinion shall contain:
>
> (1) the name and address of the expert, a statement regarding his/her relationships with the parties, and his/her professional background;
> (2) the facts, documents and other sources of information on which the expert's opinion is based;
> (3) the expert's personal opinions and conclusions, including the methods employed and grounds relied upon in forming the opinions and arriving at the conclusions; and
> (4) the date of the expert opinion and the signature of the expert.[78]

With regard to tribunal-appointed experts, CIETAC Guidelines on Evidence provides that:

> the tribunal may appoint one or more experts on its own initiative. The parties shall assist the tribunal-appointed expert, and provide any documents and information that the expert requests. The expert shall issue his/her opinion which shall be forwarded to the parties for comments.[79]

The concept of electronic evidence has also been widely accepted by international arbitration rules and institutional arbitration procedures. For example, the UNCITRAL Arbitration Rules specify that 'the arbitral tribunal may direct that witnesses, including expert witnesses, be examined through means of telecommunication that do not require their physical presence at the hearing (such as

---

75. Greenberg, S., Kee, C. and Weeramantry, J.R. (2011), International Commercial Arbitration (New York: Cambridge University Press, 2011), p. 520.
76. Greenberg, S., Kee, C. and Weeramantry, J.R. (2011), International Commercial Arbitration (New York: Cambridge University Press, 2011), p. 351.
77. Please refer to further discussion in Chapter 4.
78. CIETAC Guidelines on Evidence, effective 1 March 2015, Article 9.1, available at www.cietac.org/index.php?m=Page&a=index&id=107&l=en (last accessed 30 March 2017).
79. CIETAC Guidelines on Evidence, effective 1 March 2015, Article 9.2.

videoconference)'.[80] The CIETAC Online Arbitration Rules also provide conditions for admitting electronic evidence:

> the evidence submitted by the parties may be electronic evidence that is generated, sent, received or stored by electronic, optical, magnetic or other similar means. The following factors shall be taken into consideration when the authenticity of electronic evidence is examined:
>
> (a) The reliability of the methods used to generate, store or transmit the data message;
> (b) The reliability of the methods used to maintain the integrity of the contents of the data message;
> (c) The reliability of the methods used to identify the sender of the data message;
> (d) Other relevant factors.
>
> Electronic evidence with a reliable electronic signature shall have the same admissibility and weight as evidence with a handwritten signature or affixed seal.[81]

Accordingly, expert opinions are accepted in any electronic form and in any way of electronic communications as long as the expert witness records are authentic, reliable and durable. The CIETAC Online Arbitration Rules 2015 also accept that the witnesses may testify by online video conferencing, by regular oral hearing in person or by any other appropriate manner as decided by the arbitral tribunal where an oral hearing is to be held.[82] In accordance with the CIETAC Online Arbitration Rules, there are three virtues that qualified electronic evidence should present: authenticity, reliability and appropriateness. Authenticity can be understood as originality of evidential records and identity of their ownership. Reliability can be understood as integrity and durability of evidential records. Appropriateness can be understood as suitable technological means for gathering and presenting evidential records.

The revised IBA Rules of Evidence in 2010, as opposed to its earlier versions in 1999 and 1983, also accept evidential hearing via electronic communications. The IBA Rules of Evidence define 'evidentiary hearing' as 'any hearing, whether or not held on consecutive days, at which the Arbitral Tribunal, whether in person, by teleconference, videoconference or other method, receives oral or other evidence'.[83] Moreover, IBA Rules of Evidence 2010 provide the requirements of the form of submission or production of documents that:

---

80. UNCITRAL Arbitration Rules (Revised 2013), Article 28(4) available at www.uncitral.org/pdf/english/texts/arbitration/arb-rules-2013/UNCITRAL-Arbitration-Rules-2013-e.pdf (last accessed 30 March 2017).
81. CIETAC Online Arbitration Rules 2015, Article 29.
82. CIETAC Online Arbitration Rules 2015, Article 36, available at www.cietac.org/index.php?m=Article&a=show&id=2770&l=en (last accessed 30 March 2017).
83. IBA Rules on the Taking of Evidence in International Arbitration (2010), available at www.ibanet.org/Publications/publications_IBA_guides_and_free_materials.aspx (last accessed 30 March 2017).

(a) copies of Documents shall conform to the originals and, at the request of the Arbitral Tribunal, any original shall be presented for inspection; (b) Documents that a Party maintains in electronic form shall be submitted or produced in the form most convenient or economical to it that is reasonably usable by the recipients, unless the Parties agree otherwise or, in the absence of such agreement, the Arbitral Tribunal decides otherwise.[84]

The IBA Rules of Evidence require the format of electronic evidence documents to be the most convenient or economical, which means that the format will generally not be the native format with full metadata, as submission in this format can be unduly expensive and inconvenient.[85] However, there is no explanation as to the technological measures of producing electronic evidence by arbitration institutions except for the confirmation of the effect of electronic signature to electronic evidential documents and the acceptance to electronic evidential records in general. There is need for further regulatory development relating to generating, presenting, admitting and storing electronic evidential records for online arbitration across the globe.[86]

3.6 Format of arbitration agreements

An effective dispute resolution process starts with a well-constructed dispute resolution clause or agreement. It is important to arrange and set out appropriate arbitration agreements and clauses.[87] It is suggested that when writing a dispute resolution clause, parties should keep in mind that its purpose is to resolve disputes, not create them.[88]

In the ODR environment, there are three most common ways that parties may generate or submit their agreements and clauses. The straightforward way is that parties upload a signed and scanned copy of their agreements and clauses. The second way is also simple if the ODR service providers provide an online arbitration agreement form that parties can fill in online. The third way is to use an online arbitration clause builder tool. A well-built ODR system may provide clause-builder tools that enable parties to create custom ADR clauses. For example, the American Arbitration Association (AAA) and the International Centre for Dispute Resolution (ICDR) offer a ClauseBuilder tool, which is designed to assist individuals and organisations develop customised, clear and

---

84. IBA Rules on the Taking of Evidence in International Arbitration (2010), Article 3(12).
85. Commentary on the revised text of the 2010 IBA Rules on the Taking of Evidence in International Arbitration (2010), p. 12.
86. Please refer to further discussion on technological measures on electronic evidence.
87. See Introduction of American Associate Arbitration (AAA) Alternative Dispute Resolution ClauseBuilder Tool, available at www.clausebuilder.org (last accessed 30 March 2017).
88. Drafting Dispute Resolution Clauses: A Practical Guide by AAA (this Guide has been updated to correspond with the AAA®'s Commercial Arbitration Rules in effect on 1 October 2013), available at www.adr.org/aaa/ShowPDF?doc=ADRSTG_002540 (last accessed 30 March 2017), p. 36.

effective arbitration and mediation agreements or clauses.[89] The ClauseBuilder Tool provides steps as follows:

- a) As a starting point for the ClauseBuilder, select the nature of the contract or dispute type for which the clause is being built, i.e. commercial, construction or international/transnational commercial contracts.
- b) Select future or existing arbitration agreement, i.e. I want to include a mediation and/or arbitration agreement in a contract so that all future disputes arising out of that contract will be resolved by mediation or arbitration. Or I am in a dispute with another party that I would like to submit to arbitration. However, there is no contract between the parties that provides for mediation or arbitration.
- c) Select the clause you would like to create, i.e. arbitration or mediation; and then, if necessary, arbitration.
- d) Choose one of two options to proceed, i.e. to utilise a Standard ICDR Clause without viewing optional clause provisions, please click on the 'Finish and Choose this Clause'. Contracting parties should add language regarding the number of arbitrators, the place of arbitration and the language of arbitration to the standard clause, except where the Expedited Procedures apply, in which case one arbitrator is provided for in all cases. To see these and other clause drafting options, please select the 'Proceed to Other Options' button. If parties select the 'Proceed to Other Options' button, it also offers parties opportunity to specify arbitration qualifications, information exchange, documents only hearing, duration arbitration proceedings, confidentiality and appeal.

If parties fill in the form with information for each option, the system will automatically generate a dispute resolution clause that should address the special needs of the parties involved.[90] For example, the system may generate a clause as follows:

> In the event of any controversy or claim arising out of or relating to this contract, or the breach thereof, the parties hereto agree first to try and settle the dispute by mediation, administered by the International Centre for Dispute Resolution under its Mediation Rules. If settlement is not reached within 60 days after service of a written demand for mediation, any unresolved controversy or claim arising out of or relating to this contract shall be settled by arbitration in accordance with the International Arbitration Rules of the International Centre for Dispute Resolution.
> All disputes shall be heard by a panel of three arbitrators. The place of arbitration shall be London. The language of the arbitration shall be English. Within 30 days after the commencement of arbitration, each party shall select a person to serve as an arbitrator. The parties shall then select the presiding arbitrator within 40 days

---

89. See www.clausebuilder.org (last accessed 30 March 2017).
90. Drafting Dispute Resolution Clauses: A Practical Guide by AAA (this Guide has been updated to correspond with the AAA®'s Commercial Arbitration Rules in effect on 1 October 2013), available at www.adr.org/aaa/ShowPDF?doc=ADRSTG_002540 (last accessed 30 March 2017), p. 36.

after completion of the appointment of the party selections. If any arbitrators are not selected within these time periods, the International Centre for Dispute Resolution shall, at the written request of any party, complete the appointments that have not been made. The arbitrator(s) shall be commercial lawyer. Consistent with the expedited nature of arbitration, pre-hearing information exchange shall be limited to the reasonable production of relevant non-privileged documents explicitly referred to by a party for the purpose of supporting relevant facts presented in its' case, carried out expeditiously. Regardless of the amount in dispute, evidence will be taken by the submission of documents only. The award shall be rendered within 3 months of the commencement of the arbitration, unless such time limit is extended by the arbitrator. Failure to adhere to this time limit shall not constitute a basis for challenging the award. Except as may be required by law, neither a party nor its representatives may disclose the existence, content, or results of any arbitration hereunder without the prior written consent of (all/both) parties. Notwithstanding any language to the contrary in the contract documents, the parties hereby agree that a Final Award issued may be appealed pursuant to the American Arbitration Association's Optional Appellate Arbitration Rules ('Appellate Rules'). Appeals must be initiated within thirty (30) days of receipt of a Final Award, as defined by Rule A-3 of the Appellate Rules, by filing a Notice of Appeal with the International Centre for Dispute Resolution. Following the appeal process the decision rendered by the appeal tribunal may be entered in any court having jurisdiction thereof.

Finally, the ClauseBuilder Tool offers users a tool to print or download the customised clauses. Users are then advised to use AAA Case Filing Services – AAA WebFile – which provide customers with an easy, fast and efficient process for filing any type of dispute resolution case, regardless of geographical location.[91] It is helpful that users use the ClauseBuilder Tool before filing a case on AAA WebFile, because an inadequate ADR clause can produce as much delay, expense, and inconvenience as a traditional lawsuit.[92]

3.7 Process of hearing/commencement of arbitration proceedings

The preliminary hearing of arbitration is a management meeting conducted between arbitrators and parties. It is usually the first time the parties and the arbitrator discuss the case and agree on a scheduling order. Nowadays, preliminary hearing is often allowed to be conducted via conference call or video conferencing. During the preliminary hearing, parties usually work with arbitrators to identify necessary procedural steps and actions in preparation of the evidentiary hearing and establish a schedule/timetable for those steps and actions. Parties and arbitrators also set timeframes for the hearing process including dates for the submission of final witness lists and the evidentiary hearing.

---

91. See www.clausebuilder.org and Case Filing Services, www.adr.org/fileacase (last accessed 30 March 2017).
92. Drafting Dispute Resolution Clauses: A Practical Guide by AAA (this Guide has been updated to correspond with the AAA®'s Commercial Arbitration Rules in effect on 1 October 2013), available at www.adr.org/aaa/ShowPDF?doc=ADRSTG_002540 (last accessed 30 March 2017), p. 36.

Rules concerning preliminary hearings are similar in all arbitration institutions, although there may be variations concerning schedules and fees. According to the AAA Arbitration Roadmap, the parties are required to pay a deposit within 30 days prior to the first evidentiary hearing to cover the arbitrator's estimated fees and expenses for the scheduled hearings and anticipated study time.[93] At the preliminary hearing, parties exchange information, prepare their document submissions including presentation of evidence and arguments and submit final witness lists, while arbitrators address any issues raised during this process.[94]

Hearings in international commercial arbitration usually take place once information has been exchanged including the written submissions, evidence, witness statements and expert reports. There may be several hearings depending on the complexity of the case. At the hearings, parties present evidence and testimony to arbitrators in a format that is similar to, but less formal than, a court proceeding.[95] The hearing usually includes the following steps:

- Opening of the hearing. The sole arbitrator or chairman explains his/her role, organisational matters and the manner in which the hearing is to be run. Parties and representatives will be introduced.
- Opening statements. Each party provides a summary presentation of the case, highlighting all key issues backed up by the documentary evidence or other evidence that is to follow.
- Hearing of witnesses and expert witnesses. Usually the claimant's witnesses will present first, followed by the respondent's witnesses. The arbitrators or arbitral tribunal may question witnesses at any time during this process. Then, expert witnesses will present and also be examined and cross-examined.
- Stage of closing arguments. Parties or their representatives are usually asked to sum up their case taking into consideration all the evidence presented.
- Closing of the hearing. The sole arbitrator or chairman may address any outstanding procedural issues such as the dates of the availability of the full transcript/record of the hearing. The arbitration panel may also require the parties to provide additional evidence or information and will set a deadline or additional hearing for the submission of such information.

In the ODR environment, conducting an arbitration meeting via video conference may present challenges, compared with a face-to-face meeting. Internet-based video conferencing applications must cope with bandwidth limitations, poor latency and packet-loss by allowing degradation of video/audio quality.

---

93. AAA Arbitration Roadmap, 14 November 2011, available at www.adr.org/aaa/ShowPDF?doc=ADRSTG_003838 (last accessed 30 March 2017), p. 6.
94. AAA Arbitration Roadmap 2011, p. 7.
95. AAA Arbitration Roadmap 2011, p. 8.

This means there is no guarantee that each party will receive exactly what is transmitted. An audio drop-out of an important word or sentence may alter the understanding for one or more parties. As Internet connections become faster and more reliable due to technological advances, these issues may diminish. If a recording of the video conference is required as expert and witness evidence, it may be preferable to make the recording on the central server hosting the video conferencing call (i.e. specially designed and integrated video call service within ODR systems or generic video conference service such as Skype for Business), known as server-side recording, as this may prove the most reliable. It is noteworthy that general consumer video conferencing facilities are not ideal for conducting and recording an online hearing as auto drop-out of words or sentences are common in those systems.

3.8 Format and issuance of online arbitral awards

Institutional rules provide similar basic requirements as to the format and issuance of arbitral awards, which include the need for an arbitral award to be in writing, the names and addresses of all parties, representatives and arbitrators; the facts, procedure and claims of the dispute; the reasons on which the arguments are based, the date and place of arbitration where the award was made, the result of hearings (i.e. the decision of the award) and signatures by the arbitrators. The formality of the award and the scope for the award are crucial as the award may not be recognised and enforced if at the time of the application for recognition and enforcement, the award is not a 'duly authenticated original award or a duly certified copy';[96] or 'the award deals with a difference not contemplated by or not falling within the terms of the submission to arbitration, or it contains decisions on matters beyond the scope of the submission to arbitration'.[97] As to the standard of reasoning, it is debatable whether arbitrators should provide the same level of reasoning compared to judges in courts. It has been argued that a commercial arbitrator's role is not that of a national judge who may need to make decisions to accord with notions of fairness applicable to the community at large or set a precedent for future reference.[98] According to the UNCITRAL Model Law on International Commercial Arbitration, the award shall state the reasons upon which it is based, unless the parties have agreed that no reasons are to be given or the award is an award on agreed terms under Article 30.[99] According to the UK Arbitration Act 1996, if on an application or appeal it

---

96. Convention on the Recognition and Enforcement of Foreign Arbitral Awards (New York, 1958) (the 'New York Convention'), Article IV(1)(a).
97. Convention on the Recognition and Enforcement of Foreign Arbitral Awards (New York, 1958) (the 'New York Convention'), Article V(1)(c).
98. Greenberg, S., Kee, C. and Weeramantry, J.R. (2011), International Commercial Arbitration (New York: Cambridge University Press, 2011), p. 385.
99. UNCITRAL Model Law on International Commercial Arbitration 1985 With amendments as adopted in 2006, Article 31(2).

appears to the court that the award (a) does not contain the tribunal's reasons, or (b) does not set out the tribunal's reasons in sufficient detail to enable the court properly to consider the application or appeal, the court may order the tribunal to state the reasons for its award in sufficient detail for that purpose.[100] In the English Court of Appeal case of *Bremer Handelsgesellschaft mbH v Westzucker*, it defined the meaning of a 'reasoned award' as 'all that is necessary is that the arbitrators should set out what, on their view of the evidence, did or did not happen and should explain succinctly why, in the light of what happened, they have reached their decision and what that decision is'.[101] The Victorian Court of Appeal decision of *Oil Basins Ltd v BHP Billiton Ltd* even upheld the judgment that set aside an arbitral award on the basis of inadequate reasons.[102] In view of the legal requirements of arbitral awards, major arbitration institutions provide practical guidelines on how to draft arbitral awards. For example, in 2015 the UK Chartered Institute of Arbitrators (CIArb) provided the International Arbitration Practice Guideline on Drafting of Arbitral Awards, which sets out the current best practice in international commercial arbitration for drafting arbitral awards.[103] There is an exemption clause in this guideline concerning reasons for consent or agreed awards that 'if the arbitrators are satisfied that they should make a consent award, they do not need to include any reasons for the award'.[104] The Guideline on Drafting of Arbitral Awards explains the requirements of 'reasons' for an arbitral awards in detail as follows (emphasis added):

> a) All arbitral awards should contain reasons, unless otherwise agreed by the parties or where the award records the parties' settlement. The inclusion of reasons is necessary to demonstrate that arbitrators have given full consideration to the parties' respective submissions and **to explain to the parties why they have won or lost**. Most national laws and arbitration rules expressly require arbitrators to include reasons in their awards. Even where they are silent on the matter, it is good practice to provide reasons, unless the parties agree otherwise or where the award records the parties' settlement.
>
> b) Arbitrators have a wide discretion to decide on the length and the level of detail of the reasons but it is good practice to keep the reasons **concise and limited to what is necessary**, according to the particular circumstances of the dispute. In any event, arbitrators need to set out Chartered Institute of Arbitrators their findings, based on the evidence and arguments presented, as to what did or did not happen. They should explain why, in the light of what they find happened, they have reached their decision and what their decision is.

---

100. UK Arbitration Act 1996, s 70(4).
101. *Bremer Handelsgesellschaft mbH v Westzucker* [1981] 2 Lloyd's Rep 130 at 132–133.
102. *Oil Basins Ltd v BHP Billiton Ltd* [2007] VSCA 255.
103. Chartered Institute of Arbitrators (CIArb) International Arbitration Practice Guideline on Drafting of Arbitral Awards, 2015, available at www.ciarb.org/docs/default-source/ciarbdocuments/guidance-and-ethics/practice-guidelines-protocols-and-rules/international-arbitration-guidelines-2015/drafting-arbitral-awards-part-i-general-8-june-2016.pdf?sfvrsn=16 (last accessed 30 March 2017).
104. Chartered Institute of Arbitrators (CIArb) International Arbitration Practice Guideline on Drafting of Arbitral Awards, 2015, p. 10, (iv)(d).

c) Arbitrators should also consider whether it is appropriate to include a statement that the parties have had a fair and equal opportunity to present their respective cases and deal with that of their counterparty.[105]

As shown above, the Guideline on Drafting of Arbitral Awards does not encourage developing extensive reasoning, which may reduce the efficiency of international arbitration. Instead, it promotes concise and necessary reasoning with clarity to submitted issues and arbitral decision.

It is noteworthy that in practice there are also time limits for making arbitral awards; national laws and arbitration rules may not specify time limits. Time limits for issuing a final award are usually specified in the arbitration agreement or defined by arbitration institutions. For example, according to the AAA Arbitration Roadmap, an arbitral award is due 30 days after the arbitrator closes the record and should address all claims raised in the arbitration. It is possible that the award may direct one or more parties to pay another party a monetary amount or direct parties to take specific actions based on how the arbitrator decided the matters in the case.[106]

According to online arbitration procedures as discussed above, the design of an ODR platform should take into consideration appropriate technological measures to enhance the fairness of arbitration procedures and make sure that it is secure and user-friendly. The development of a sophisticated ODR system is a complicated and ongoing process. It is suggested that the ODR platform should offer a variety of optional case management tools, which could even be licensed to ADR entities for a fee in order to share developmental costs and economies of scale.[107]

In general, a harmonised standard of technological measures should be deployed to build an ODR system. An ODR platform should provide a common location for parties to, where possible, fully manage all parts of the dispute process. Users should be authenticated with unique credentials and uploaded documents should be versioned and timestamped. Users should be granted read-only or read/write access depending on their roles. A case administrator will have responsibility for setting the access privileges of each party. All actions in the system should be logged to provide a chronologically accurate audit trail, only accessible by a system administrator, in the event that the platform software is called into question. The platform should indicate the current state of the arbitration process and provide a messaging system for secure communications between parties.

---

105. Chartered Institute of Arbitrators (CIArb) International Arbitration Practice Guideline on Drafting of Arbitral Awards, 2015, pp. 16–17.
106. AAA Arbitration Roadmap 2011, p. 10.
107. Cortes, P. and Lodder, A. R. (2014), Consumer Dispute Resolution Goes Online: Reflections on the Evolution of European Law for Out-of-Court Redress, *Maastricht Journal of European and Comparative Law*, Volume 1, p. 21.

In addition, the platform should present a number of arbitration bodies, ideally several with specialisations in each of the supported subjects. Supplied information may include fees, testimonials and details of arbitration procedures. The platform should provide a private and group messaging service, with emphasis on durability of data. At any time before the arbitrator commences the decision-making processes, it should be possible for either party to offer a settlement via the platform. The platform may allow parties to withdraw from the arbitration process altogether, depending upon the agreed-upon arbitration rules. There must be a cut-off point for uploading or changing submitted documents and evidentiary evidence. When the decision is made, it should be possible for the outcome to be transmitted simultaneously to both parties. The platform may offer an online payment system to allow payment of fees to the arbitration body and, depending on the nature of the dispute, it may be also desirable for any award to be settled in the same manner.

CHAPTER 4

Systematic legal and technological development for online arbitration procedures

4.1 The expansion of general ODR systems

Since the advent of the Online Dispute Resolution (ODR) system in late 1990s and early 2000s, it has been commonly known that there are two additional elements involved in the process compared with traditional ADR (i.e. two disputing parties and third parties such as mediators or arbitrators): technology and providers of technology.

The ODR process, as a dispute resolution medium, is desired to be secure, efficient, flexible and user-friendly. It must be able to deal with the initial filing, neutral appointment, evidentiary processes, oral hearings, neutral executive sessions, and the rendering and transmittal of an award in binding processes.[1] It should be envisioned as a virtual space in which disputants have a variety of dispute resolution tools at their disposal. Participants can select any tool they consider appropriate for the resolution of their conflict and use the tools in any order or manner they desire, or they can be guided through the process.[2] At the initial stage of ODR development, it was suggested that the most effective non-human assisted negotiation environment can be created by a three-step model where each step can be reversed and repeated until parties are satisfied with the results. The three steps are: 1) estimated outcomes generated by the negotiation support tools; 2) dialogue techniques facilitating negotiation; and 3) compensation/trade-off strategies employed to facilitate resolution of the dispute.[3] Such system is known as a basic 'bidding system' which is particularly suitable for money claims such as bidding for payment, refund or compensation. With regard to resolving other types of disputes, Lodder developed a basic ODR software called 'DiaLaw', a two-player dialogue game designed to establish justified

---

1. Alvaro, J. A. G. (2003), Online Dispute Resolution – Unchartered Territory, VJ, Volume 7, pp. 187–98, p. 188.
2. Lodder, A. R. & Zeleznikow, J. (Spring 2005), Developing An Online Dispute Resolution Environment: Dialogue Tools and Negotiation Support Systems in a Three-Step Model, *Harvard Negotiation Law Review*, Volume 10, pp. 287–338, p. 300.
3. Lodder, A. R. & Zeleznikow, J. (Spring 2005), Developing An Online Dispute Resolution Environment: Dialogue Tools and Negotiation Support Systems in a Three-Step Model, *Harvard Negotiation Law Review*, Volume 10, pp. 287–338, p. 301.

statements, which can clearly explain the basic logic of the ODR environment.[4] A dialogue in DiaLaw starts when a player introduces a statement he/she wants to justify. The dialogue ends if the opponent accepts the statement (justified), or if the statement is withdrawn (not justified).

Such advanced ODR systems encompass a broad array of artificial intelligence technologies to resolve a growing variety of domestic and cross-border commercial and consumer disputes. It was estimated that the eBay Resolution Centre resolved over 60 million consumer disputes per year, making it one of the biggest ODR systems in the world, where most of the cases were settled without a neutral and 90% of the cases were resolved without going to court.[5] ODR has also been used to resolve other types of domestic disputes such as small claims, traffic and parking disputes and landlord–tenant disputes in some countries. Some of the countries and regions such as the US and EU have been working on deploying innovative ODR services with a broad suite of technologies to the judiciary. For example, in the EU, some European countries' (such as Austria) courts have been employing dispute resolution technology through online court forms, case-management and e-filing systems. The Austrian judicial system provides a court e-portal system where citizens can log in by citizen cards and mobile phone signature to manage their cases online.[6] The Austrian online court portal system is considered as a concise and complete integrated system 'for direct assistance of the judges/court clerk (word processing, electronic database of case law, electronic files, e-mail, internet connection), for administration and management (case registration system, court management information system, financial information system, videoconferencing) and for electronic communication and exchange of information between the courts and their environment'.[7] It is reported that the computer facilities used within/by the Austrian courts are involved in the entire litigation process, and videoconferencing is used in all type of cases for hearing.[8] Other non-EU members such

---

4. Lodder, A. R. & Zeleznikow, J. (Spring 2005), Developing An Online Dispute Resolution Environment: Dialogue Tools and Negotiation Support Systems in a Three-Step Model, *Harvard Negotiation Law Review*, Volume 10, pp. 287–338, p. 305.

5. Petreikyte, G., ODR Platforms: EBay Resolution Center, the 15th ODR Conference, 23–24 May 2016, available at https://20160dr.wordpress.com/2016/04/14/odr-platforms-ebay-resolution-center/ (last accessed 30 March 2017).

6. Judicial system – Austria, available at https://webportal.justiz.gv.at (last accessed 30 March 2017).

7. European Commission for the Efficiency of Justice (CEPEJ) Study on the functioning of judicial systems in the EU Member States, Facts and figures from the CEPEJ 2012–2014 evaluation exercise, Study prepared by scientific experts of the CEPEJ under the authority of the Working Group on the evaluation of judicial systems (CEPEJ-GT-EVAL) for the attention of the European Commission (Directorate General Justice), CEPEJ(2014)4final, available at http://ec.europa.eu/justice/effective-justice/files/cepj_study_scoreboard_2014_en.pdf (last accessed 30 March 2017), p. 268.

8. European Commission for the Efficiency of Justice (CEPEJ) Study on the functioning of judicial systems in the EU Member States, Facts and figures from the CEPEJ 2012–2014 evaluation exercise, Study prepared by scientific experts of the CEPEJ under the authority of the Working Group on the evaluation of judicial systems (CEPEJ-GT-EVAL) for the attention of the European Commission (Directorate General Justice), CEPEJ(2014)4final, p. 269.

as Switzerland and Norway have also widely used information technology in their judicial systems.[9]

In the US, since 2012 when Oregon eCourt was introduced, the Oregon eCourt's integrated case management system (OECI) has been fast developing. By 2016 there were 36 Oregon circuit courts and Oregon Tax Courts employing OECI.[10] Moreover, Franklin County, Ohio's Small Claims Court offers a pre-trial ODR process where parties can negotiate a settlement before initiating any court proceedings.[11] In Canada, the Civil Resolution Tribunal (CRT) is the country's first online tribunal with a fully integrated dispute resolution system called the Solution Explorer for resolving strata and small claims disputes.[12] The CRT online court system is timely (60–90 days' process), flexible (range of ADR options), accessible (24/7), affordable (staged fees) and effective (active case management and tailored timelines and processes).[13]

The utilisation of ODR technology in courts may have the potential to dramatically expand the public's access to the court and to improve the services courts provide and the way they function as businesses. Research on Online Dispute Resolution and the Courts was conducted by the Joint Technology Committee (JTC) to improve the administration of justice through technology in the US. According to JTC's first report on 30 November 2016, the basic form of ODR 'not only enables people to interact and communicate about disputes at a distance, but also facilitates resolution by improving the flow and character of information and reducing conflict, as well as minimizing financial and time costs through the creative use of technology'.[14] Advanced technologies for ODR may increasingly shape online written communication to avoid escalating conflict by blocking foul language and other communication patterns that may worsen the situation. Artificial intelligence may also be able to provide automated diagnostics and guidance as to where parties should file the case (known as 'diagnostic

---

9. Thematic report: Use of information technology in European courts by CEPEJ Studies No.24, European Judicial Systems: Efficiency and quality of justice, Strasbourg, 30 June-1 July 2016, available at http://www.coe.int/t/dghl/cooperation/cepej/evaluation/2016/publication/REV1/2016_2%20-%20CEPEJ%20Study%2024%20-%20IT%20Report%20-%20EN.pdf (last accessed 30 March 2017).

10. Oregon eCourt's integrated case management system, available at www.courts.oregon.gov/Oregonecourt/pages/oregoneCourtMap.aspx (last accessed 30 March 2017).

11. Franklin County Municipal Court ODR, available at www.courtinnovations.com/ohfcmc (last accessed 30 March 2017).

12. The Civil Resolution Tribunal (CRT) Canada, available at www.civilresolutionbc.ca/disputes/ (last accessed 30 March 2017).

13. CHOA Forum, January 2017, available at https://vanity.blog.gov.bc.ca/app/uploads/sites/5/2017/01/CHOA-Forum-Vancouver-January-2017.pdf (last accessed 30 March 2017).

14. Online Dispute Resolution and the Courts, Version 1.0, 30 November 2016, Joint Technology Committee (JTC) established by the Conference of State Court Administrators (COSCA), the National Association for Court Management (NACM) and the National Center for State Courts (NCSC), available at www.ncsc.org/~/media/Files/PDF/About%20Us/Committees/JTC/ODR%20QR%20final%20V1%20-%20Nov.ashx (last accessed 30 March 2017), p. 3.

capabilities'),[15] navigate procedures[16] and offer mock response to help parties understand their positions. It is suggested that the design of a three-tier system with a diagnosis phase, a conciliation phase and a decision phase may provide a user-centred online justice service.[17]

With the deployment of big data and automated computing, machine analysis of types of disputes resolved by ODR services and statistics on length and cost of each dispute may be able to optimise resources on ODR platforms and improve efficiency. For example, there is a big data and dispute resolution project analysing the frequency, location, sentimentality (categorisation of the feeling), and timing of 52,203 unique conflict-related search terms over time within each of the 3,143 US counties and county-equivalent geographies.[18] It was suggested that the resulting dataset was able to provide a chronological review of the collective interests and conflict intensities of hundreds of distinct conflict contexts (i.e. 33% family-related conflict and 32% market-related conflict), which may be used to inform future resource development and deployment efforts.[19]

Taking advantage of technological developments in recent years, a smart ODR system may be built. Compared with current ODR systems, smart ODR systems deploy smart technology and service-oriented computing applications to create virtual robots such as smart administrators, arbitrators, mediators and negotiators. When building the next generation of robotic ODR systems, psychological management for resolving conflicts should be considered to increase the chance of the outcome of settlement being accepted by parties. In the traditional mediation process, it is suggested that certain factors may contribute to successful mediation: (1) whether parties were given an opportunity to 'tell their story' ('opportunity for voice'), (2) whether the third party considered the parties' views, (3) whether the third party treated the parties in an even-handed and dignified manner; and (4) whether the third party is impartial.[20] The process for dispute resolution is often a three-stage process – colloquially known as

---

15. Online Dispute Resolution and the Courts, Version 1.0, 30 November 2016, p. 7.
16. ODR and the Courts: The promise of 100% access to justice?, HiiL TREND REPORT IV (2016), available at www.onlineresolution.com/hiil.pdf (last accessed 30 March 2017), p. 34.
17. Susskind, R. (2015). Online Dispute Resolution for Law Value Civil Claims, by Online Dispute Resolution Advisory Group, Civil Justice Group, UK, February 2015, available at www.judiciary.gov. uk/wp-content/uploads/2015/02/Online-Dispute-Resolution-Final-Web-Version1.pdf (last accessed 30 March 2017).
18. Corbett, J.R. (2016) At the Nexus of Big Data and Dispute Resolution: A Case Study on Conflict-Related Search Data, Mediation Theory and Practice, Volume 1, No. 1, pp. 5–33, available at https://doi.org/10.1558/mtp.v1i1.29197 and www.advancingdr.org/research/search (last accessed last accessed 30 March 2017).
19. Corbett, J.R. (2016) At the Nexus of Big Data and Dispute Resolution: A Case Study on Conflict-Related Search Data, Mediation Theory and Practice, Volume 1, No. 1, pp. 5–33, available at https://doi.org/10.1558/mtp.v1i1.29197 and www.advancingdr.org/research/search (last accessed last accessed 30 March 2017).
20. Welsh, N. (2001), Making Deals in Court-Connected Mediation: What's Justice Got to Do With It?, *Washington University Law Review*, Vol. 79, p. 817.

naming, blaming and claiming.[21] Accordingly, a robotic arbitrator, mediator or negotiator needs to have the ability to recognise the type of the case, connect the case to particular sources of arguments and calculate appropriate compensations for the winning party. The dispute resolution procedure that a robotic arbitrator, mediator or negotiator follows should be rigorous and the decision should also be consistent. It was advised that the procedural elements may have an impact on disputants' impression of the fairness of the substantive outcome, meaning that if a party thought the procedure was unfair, she/he would not be happy even when winning the case. Likewise, a party may feel alright when losing the case, if he/she thought procedural fairness was firmly displayed during the process.[22] Procedural justice should be strengthened and justified both on a design level (justifying a certain mix of procedural traits) and on an individual level (justifying choice of one process over another).[23]

4.2 Expertise, authority, reputation and strategic alliance

The success of deployment of ODR services, either public services or private services, relies on various factors. It requires technology and knowledge expertise, trusted authorities for technological and regulatory guidance, good reputation to build users' trust and confidence, and effective strategic alliances to strengthen their expertise, authority and reputation in the field. In recent years, some governments and courts also invest money to deliver 'a more effective, efficient and high performing courts and tribunal administration' through the use of modern technology;[24] outsource private companies to build integrated ODR services, case filing or management systems for courts; or subcontract ODR services for courts (though it is more controversial due to security, confidentiality and data protection). With regard to ODR private services, there are a number of past and current examples where ODR service providers and arbitration institutions have formed successful strategic alliances; likewise ODR service providers and e-commerce marketplaces have also formed positive

---

21. Senft, L.P. & Savage, C. A. (2003), ADR in the Courts: Progress, Problems and Possibilities, *Penn State Law Review* Vol. 108, p. 328.
22. Connely, J. M. & O'Barr, W. M. (1998), Hearing the Hidden Agenda: The Ethnographic Investigation of Procedure, *Law & Contemporary Problems* Vol. 51, pp. 184–8.
23. Rabinovich-Einy, O. & Katsh, E. (2014), Reshaping Boundaries in Online Dispute Resolution Environment, *International Journal of Online Dispute Resolution*, Volume 1, No. 1, pp. 5–36, p. 15–17.
24. For example, 'On 28 March 2014, the Lord Chief Justice announced a reform programme to deliver "a more effective, efficient and high performing courts and tribunal administration" through the use of modern technology. This is to be enabled by a new one-off investment, averaging up to £75m per annum over five years from 2015/16. It was said that the investment would enable the legal profession and other justice agencies to adopt more efficient and cost-saving working practices by using digital technology in their dealings with the courts and tribunals, and that users should only need to attend at a court or tribunal when absolutely necessary.' See The e-court service – a vision of the future, 29 January 2015, available at www.lawsociety.org.uk/communities/solicitor-judges-division/articles/e-court-service/ (last accessed 30 March 2017).

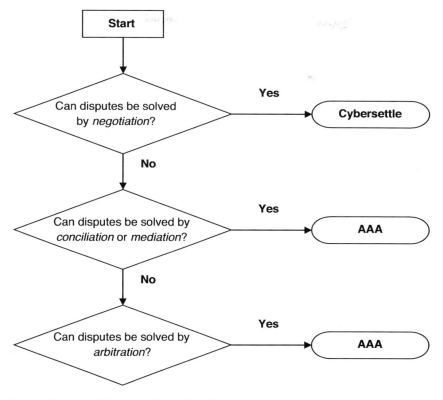

Figure 4.1 AAA–Cybersettle Strategic Alliance

partnership. As discussed in Chapter 2, some typical examples of ODR service collaboration are as follows:

- eBay and SquareTrade (past experience); and eBay, PayPal and Modria;
- AAA (the American Arbitration Association) and Cybersettle (ODR private service);
- WIPO (World Intellectual Property Organization) and ICANN (the Internet Corporation for Assign Names and Numbers) – UDRP (Domain Name Dispute Resolution Policy).

Whilst WIPO and ICANN-UDRP provide a specialised domain dispute resolution service with a self-enforcement mechanism (that the ICANN accredited-registrars reserve the rights to transfer or cancel a domain name directly), AAA and Cybersettle provide one of the most distinctive Med-Arb alliance service between an arbitration institution and a private ODR company since 2006. Cybersettle, a patented online and double-blind bidding process, provides the competence and capacities to complement AAA's abilities.[25] With the goal of 'ensuring that no one walks away without a resolution', AAA clients using the AAA's online case management tools will be able to attempt settlement with Cybersettle before AAA neutrals are selected. And Cybersettle clients who have not been able to reach settlement through online negotiation will be able to switch to the AAA's dispute resolution processes, including conciliation, mediation, and arbitration.[26]

The benefits of the cooperation between AAA and Cybersettle are fourfold:

(1) **Reputation and merits**. The AAA is a non-profit making public service organisation. It also serves as a centre for education and training, issues specialised publications, and conducts research on all forms of out-of-court dispute settlement. Cybersettle, founded in 1996 as a pioneer in online negotiation, is the inventor and patent-holder of the online double-blind bidding system.

(2) **Experience**. AAA offers a broad range of dispute resolution services to business executives, attorneys, individuals, trade associations, unions, management, consumers, families, communities, and all levels of government, while between 1996 and 2008 Cybersettle had already handled more than 200,000 transactions, with more than 1.46 billion USD in settlements.[27]

(3) **Professional regulations**. AAA has the Commercial Arbitration Rules and Mediation Procedures, including Procedures for Large, Complex Commercial Disputes; as well as Supplementary Rules for the Resolution of Patent Disputes and a Practical Guide on Drafting Dispute Resolution Clauses, including negotiation, mediation, arbitration and large, complex cases. Cybersettle can contribute its private practices and work with AAA to promote other services when appropriate and to make joint proposals and business presentations under certain circumstances.

(4) **Advanced case filing and management systems**. In addition to Cybersettle's web-assisted claim settlement, AAA has provided a sophisticated case-filing system called AAA WebFile/Panelist eCenter[28] and a case

---

25. Institutional ADR Today: The Comprehensive, Cost-Effective Alternative, (August 2011) *The Metropolitan Corporate Counsel, Inc*, Volume 19, No. 8, available at www.adr.org/aaa/ShowPDF?doc=ADRSTG_004012 (last accessed 30 March 2017).

26. AAA and Cybersettle Sign Unique Partnership Agreement, 2006; see also Institutional ADR Today: The Comprehensive, Cost-Effective Alternative, (August 2011) *The Metropolitan Corporate Counsel, Inc*, Volume 19, No. 8, available at www.adr.org/aaa/ShowPDF?doc=ADRSTG_004012 (last visited 17 January 2017).

27. Cybersettle makes the case for resolving disputes online, posted 20 February 2008, available at https://mediationchannel.com/2008/02/20/cybersettle-makes-the-case-for-resolving-disputes-online/ (last accessed 30 March 2017).

28. AAA WebFile/Panelist eCenter, available at www.adr.org/webfile/faces/home (last accessed 30 March 2017).

management tool called online À La Carte Services[29] in conjunction with an online case analysis tool known as CaseXplorer® Arbitration™.[30]

When comparing the examples of WIPO and ICANN-UDRP, AAA with Cybersettle and the past experience of SquareTrade with eBay, what is striking is that these three ODR services do not only make a very attractive offer for easy accessible, quick, effective, and low-cost dispute resolution, but most importantly have succeeded in integrating their offer to the primary markets for Internet-related disputes such as domain names disputes and online purchase/service disputes.[31]

This integration is brought about in all these three cases by cooperation agreements with the primary market makers, for example, WIPO with ICANN; SquareTrade with eBay, and Cybersettle with AAA, and by creating socio-legal bonds for potential dispute parties to commit to the process.[32] That is, the ICANN UDRP administrative procedure is mandatory to domain name holders, whilst the SquareTrade mediation process was mandatory to eBay-sellers before eBay and PayPal established their own dispute resolution centre with technological help from Modria. Modria, a private company that was founded in 2011, created ODR systems at eBay and PayPal using a software-as-a-service (SaaS) platform which easily integrates with the back-end architecture and front-end user experience.[33]

In recent years, notice and takedown procedures (NTD), known as notice-and-action procedures (N&A), have also been developed to resolve online infringement issues. They are also called 'takedown procedures' or 'takedown notice' in the Digital Millennium Copyright Act in the US.[34] The notice and takedown procedures can be conducted entirely online, which may be deemed as the 'negotiation' stage in an ODR system. In other words, the notice and take down procedure can be embedded in an ODR platform, which provides guided negotiation to disputed parties. When disputes cannot be resolved to parties' satisfaction, parties may bring claims forward in arbitration or court litigation. The NTD procedures are commonly understood as: starting whenever someone notifies a hosting service about illegal content on the internet and concluding when an online intermediary takes down (i.e. blocking or deleting) the alleged

---

29. À La Carte Services, 'available at http://info.adr.org/a-la-carte-services/ (last accessed 30 March 2017).

30. CaseXplorer® Arbitration™, available at http://info.adr.org/cxa/ (last accessed 30 March 2017).

31. Calliess, G. P. (2006), Online Dispute Resolution: Consumer Redress in a Global Market Place, *German Law Journal*, Volume 7, No.8, pp. 647–60, p. 653.

32. In the author's view, 'social-legal bones' means the combination of the powers between social organizations and legislation. The term 'legal bond' is being used in a very broad sense, including not only contractual design but also all kinds of 'private ordering'.

33. Modria, available at http://modria.com/about-us/ (last accessed 30 March 2017).

34. Pallas, L. (2011), Deterring Abuse of the Copyright Takedown Regime by Taking Misrepresentation Claims Seriously, 46 *Wake Forest Law Review* pp. 745–82, 745.

illegal content.[35] The NTD procedures are deemed to be 'indispensable measures in the fight against the sale of Counterfeit Goods over Internet Platforms'.[36] It was also popularly used to fight again other IP rights infringement, defamatory content, terrorism-related content, illegal online gambling, child abuse content, misleading advertisements or incitement to hatred or violence on the basis of race, origin, religion, gender, sexual orientation etc.[37] The NTD procedures have been horizontally applied across a variety of legal subject matters including Internet-related consumer disputes. In practice, some hosting service providers have voluntarily put in place technical mechanisms/systems for the 'notice and takedown' process. For example, it is notable that eBay has developed a NTD system called 'VeRO' (Verified Rights Owner) – a filter program – that is intended to provide IP owners with assistance in removing infringing listings from the marketplace. It requires that the complainant fill out the standard notice of infringement form specifying the allegedly infringing listings and infringed works, completing with an original authorised signature, and faxing it to eBay.[38] Amazon have also introduced their self-regulated 'notice and takedown' procedures to deal with rights infringements. Different from eBay, Amazon sets up separate formats for different rights infringement such as 'notice and procedure for notifying Amazon of defamatory content' and 'notice and procedure for making claims of right infringements'. The complainant will need to send to Amazon a printed and signed copy of the defamatory content notice after filling in a downloadable form.[39] Different from notification of defamatory content, the complainant is only required to fill in an online form regarding alleged infringements such as copyright and trademarks concerns and click the 'submit' button to complete the report infringement process.[40] Evidential materials gathered during the 'notice and takedown' process may be served as evidence for arbitration if parties bring claims forward in arbitration.

In order to build a successful ODR system, trust is the most crucial factor. In the early days, it was suggested that there are three fundamental factors for a successful ODR system: trust, convenience and expertise. It is important to

---

35. A Clean and Open Internet: Public Consultation on Procedures for Notifying and Acting on Illegal Content hosted by Online Intermediaries, available at http://ec.europa.eu/yourvoice/ipm/forms/dispatch?form=noticeandaction (last accessed 30 March 2017).

36. Memorandum of Understanding on the sale of counterfeit goods over the internet (hereafter, 'the MoU'), 4 May 2011, European Commission, Brussels, available at http://ec.europa.eu/internal_market/iprenforcement/docs/memorandum_04052011_en.pdf (last accessed 30 March 2017), Article 11.

37. A Clean and Open Internet: Public Consultation on Procedures for Notifying and Acting on Illegal Content hosted by Online Intermediaries, available at http://ec.europa.eu/yourvoice/ipm/forms/dispatch?form=noticeandaction (last accessed 30 March 2017).

38. eBay VeRo Program information, available at http://pages.ebay.co.uk/vero/notice.html (last accessed 30 March 2017).

39. Notice and Procedure for Notifying Amazon of Defamatory Content, available at www.amazon.co.uk/gp/help/customer/display.html?nodeId=1040616#defame (last accessed 30 March 2017).

40. Notice and Procedure for Making Claims of Right Infringements – Report Infringement, available at www.amazon.co.uk/gp/help/reports/infringement (last accessed 30 March 2017).

strike the balance among these factors depending on the intended usage of an ODR system.[41] The design of the system will depend on who the parties are and what the context is. This is the case in particular for a combined ADR and ODR service, which needs to be assessed in order to enhance a successful dispute resolution process.[42] There is often a trade-off between the power of an application (expertise) and how complicated it is to use (convenience).[43] There is a relationship between expertise and trust, as a seemingly competent system is more likely to be trustworthy. Consequently, convenience and trust may be inversely related. With the deployment of advanced ODR systems embedded with artificial intelligence and even robotic technology, the fundamental factors of trust, convenience and expertise may need to be expanded to a wider scope of factors such as: authenticity, reliability, durability, efficiency and flexibility. In both basic and advanced/intelligent ODR systems, trust is of paramount importance, in particular in advanced ODR systems where a higher level of trust is desired due to the fact that users are less willing to trust computer algorithms to make automated decisions.

4.3 Appointment of online arbitrators

Following the discussion on the concept and selection of online arbitrators by parties, appointing authorities and national courts in the previous chapter, the next step is to seek for the establishment of a harmonised legal framework with legal and technological measures for appointing online arbitrators across the globe.

The United Nations Commission on International Trade Law (UNCITRAL) Online dispute resolution for cross-border electronic commerce transactions draft procedural rules have provided procedural requirements concerning appointment of neutrals.[44] However, the UNCITRAL Draft Procedural Rules do not specify types of neutrals such as negotiators, mediators or arbitrators and the qualifications of neutrals, but generally concern any individual that assists the parties in settling or resolving the dispute.[45] Draft Article 9 of the UNCITRAL draft procedural rules stipulates appointment of neutrals as follows:[46]

---

41. Katsh, E. M. & Rifkin, J. (2001), Online Dispute Resolution: Resolving Conflicts in Cyberspace (San Francisco: Jossey-Bass, 2001), p. 73.
42. Katsh, E. M. & Rifkin, J. (2001), Online Dispute Resolution: Resolving Conflicts in Cyberspace (San Francisco: Jossey-Bass, 2001), p. 75.
43. Katsh, E. M. & Rifkin, J. (2001), Online Dispute Resolution: Resolving Conflicts in Cyberspace (San Francisco: Jossey-Bass, 2001), p. 76.
44. A/CN.9/WG.III/WP.133 – Online dispute resolution for cross-border electronic commerce transactions: draft procedural rules, United Nations Commission on International Trade Law, Working Group III (Online dispute resolution), Thirty-first session, New York, 9–13 February 2015, available at https://documents-dds-ny.un.org/doc/UNDOC/LTD/V14/080/65/PDF/V1408065.pdf?OpenElement (last accessed 30 March 2017).
45. UNCITRAL Draft ODR Procedural Rules 2014 (A/CN.9/WG.III/WP.133), Articles 2(6) and 9.
46. UNCITRAL Draft ODR Procedural Rules 2014 (A/CN.9/WG.III/WP.133), Article 9.

1. The ODR administrator shall appoint the neutral promptly following commencement of the facilitated settlement stage of proceedings. Upon appointment of the neutral, the ODR administrator shall promptly notify the parties of the name of the neutral and any other relevant or identifying information in relation to that neutral.
2. The neutral, by accepting appointment, confirms that he or she can devote the time necessary to conduct the ODR proceedings diligently, efficiently and in accordance with the time limits in the Rules.
3. The neutral shall, at the time of accepting his or her appointment, declare his or her impartiality and independence. The neutral, from the time of his or her appointment and throughout the ODR proceedings, shall without delay disclose any circumstances likely to give rise to justifiable doubts as to his or her impartiality or independence to the ODR administrator. The ODR administrator shall promptly communicate such information to the parties.
4. Either party may object to the neutral's appointment within [two (2)] calendar days (i) of the notification of appointment without giving reasons therefor; or (ii) of a fact or matter coming to its attention that is likely to give rise to justifiable doubts as to the impartiality or independence of the neutral, setting out the fact or matter giving rise to such doubts, at any time during the ODR proceedings.
5. Where a party objects to the appointment of a neutral under paragraph 4(i), that neutral shall be automatically disqualified and another appointed in his or her place by the ODR administrator. Each party shall have a maximum of [three (3)] challenges to the appointment of a neutral following each notice of appointment, following which the appointment of a neutral by the ODR administrator will be final, subject to paragraph 4(ii). Alternatively if no challenges are made within two (2) days of any notice of appointment, the appointment will become final, subject to paragraph 4(ii).
6. Where a party objects to the appointment of a neutral under subparagraph 4(ii) above, the ODR administrator shall make a determination within [three (3)] calendar days, regarding whether that neutral shall be replaced.
7. In the event both parties object to the appointment of a neutral under paragraph 4(i) or 4(ii), that neutral shall be automatically disqualified and another appointed in his or her place by the ODR administrator, notwithstanding the number of challenges that has been made by either party.
8. Either party may object, within three (3) calendar days of the final appointment of the neutral, to the provision by the ODR administrator to the neutral of information generated during the negotiation stage. Following the expiration of this three-day period and in the absence of any objections, the ODR administrator shall convey the full set of existing information on the ODR platform to the neutral.
9. The number of neutrals shall be one.

In relation to the rules above, they may contradict common practice and national arbitration legislation concerning party autonomy in selection and appointment of arbitrators if parties have not been given any chance to recommend their own arbitrators and decide the number of arbitrators. According to the UNCITRAL Draft ODR Procedural Rules, the ODR administrator[47] has the power to appoint

---

47. UNCITRAL Draft ODR Procedural Rules 2014 (A/CN.9/WG.III/WP.133), Article 2(2). It provides 'ODR administrator means the entity [specified in the dispute resolution clause] that administers

arbitrators but the number of such arbitrators is only one, who will be accepted in arbitration procedure, though parties have the right to object to ODR administrator's recommendation of the arbitrator within two calendar days without the need of giving any reason. One of the perceived advantages of international arbitration is that it allows parties to choose neutrals (i.e. negotiators, mediators or arbitrators).[48] Harmonised best practices for the appointment of arbitrators would be to give parties an option to decide the required number of arbitrators and select arbitrators other than to have a restricted scope of selection and number within recommendations by the ODR administrator suggested by the UNCITRAL Draft ODR Procedural Rules. The wording of 'ODR administrator', which is compatible with an equivalent concept in other legislation such as the EU Regulation on Consumer ODR, refers to any entity including a natural person, a legal person or an authority/public body, however named or referred to, which is established on a durable basis and offers the resolution of a dispute through an ADR procedure.[49]

With regard to the ethical requirements and power of online neutrals, Article 10 of the UNCITRAL Draft ODR Procedural Rules complements Article 9(3) concerning neutrals' ethics and further stipulates the power of the neutral as follows:[50]

1. Subject to the Rules, the neutral may conduct the ODR proceedings in such manner as he or she considers appropriate.

    1 bis. The neutral, in exercising his or her functions under the Rules, shall conduct the ODR proceedings so as to avoid unnecessary delay and expense and to provide a fair and efficient process for resolving the dispute. In doing so, the neutral shall remain at all times wholly independent and impartial and shall treat both parties equally.

2. Subject to any objections under article 9, paragraph 8, the neutral shall conduct the ODR proceedings on the basis of all communications made during the ODR proceedings [, the relevance of which shall be determined by the neutral. The ODR proceedings shall be conducted on the basis of these materials only unless the neutral decides otherwise.]

3. At any time during the proceedings the neutral may [require] [request] or allow the parties (upon such terms as to costs and otherwise as the neutral shall determine) to provide additional information, produce documents, exhibits or other evidence within such period of time as the neutral shall determine.

4. The neutral shall have the power to rule on his or her own jurisdiction, including any objections with respect to the existence or validity of any agreement to refer the dispute to ODR. For that purpose, the dispute resolution clause

---

and coordinates ODR proceedings under these Rules, including where appropriate, by administering an ODR platform.'

48. Born, G., International Arbitration: Cases and Materials (New York: Aspen Publishers, 2011), p. 99.

49. Directive 2013/11/EU of the European Parliament and of the Council of 21 May 2013 on alternative dispute resolution for consumer disputes and amending Regulation (EC) No 2006/2004 and Directive 2009/22/EC (Directive on consumer ADR), OJ L 165, 18.6.2013, pp. 63–79, Articles 4(1)(h), 4(3) and 20(2).

50. UNCITRAL Draft ODR Procedural Rules 2014 (A/CN.9/WG.III/WP.133), Article 11.

that forms part of a contract shall be treated as an agreement independent of the other terms of the contract. A determination by the neutral that the contract is null shall not automatically entail the invalidity of the dispute resolution clause.

5. The neutral, after making such inquiries as he or she may deem necessary, may, in his or her discretion, extend any deadlines under these Rules.

In accordance with the rules above, the arbitrator shall conduct the arbitral proceedings fairly, diligently, efficiently, independently and impartially, which is mostly in line with the majority of institutional rules, national law and international arbitration legislation. Procedural rules in some countries or regions concerning arbitrators may also require arbitrators with specific knowledge or expertise. For example, the EC Directive on Consumer ADR provides that 'member States shall ensure that the natural persons in charge of ADR [. . .] possess the necessary knowledge and skills in the field of alternative or judicial resolution of consumer disputes, as well as a general understanding of law'.[51] The China Arbitration Law also stipulates that an arbitrator shall have acquired the knowledge of law, engaged in the professional work in the field of economy and trade, etc.[52]

With regard to the design of a more sophisticated ODR system, in addition to building in credit rating systems for the selection of arbitrators according to customers' reviews as discussed in the previous chapter, the system may be able to automatically recommend qualified arbitrators through aggregated data according to the criteria of required arbitrators that parties input in the system. It is common knowledge that arbitration is confidential and arbitral awards are usually unpublished. It is hard to know the actual experience of arbitrators and their standard of decision-making. In order to increase and equalise access to critical information in the arbitrator selection process, in 2015 Arbitrator Intelligence – a non-profit, interactive informational network – concluded its preliminary start-up phrase to set up a pilot project to collect arbitrators' past decision-making information.[53] Arbitrator Intelligence has designed a feedback questionnaire called 'Arbitrator Intelligence Questionnaire (AIQ)' to facilitate systematic collection of information about arbitrators' past case management and decision-making.[54] They are also collecting published and unpublished international arbitrator award submissions.[55] The initiative is an excellent idea; however it is unpredictable how many arbitrators in the world may participate in the questionnaire and contribute their awards to the system. On 1 June 2017 the Singapore International Arbitration

---

51. EC Directive on Consumer ADR, Article 6(1)(a).
52. Arbitration Law of People's Republic of China, 1994, Article 13.
53. Arbitrator Intelligence, available at www.arbitratorintelligence.org/about/ (last accessed 30 March 2017).
54. Arbitrator Intelligence Questionnaire (AIQ), available at www.arbitratorintelligence.org/aiq-frequently-asked-questions/ (last accessed 30 March 2017).
55. Award Progress Bar, available at www.arbitratorintelligence.org/project-updates/ (last accessed 30 March 2017).

Centre (SIAC) entered into a cooperation agreement with Arbitrator Intelligence to encourage their arbitrators to participate in AIQ.[56] Although the use of AIQ has been promoted across the globe, it is still not clear how reliable the result data will be and how useful such data can be. Nevertheless, if ODR service providers use their published and unpublished arbitral awards in their database to analyse the quality and standard of arbitrators' past decision-making, it may provide parties with helpful recommendations. It will be even more helpful if the majority of ODR service providers establish partnerships to share their data of arbitrators' past decision-making in an aggregated form without revealing parties' personal data and confidential information by means of data anonymisation. Such aggregated data may provide factors for consideration of the selection of arbitrations such as arbitrators' speed of resolving disputes in each phrase of the arbitration process, qualifications, special knowledge, experience and skills of arbitrators, successful rates of arbitral awards and customers' review etc. ODR service providers must take care to ensure information is original and unmodified before inclusion in their system. False reviews or modified awards could skew the impression of an arbitrator, and result in a poor choice being made for a given dispute. The person or body submitting information should not be anonymous, and their relationship to the case should be noted.

4.4 The admission of electronic evidence

The conditions for taking and admitting electronic evidence in international arbitration depends on various factors such as the parties' arbitration agreement, institutional rules and procedural laws. Arbitral tribunals or national courts may also exercise their discretion in taking and admitting evidential materials depending on their adopted procedural rules. It is suggested that the evaluation of the evidence is entirely within the discretion of tribunals across the globe,[57] though rules and principles of admissibility of evidence are different between civil law and common law systems in procedures and practices. In the civil law system, the rules of admissibility of evidence for arbitration may give priority to documentary evidence, depend on the examination of witnesses conducted by tribunals and permit the freedom from technical and restrictive rules of evidence.[58] Whereas, in the common law system, in addition to admitting evidence of witness being examined and cross-examined by tribunals at the hearing, the rules of admissibility of evidence have mainly come from jury trials determining competence, relevance and materiality and testimonial evidence by oral testimony is generally

---

56. SIAC Signs Cooperation Agreement with Arbitrator Intelligence, posted on 1 June 2017, available at http://www.siac.org.sg/ (last accessed 1 June 2017).
57. Pietrowski, R. (2006), Evidence in International Arbitration, *Arbitration International*, Volume 22 Issue 3, pp. 373–410, p. 374.
58. Pietrowski, R. (2006), Evidence in International Arbitration, Arbitration International, Volume 22 Issue 3, pp. 373–410, p. 375.

proved.[59] In both civil law and common law systems, evaluation of evidence often relies on the weight of evidence rather than its admissibility. Direct evidence and documentary evidence usually carry more weight than indirect evidence and testimonial evidence. International legislation and arbitration institutional rules have been reflecting on the combination of civil law and common law arbitration procedures such as the UNCITTRAL Arbitration Rules and IBA Rules on the Taking of Evidence in International Commercial Arbitration. For example, the UNCITRAL Arbitration Rules stipulate that 'the arbitral tribunal shall determine the admissibility, relevance, materiality and weight of the evidence offered'.[60]

International organisations, national law and arbitration institutions have also been working on updating their arbitration procedural rules and regulations concerning admission of electronic evidence to keep up with resolving disputes online. For example, as identified and discussed in the previous chapter, the CIETAC Guideline on Evidence and CIETAC Online Arbitration Rules both accept a wide range of electronic evidence including electronic documentary evidence and online testimonial evidence from both parties' witnesses and expert witnesses.[61] The revised IBA Rules on the Taking of Evidence in International Commercial Arbitration also recognise the admission of electronic evidence.[62] The major development of procedures for taking electronic evidence is the UNCITRAL Draft ODR Procedural Rules. In recent years, the UNCITRAL online dispute resolution working group has also been working on the UNCITRAL Draft ODR Procedural Rules in terms of the procedures for taking evidence at the notice and response stages during dispute resolution proceedings. For example, Article 4A(1) of the UNCITRAL Draft ODR Procedural Rules provides that 'The notice should, as far as possible, be accompanied by all documents and other evidence relied upon by the claimant, or contain references to them.' Article 4A(5) further explains that 'the claimant may provide, at the time it submits its notice, any other relevant information, including information in support of its claim, and also information in relation to the pursuit of other legal remedies'. With regard to admission of evidence at the response stage, Article 4B(1) provides that:

> The respondent shall communicate to the ODR administrator a response to the notice in accordance with paragraph 2 within [seven (7)] calendar days of being notified of the availability of the notice on the ODR platform. [The response should, as far

---

59. Pietrowski, R. (2006), Evidence in International Arbitration, Arbitration International, Volume 22 Issue 3, pp. 373–410, p. 375.
60. UNCITRAL Arbitration Rules (Revised 2013), Article 27(4) available at www.uncitral.org/pdf/english/texts/arbitration/arb-rules-2013/UNCITRAL-Arbitration-Rules-2013-e.pdf (last accessed 30 March 2017).
61. CIETAC Guidelines on Evidence, effective 1 March 2015, Article 9, available at www.cietac.org/index.php?m=Page&a=index&id=107&l=en (last accessed 30 March 2017); and CIETAC Online Arbitration Rules 2015, Articles 29 and 36, available at www.cietac.org/index.php?m=Article&a=show&id=2770&l=en (last accessed 30 March 2017).
62. IBA Rules on the Taking of Evidence in International Arbitration (2010), Article 3(12), available at www.ibanet.org/Publications/publications_IBA_guides_and_free_materials.aspx (last accessed 30 March 2017).

as possible, be accompanied by all documents and other evidence relied upon by the respondent, or contain references to them.

Article 4B(3) further clarifies that 'The respondent may provide, at the time it submits its notice, any other relevant information, including information in support of its response, and also information in relation to the pursuit of other legal remedies.' As discussed previously, neutrals also have power to determine the relevance of materials submitted and request or allow the parties to provide additional information, produce documents, exhibits or other evidence within such period of time.[63] While the UNCTIRAL Draft Procedural Rules are helpful with regard to the timing of the submission of electronic evidence, the UNCTIRAL Draft Procedural Rules do not specify as to the technological standard of admitting electronic evidential records but leave the burden on the neutrals to determine the relevance of materials submitted from a legal perspective.

As none of the institutional rules, national and international regulations provide specific legal and technological measures in relation to generating, presenting, taking, admitting and storing/keeping electronic evidential records for online arbitration, inconsistent quality and unfair requirements towards electronic evidence is alarming. There is need for a harmonised legal framework or at least a set of well-recognised best practices concerning technological and legal measures for generating, presenting, taking, admitting and storing/keeping electronic evidential records.

How to produce and keep an electronic evidential record is the most crucial point of the matter in question. In absence of specific regulations on legal and technological measures for producing and keeping electronic evidence, relevant rules and legislation concerning electronic communications for consumer and commercial transactions may be transplanted to the interpretation and practice of format requirements of electronic evidence in arbitration. There are a number of common virtues that qualified electronic evidence should present as required by institutional arbitrational rules and relevant national and international legislation: authenticity, reliability, appropriateness, convenience and economical cost.[64] Authenticity usually refers to originality of evidential records and identity of their ownership. Reliability usually refers to integrity and durability of evidential records. Appropriateness usually refers to suitable technological means for gathering and presenting evidential records, which should be convenient and economical.

The principle of authenticity sometimes intertwines with the principle of reliability in that electronic evidential records should be generated, produced, transmitted, presented and stored by any reliable means that enhance the authenticity of evidence. Inside the principles of authenticity and reliability, durability of

---

63. UNCITRAL Draft ODR Procedural Rules 2014 (A/CN.9/WG.III/WP.133), Article 11(2),(3).
64. CIETAC Online Arbitration Rules 2015, Article 29; and IBA Rules on the Taking of Evidence in International Arbitration (2010), Article 3(12).

electronic evidential records should be the cornerstone. For example, in the EU, the EC Directive on Consumer ADR requires that ADR entities make publicly available on their websites, on a durable medium upon request, and by any other means they consider appropriate, clear and easily understandable information on the entities and their annual activity reports.[65] In the UK, the Consumer Contracts Regulations provide a systematic and constructive explanation of the meaning of 'durable medium', defining 'durable medium' as

> paper or email, or any other medium that (a) allows information to be addressed personally to the recipient; (b) enables the recipient to store the information in a way accessible for future reference for a period that is long enough for the purposes of the information; and (c) allows the unchanged reproduction of the information stored.[66]

At the international level, the UN Convention on the Use of Electronic Communications in International Contracts (hereafter 'the UN Convention') also emphasises that 'where the law requires that a communication or a contract should be in writing, or provides consequences for the absence of a writing, that requirement is met by an electronic communication if the information contained therein is *accessible* so as to be usable *for subsequent reference*'.[67] The UN Convention further establishes two benchmarks for a communication or a contract to be validly 'made available or retained in its original form', namely, the 'integrity of information' and the capability of 'being displayed'.[68] With regard to electronic signatures affixed with electronic evidential documents in arbitration, the general effect of electronic record and electronic signatures have been widely accepted by international, regional and national legislation.[69] The most recent legislation concerning electronic signatures is the EU Regulation on Electronic Identification and Trust Services for Electronic Transactions 2014 (in force from 1 July 2016), which repealed the EC Directive on Electronic Signatures 1999.[70] The EU Regulation on Electronic Identification and Trust Services for

---

65. Directive 2013/11/EU of the European Parliament and of the Council of 21 May 2013 on alternative dispute resolution for consumer disputes and amending Regulation (EC) No 2006/2004 and Directive 2009/22/EC (Directive on consumer ADR), Article 7.
66. The Consumer Contracts (Information, Cancellation and Additional Charges) Regulations 2013, UK, available at www.gov.uk/government/uploads/system/uploads/attachment_data/file/265898/consumer-contracts-information-cancellation-and-additional-payments-regulations-2013.pdf (last accessed 30 March 2017), WLR 5.
67. The UN Convention on the Use of Electronic Communications in International Contracts 2005, Article 9(2).
68. The UN Convention on the Use of Electronic Communications in International Contracts 2005, Article 9(4).
69. See for example the UN Convention on the Use of Electronic Communications in International Contracts 2005; UNCITRAL Model Law on Electronic Signatures 2001; Electronic Signature Law of the People's Republic of China 2005; the Uniform Electronic Transactions Act (UETA) 1999; the Electronic Signatures in Global and National Commerce Act 2000; and Regulation (EU) No 910/2014 of the European Parliament and of the Council of 23 July 2014 on electronic identification and trust services for electronic transactions in the internal market and repealing Directive 1999/93/EC.
70. Regulation (EU) No 910/2014 of the European Parliament and of the Council of 23 July 2014 on electronic identification and trust services for electronic transactions in the internal market and repealing Directive 1999/93/EC, OJ L 257, 28.8.2014, pp. 73–114.

Electronic Transactions affirms the definition of 'electronic signature' as 'data in electronic form which is attached to or logically associated with other data in electronic form and which is used by the signatory to sign'.[71] It introduces new concepts of 'qualified electronic signature', 'electronic seal', 'advanced electronic seal' and 'qualified electronic seal'. The definitions and conditions concerning electronic seal endorse the form requirements of electronic records including electronic documents and any other forms of electronic records. According to the EU Regulation on Electronic Identification and Trust Services for Electronic Transactions, 'electronic seal' means 'data in electronic form, which is attached to or logically associated with other data in electronic form to ensure the latter's origin and integrity',[72] whilst 'qualified electronic seal' means 'an advanced electronic seal, which is created by a qualified electronic seal creation device, and that is based on a qualified certificate for electronic seal'.[73] 'An advanced electronic seal' shall meet all requirements that:

> (a) it is uniquely linked to the creator of the seal; (b) it is capable of identifying the creator of the seal; (c) it is created using electronic seal creation data that the creator of the seal can, with a high level of confidence under its control, use for electronic seal creation; and (d) it is linked to the data to which it relates in such a way that any subsequent change in the data is detectable.[74]

The key purpose of an electronic seal is to ensure the origin and integrity of an electronic record, which is compatible with the requirements of electronic documents to be kept in a durable medium provided by the EC Directive on Consumer Rights 2011 (implemented in 2014).[75]

Accordingly, records of online video conferencing during online arbitration hearings may be admitted as electronic evidence provided that they are kept in a durable medium. In other words, expert opinions provided by electronic means should be stored safely for unchanged reproduction in a sense that integrity and authenticity can be maintained.[76] At the same time, electronic records of evidence for arbitration should be signed and encrypted to enhance confidentiality and security.

---

71. The EU Regulation on Electronic Identification and Trust Services for Electronic Transactions 2014, Article 3(10).
72. The EU Regulation on Electronic Identification and Trust Services for Electronic Transactions 2014, Article 3(25).
73. The EU Regulation on Electronic Identification and Trust Services for Electronic Transactions 2014, Article 3(27).
74. The EU Regulation on Electronic Identification and Trust Services for Electronic Transactions 2014, Article 36.
75. EC Directive on Consumer Rights 2011, Article 2(10). See also ECJ Case C-49/11, *Content Services Ltd. v Bundesarbeitskammer*, 5 July 2012.
76. Wang, F. (2015), The Incorporation of Terms into Commercial Contracts: A Reassessment in the Digital Age, *Journal of Business Law*, (2015) Issue 2, pp. 87–119, p. 103.

4.5 The attendance/testimony of witnesses online in arbitral proceedings

CIETAC Guideline on Evidence, CIETAC Online Arbitration Rules and the revised IBA Rules on the Taking of Evidence in International Commercial Arbitration all acknowledge the valid means of online attendance and testimony of parties' witnesses and expert witnesses during arbitral proceedings and admission of electronic evidence.[77] The challenges of the attendance and testimony of witnesses on the ODR platform may be similar to the challenges that have already existed in the traditional environment. One of the major issues is about the treatment concerning witness interviews and preparation for testimony. It is advised that it is a basic requirement in US litigation that lawyers have an obligation to carefully interview potential witnesses and prepare them for testimony.[78] However, this is an opposite approach compared with some approaches in some civil law systems. In some civil law systems, it is unethical or even potentially criminal to assist witnesses in preparing their testimonies and familiarising the disputes.[79] This may cause difficulties in determining which approach to apply when there are disputes among parties from different nations. Some institutional arbitration rules may try to harmonise different approaches between different legal systems by allowing witnesses interview without explicitly mentioning the wording of assisting the preparation for testimonies. For example, in the US, the IBA Rules on the Taking of Evidence 2010 provides that 'It shall not be improper for a Party, its officers, employees, legal advisors or other representatives to interview its witnesses or potential witnesses and to discuss their prospective testimony with them.'[80] However, it raised a question as to whether it would be possible for institutional rules to override national law with regard to professional responsibility.[81] It is most unlikely that institutional rules could ever overrule national law. Some institutional rules point out that whether it is proper to interview witnesses is subject to the mandatory provisions of any applicable law. For instance, in the UK, the London Court of International Arbitration (LCIA) Arbitration Rules 2014 provides that:

> Subject to the mandatory provisions of any applicable law, rules of law and any order of the Arbitral Tribunal otherwise, it shall not be improper for any party or its legal representatives to interview any potential witness for the purpose of presenting his

---

77. CIETAC Guidelines on Evidence, effective 1 March 2015, Article 9; CIETAC Online Arbitration Rules 2015, Articles 29 and 36; and IBA Rules on the Taking of Evidence in International Arbitration (2010), Article 3(12).
78. Born, G. (2011), International Arbitration: Cases and Materials (New York: Aspen Publishers, 2011), p. 990.
79. Born, G. (2011), International Arbitration: Cases and Materials (New York: Aspen Publishers, 2011), p. 990; see also Damaska, M. (1975), Presentation of Evidence and Fact-finding Precision, *University of Pennsylvania Law Review* Volume 123, pp. 1083–106, pp. 1088–9.
80. IBA Rules on the Taking of Evidence 2010, Article 4(3).
81. Born, G. (2011), International Arbitration: Cases and Materials (New York: Aspen Publishers, 2011), p. 991.

or her testimony in written form to the Arbitral Tribunal or producing such person as an oral witness at any hearing.[82]

Some institutional rules remain silent on this issue. For example, in China, the China International Economic and Trade Arbitration Commission (CIETAC) Guidance on Evidence 2015 mentions nothing about interviewing witnesses.

In the ODR systems, the issue of interviewing witnesses and assisting preparation of testimonies may become more complicated, because on most of the current ODR platforms, parties may not be aware of different institutional rules concerning witnesses' interview matters until they agree on an arbitration institution. Thus, a sophisticated ODR system should offer parties to choose a few arbitration institutions from a list of arbitration institutions for comparative purposes. Once arbitration institutions are chosen, the ODR system should outline the most significant differences of those institutional rules so that parties can make informed decisions.

4.6 Security, integrity and accessibility of online arbitration platforms

ODR systems may be categorised into the two areas of basic ODR and intelligent/advanced ODR. In basic ODR, the arbitrator is a natural person, or persons, usually within an organisation such as arbitral tribunals. The disputing parties are typically guided through a structured process such as the arbitration procedures. Certain types of disputes may have a narrower range of disputed issues and outcomes. For example, in B2C online purchase of goods, the scope of dispute may be limited. In such cases, communication may be limited to predetermined choices in order to simplify the process and reduce the scope for misunderstanding between the parties, particularly when the parties do not speak a common language. In this situation, the consumer may be provided with a list of possible complaints such as goods incorrectly described, goods damaged, goods missing etc. The seller may be provided with a list of possible solutions such as request return and refund, ship replacement item etc. The system may allow evidence to be submitted such as proof of delivery, where it may be possible for it to be validated with no human input. Where a dispute is more complex, the parties may be invited to explain their issue in more detail. This model is less likely to fit B2B disputes where the product or service being purchased may have additional complexity such as multiple deliverables and negotiated timescales, organised with a formal contract. The technological measures for the above can include a web-based and double-blind bidding system. Double-blind bidding is

> a form of confidential dispute resolution where opponents' offers and demands are compared in the blind by a neutral third party system: neither side knows the other side's position. If the submitted numbers meet the agreed to settlement criteria, that

---

82. The London Court of International Arbitration (LCIA) Arbitration Rules 2014, Article 20.5.

is, one side's offer is greater than or equal to the other side's demand, the third party system declares a settlement and the dispute is considered resolved.[83]

It is suggested that there are three merits in using double-blind bidding system: 1) eliminating unnecessary posturing as both parties enter realistic numbers; 2) being non-confrontational as there is no need for hostile negotiations or emotional arguments; 3) protects both parties' bargaining position, because if the dispute does not settle, bidding numbers are kept confidential and are never revealed to the other party.[84]

Intelligent ODR replaces or supplements the arbitrator in the basic ODR model with artificial intelligence. Artificial intelligence is the science and engineering of making intelligent machines, especially intelligent computer programs.[85] For an artificial intelligence model to replace the arbitrator, the machine itself must understand the nature of the dispute and the associated rules and laws relating to the case. It may need to have knowledge of previous cases, and if such cases are similar but not identical, it needs to understand how any differences affect the relevance to the case in question.[86] It may also help to have the ability to apply heuristics, known as guidelines or rules-of-thumb that an experienced arbitrator will have gained from a long career. This approach can provide faster decisions when there is too much information to realistically analyse. For artificial intelligence to replace the arbitrator, all factors in the case must be represented in the system such that an outcome can be produced. For artificial intelligence to supplement the arbitrator, only an appropriate subset of this work needs to be done. In a real-life application, it is likely that, as the model is developed, it gains complexity, experience and skill, and gradually solves more tasks to take the workload off the arbitrator, perhaps with the eventual goal of replacing the arbitrator altogether.

Whilst artificial intelligent is multidisciplinary and can be divided into multiple subfields, it is helpful to divide it into two distinct areas. The first is machine learning, a type of artificial intelligence that allows computers to learn to perform a task from studying a set of example data without being explicitly programmed. Machine-learning techniques help to perform recognition tasks, such as faces and text, classification tasks such as cancer screening and detection of unsolicited email, and robotic tasks such as automation in manufacturing. Machine learning is perhaps the most commonly thought of area when artificial intelligence is mentioned.

---

83. American Arbitration Association (AAA) International Centre for Dispute Resolution (ICDR) Manufacturer/Supplier Online Dispute Resolution Program, 2011.
84. AAA ICDR Manufacturer/Supplier Online Dispute Resolution Program, 2011.
85. McCarthy, J. (2007), What is Artificial Intelligence?, available at http://www-formal.stanford.edu/jmc/whatisai/node1.html (last accessed 30 March 2017).
86. Main, J., Dillon, T. and Shiu, S. (2001), A Tutorial on Case-Based Reasoning, Soft Computing in Case Based Reasoning, (eds.) Pal, S.K., Dillon, T. and Yeung, D. (London: Springer-Verlag, 2001), pp. 1–28, available at http://www4.comp.polyu.edu.hk/~csckshiu/pdf/shiu01scbrb2.pdf (last accessed 30 March 2017).

The secondary area is expert systems. These have been in use since the 1970s and are predominantly rule-based. Expert systems have been successfully used in numerous applications including manufacturing, planning, scheduling and medical diagnosis. Benefits may include a reduction in labour costs and the possibility of improving upon solutions obtained from a human expert.

For development of an intelligent arbitrator using artificial intelligence techniques, both machine learning and expert systems areas would have to be considered. There was debate over the suitability of employing these two technological measures for the development of ODR systems due to the ambiguous nature of relevant rules and law.[87] However, since then technologies have been further developed and given that laws and regulations may be expressed as a set of rules intended to be met by all parties, the task domain of an ODR arbitrator may perhaps be represented using a variety of high-level techniques including service-oriented computing, and automated computing, joining up with lower-level technologies such as expert systems, machine learning, argumentation theories, systems of non-monotonic logic, case-based reasoning and knowledge-based method. Service-oriented computing is a paradigm for distributed system development that allows software developers to focus on the fulfilment of the required enterprise functionalities at a conceptual level[88] and allows connections between the multiple tasks of an arbitrator and allocates resources within the ODR system.

An expert system comprises a knowledge base (KB) containing factual and heuristic knowledge and an inference engine that uses knowledge to form a line of reasoning to produce an outcome. Knowledge rules can be expressed with an IF (antecedent) THEN (consequent) structure. Development of a KB requires the input of a domain expert – a human arbitrator with expert knowledge in the field being modelled. This knowledge must be codified into an appropriate form, typically by a person other than the expert, unless the rule base is simple. The languages used are often Prolog and Lisp, which are commonly used in AI domains and are well suited for logical reasoning and natural language processing. A well-known expert system was CADIAG-2, aimed at providing support for medical diagnosis in the field of internal medicine.[89] The knowledge base comprised of approximately 40,000 rules that express the probability, or degree, to which the antecedent confirms the consequent. The inference engine can provide a diagnosis with a stated degree or certainty, having been provided

---

87. Lodder, A. R. & Zeleznikow, J. (Spring 2005), Developing An Online Dispute Resolution Environment: Dialogue Tools and Negotiation Support Systems in a Three-Step Model, *Harvard Negotiation Law Review*, Volume 10, pp. 287–338, p. 292.

88. Wang, F. & Griffiths, N. (2010), Protecting privacy in automated transaction systems: A legal and technological perspective in the European Union, *International Review of Law, Computers & Technology*, Volume 24, Number 2, pp. 153–62, pp. 156–7.

89. Muiño, D. P. (2011), A probabilistic interpretation of the medical expert system CADIAG-2, *Soft Computing*, Volume 15, Issue 10, pp. 2013–20, p. 2013.

with symptoms. This expert system, and others like it, have had success in the field of medical diagnosis.

A number of projects have attempted to replicate the success of medical expert systems in the field of law, that is, the robotisation of lawyers. This has seen limited success in cases where the domain is constrained,[90] but has not developed into large-scale, successful systems. There are various obstacles that make it difficult to build such systems, including that the law is written in natural language which is, by definition, imprecise and does not lend itself to being rewritten into unambiguous conditional statements. Also, there must be a robust mechanism to improve the information contained within the knowledge base. An end-user of the system may not be in the position to make such changes, but ODR service providers or technology providers employed by ODR service providers may be in a technical position to update the system. Customer feedback should also be taken into consideration when developing and maintaining the knowledge-based system.

An expert system can also use case-based reasoning (CBR) to produce outcomes from previous arbitral decisions. An example of such a system is UMCOURT.[91] A database of cases is developed to allow the CBR process to infer the outcome if the matter was resolved by a court. The system presents BATNA (Best Alternative to a Negotiated Agreement), WATNA (Worst Alternative to a Negotiated Agreement) and MLATNA (Most Likely Alternative to a Negotiated Agreement), which helps parties consider real-world outcomes in order to make wise decisions. In order to improve the process, the result of whether parties accept or reject the proposed outcome is fed back into the stored cases.[92] For both knowledge-based and cased-based reasoning, ongoing maintenance is required to keep rules and cases up to date and relevant.

4.7 Selection of the seat of online arbitration

In international arbitration, the location and place of arbitration, often known as the seat of arbitration, is critical and of paramount importance.[93] The seat of arbitration is an important factor to determine jurisdiction and applicable law for arbitration proceedings. According to *PT Garuda Indonesia v Birgen Air*, there is a distinction between 'place of arbitration' and the place where the arbitral tribunal carries on hearing witnesses, experts or the parties, namely, the 'venue of hearing' in that the place of arbitration does not change even though

---

90. Leith, P. (2016), The rise and fall of the legal expert system, *International Review of Law, Computers & Technology*, Volume 30, Issue 3, pp. 94–106, p. 99.

91. Carneiro, D., Novais, P., Andrade, F., Zeleznikow, J. and Neves, J. (2013), Using Case-Based Reasoning and Principled Negotiation to provide decision support for dispute resolution, *Knowledge and Information Systems*, Volume 36, Issue 3, pp 789–826, p. 795.

92. Carneiro, D., Novais, P., Andrade, F., Zeleznikow, J. and Neves, J. (2013), Using Case-Based Reasoning and Principled Negotiation to provide decision support for dispute resolution, *Knowledge and Information Systems*, Volume 36, Issue 3, pp 789–826, p. 799.

93. *Star Shipping A.S. v China National Foreign Trade Transportation Corporation* [1993] 2 Lloyd's Rep. 445, 442.

the tribunal may meet to hear witnesses or do any other things in relation to the arbitration at a location other than the place of arbitration.[94] In other words, the place or seat of arbitration is the legal place and location of arbitration proceedings but not necessarily the physical place and location of arbitration proceedings.[95] Arbitration law in most countries is territorial in scope, governing arbitration proceedings that take place within the territory of that state. It is advised that there are two categories of matters relating to arbitration proceedings stipulated under national arbitration law (the law of the arbitral seat): internal matters concerning arbitration procedural issues; and external matters concerning judicial supervision.[96] National and international arbitration legislation and rules employ the principle of party autonomy for selection of the place of arbitration and allow parties to choose the seat of arbitration by parties' agreement. In the absence of such agreement, the arbitral tribunal or arbitral institution will have the power to determine the place of arbitration at the beginning of the arbitral proceedings.[97] National and international arbitration legislation and rules normally permit arbitration hearings to be held in a location other than the legal place/seat of arbitration. For example, the UNCITRAL Model Law on International Commercial Arbitration provides that:

> (1) The parties are free to agree on the place of arbitration. Failing such agreement, the place of arbitration shall be determined by the arbitral tribunal having regard to the circumstances of the case, including the convenience of the parties.
>
> (2) Notwithstanding the provisions of paragraph (1) of this article, the arbitral tribunal may, unless otherwise agreed by the parties, meet at any place it considers appropriate for consultation among its members, for hearing witnesses, experts or the parties, or for inspection of goods, other property or documents.[98]

The UNCITRAL Arbitration Rules also recognise that the arbitral tribunal may meet at any appropriate place. The UNCITRAL Arbitration Rules also confirm that the legal place of arbitration is also the legal place of arbitral awards. The rules are written as follows:

> (1). If the parties have not previously agreed on the place of arbitration, the place of arbitration shall be determined by the arbitral tribunal having regard to the circumstances of the case. The award shall be deemed to have been made at the place of arbitration.
>
> (2). The arbitral tribunal may meet at any location it considers appropriate for deliberations. Unless otherwise agreed by the parties, the arbitral tribunal may also meet at any location it considers appropriate for any other purpose, including hearings.[99]

---

94. *PT Garuda Indonesia v Birgen Air* [2002] 1 SLR 393.
95. See also *Angela Raguz v Rebecca Sullivan* [2000] 50 NSWLR 236, para. 103.
96. Born, G., International Arbitration: Cases and Materials (New York: Aspen Publishers, 2011), p. 536.
97. UNCITRAL Notes on Organizing Arbitral Proceedings (2016), p. 11.
98. UNCITRAL Model Law on International Commercial Arbitration 1985 (With amendments as adopted in 2006), Article 20.
99. UNCITRAL Arbitration Rules (updated 2013), Article 18.

The UNCITRAL Notes on Organizing Arbitral Proceedings (2016) further explain prominent legal factors for the selection of the place of arbitration. They are: (a) the suitability of the arbitration law at the place of arbitration; (b) the law, jurisprudence and practices at the place of arbitration regarding: (i) court intervention in the course of arbitral proceedings; (ii) the scope of judicial review or of grounds for setting aside an award; and (iii) any qualification requirements with respect to arbitrators and counsel representation; and (c) whether the state where the arbitration takes place and hence where the arbitral award will be made is a party to the Convention on the Recognition and Enforcement of Foreign Arbitral Awards (New York, 1958) (the 'New York Convention') and/or to any other multilateral or bilateral treaty on enforcement of arbitral awards.[100] When hearings will be held at the legal place of arbitration, parties may also consider the convenience of the location, availability and cost of support services, the location of the subject matter in dispute and proximity and evidence and any qualification restrictions with respect to counsel representation.[101]

If parties are unable to agree on the legal place/seat of arbitration or when the agreements for the legal place/seat of arbitration are ambiguous or contradictory, parties may try to resolve this and agree on an arbitral seat after a dispute arises. If not, national courts may play a role in determining the arbitral seat.

With the deployment of the ODR system, the factors of location, availability and cost for selection of the legal and physical place of arbitration seems to be less relevant, because one of the purposes of using ODR for case filing, management and arbitral hearings is to allow parties to resolve disputes wherever they are and whenever they are available via electronic communications, which may, as a result, save cost. In the ODR system, selection of the legal place/seat of arbitration may be assisted by machine intelligence. A sophisticated ODR system may be built to generate an automated clause for the place/seat of arbitration depending on various information that parties select or provide to the ODR intelligence system. In other words, it is possible to design an online clause builder for selection of arbitral seat. For example, as discussed in the previous chapter, the American Arbitration Association (AAA) and the International Centre for Dispute Resolution (ICDR) offer a ClauseBuilder tool, which is designed to assist individuals and organisations develop customised, clear and effective arbitration and mediation agreements or clauses.[102] An arbitration agreement that is generated by the ClauseBuilder tool automatically includes a default clause of the place/seat of arbitration. A more specific online arbitral seat clause builder tool may be desired to provide a more specialised service to build a clause for selection of the place/seat of arbitration, which specifies the legal implications for choosing such a seat. This will enable parties to familiarise arbitration law in the country of that chosen seat.

---

100. UNCITRAL Notes on Organizing Arbitral Proceedings (2016), p. 12.
101. UNCITRAL Notes on Organizing Arbitral Proceedings (2016), p. 12.
102. See www.clausebuilder.org (last accessed 30 March 2017).

4.8 Users' awareness and protection in online arbitration

Traditionally when disputes arise, the common reaction from disputed parties would be going to court. ADR only became popular in the late 1990s. ODR has been new to the majority of the public. ODR tools may not even be well-known among legal practitioners.[103] It is a slow process that the public and legal practitioners get used to the idea of resolving disputes online. Users' awareness has been gradually improved by online marketplaces introducing integrated dispute resolution centres for their users or providing links to dispute resolution portals such as the EU ODR portal. Some online businesses may be reluctant to provide any information concerning dispute resolution services, hoping that customers would just walk away when problems occur. In order to tackle this issue, the EU Regulation on Consumer ODR has made it a mandatory obligation for businesses in member states to provide a link on their website to the EU ODR portal. A 'carrot and stick' approach could be taken to encourage businesses to make ODR information available. On the one hand, a trustmark could be established on the condition of the trader making appropriate information available. On the other hand, there could be penalties for businesses not fulfilling their obligations.

Whilst a country's government takes overall responsibility for ensuring compliance, they may wish to delegate responsibility to individual areas. For example, a council may be given responsibility to ensure the compliance of businesses in its local area. They may choose to advertise (such as videos or documents for users guide) on the website and in the media, send mailshots or direct personal letters to businesses. Local, central or regional consumer awareness days may also be a good channel to raise consumers' awareness to protect their rights when they encounter any issues concerning online purchases or services. Local training courses for handling conflicts and disputes may be a great addition to boost users' confidence in using one of those ODR services.

ODR service providers and courts should also provide training to users to their ODR simulation system. For example, in the EU, it is advised that 'Member States shall encourage ADR entities to provide training for natural persons in charge of ADR. If such training is provided, competent authorities shall monitor the training schemes established by ADR entities.'[104] Users' guidance, mock simulation, case/work flow chart and virtual demonstration should be offered. Policies concerning IT security and data privacy should also be transparent. Technical help should be available to users at all time by ODR service providers.

---

103. Rainey, D. (2014), Third-Party Ethics in the Age of the Fourth Party, *International Journal of Online Dispute Resolution* Volume1, Issue 1, pp. 37–56, p. 37, available at www.international-odr.com/documenten/ijodr_2014_01_01.pdf (last accessed 30 March 2017).
104. EC Directive on Consumer ADR 2013, Article 6(6).

Summary

Systematic legal and technological development for online arbitration procedures relies on continuous regulatory updates in response to technological innovation and vice versa. The expansion of general ODR systems is from basic ODR to advanced ODR and from private ODR to public ODR and court-embedded ODR. When building an ODR system, trust is the utmost important factor. The collaboration and strategic alliances among online marketplaces, technology companies and legal/arbitral institutions are the key to combine different areas of expertise for the building of a trusted ODR system. With regard to the appointment of online arbitrators, harmonised legal procedures for appointing online arbitrators are crucial. Appropriate technological measures shall be deployed to assess the reputation, competence and ethical standards of arbitrators. With reference to the admission of electronic evidence, there is a difference between civil law and common law, in which civil law gives priority to documentary evidence whilst common law depends on the jury's determination of the admissibility of evidence. They are in common in that evaluation of evidence often relies on its weight rather than its admissibility. Relating to the attendance/testimony of witnesses online, in some civil law systems, witnesses must not be assisted by parties or arbitrators to prepare testimonies and familiarise the disputes. Thus, ODR systems shall be designed to give parties clear indications when they are making decisions on which arbitration procedures to follow. The development of secure, reliable and accessible online arbitration platforms applies to both basic ODR and intelligent ODR. Traditionally, in basic ODR systems, arbitrators are natural persons. With the further development of technologies, in intelligent ODR systems, robotic arbitrators make automated decisions based on various computing technologies such as service-oriented computing and expert systems. In either system, without a physical seat in an ODR platform, it is crucial to select the seat of online arbitration as it is one of the most important factors to determine jurisdiction and applicable law for both procedures and the substance of underlying contracts. Ultimately, the success of the implementation of ODR systems heavily relies on the awareness of users and their knowledge about how to make full use of such systems.

PART III

SUBSTANTIVE LEGAL ISSUES OF ONLINE ARBITRATION

CHAPTER 5

The validity of and law applicable to online arbitration agreements

5.1 Validity of online arbitration agreements

5.1.1 The recognition of forming arbitration agreements via electronic communications

An arbitration agreement means 'an agreement to submit to arbitration present or future disputes or differences (whether or not contractual)'.[1] The UNCITRAL Model Law on International Commercial Arbitration defines an 'arbitration agreement' as 'an agreement by the parties to submit to arbitration all or certain disputes which have arisen or which may arise between them in respect of a defined legal relationship, whether contractual or not'.[2] The China International Economic and Trade Arbitration Commission (CIETAC) Online Arbitration Rules also defines an arbitration agreement as 'either an arbitration clause incorporated in a contract agreed by and between the parties or any other form of a written agreement between the parties providing for the settlement of disputes by arbitration'.[3] It further explains that an arbitration agreement shall be in writing. It is in writing 'if it is contained in a tangible form of a document, such as a contract, letter, telegram, telex, facsimile, electronic data interchange (EDI), or email'.[4] In short, an online arbitration agreement means that an arbitration agreement is formed via electronic communications. Online arbitration is one of the most complicated applications in the ODR processes as its non-localisation challenges the traditional concept of 'the arbitration agreements', 'the place of arbitration' and 'the place of arbitral awards'. It leads to the legal uncertainty of the validity, jurisdiction and applicable law, and enforceability of the arbitration agreements and arbitral awards. Consumer arbitration often encounters different interpretations of the validity of pre-dispute arbitration clauses or agreements in different countries. International commercial arbitration usually involves more

---

1. Arbitration Act 1996, s 89(1), available at www.legislation.gov.uk/ukpga/1996/23/pdfs/ukpga_19960023_en.pdf (last accessed 30 March 2017).
2. UNCITRAL Model Law on International Commercial Arbitration 1985, Article 7 (as adopted by the Commission at its thirty-ninth session, in 2006).
3. CIETAC Online Arbitration Rules 2015, Article 6.
4. CIETAC Online Arbitration Rules 2015, Article 6.

than one system of law or of legal rules and is a network of a complex interaction of laws,[5] which mainly include: 1) law applicable to the arbitration agreement and the performance of that agreement; 2) law applicable to the substantive issues in dispute; 3) procedural law applicable to the arbitral proceedings (*lex arbitri*); 4) conflict-of-laws rules applicable to the arbitral proceedings and international arbitration; and 5) law governing recognition and enforcement of arbitral awards (e.g. the New York Convention 1958).

The validity of arbitration agreements is of great importance to the arbitral process and also one of the crucial requirements to enforce arbitral awards afterwards. In order for a valid international arbitration agreement to be formed, an agreement must contain a core of essential issues such as the arbitral institution, the seat of arbitration, applicable law and procedure law. It has been suggested by certain courts that the New York Convention only applies to arbitration agreements providing for a seat in a state other than the state of the court seized with the dispute,[6] though there are some other controversial opinions.[7] The validity of arbitration agreements also relates to the recognition and enforcement of arbitral awards under the New York Convention.[8]

Traditionally, an arbitration agreement shall be recognised in writing. It is required by Article II of the 1958 Convention on the Recognition and Enforcement of Foreign Arbitral Awards (hereafter 'the New York Convention').[9] The New York Convention has been adopted by most countries, including China, the US and EU. It is considered to be one of the most successful conventions, which gives the certainty of recognition and enforcement of cross-border arbitral award. According to the New York Convention, the term 'agreement in writing' shall include an arbitral clause in a contract or an arbitration agreement, signed by the parties or contained in an exchange of letters or telegrams.[10] There are various interpretations of this 'writing' requirement of an arbitration agreement

---

5. Redfern, A., Hunter, M., Blackaby, N. and Partasides, C., Redfern and Hunter on International Arbitration (Oxford: Oxford University Press, 6th edition, 2015), p. 157.

6. 1958 Convention on the Recognition and Enforcement of Foreign Arbitral Awards (the 'New York Convention'), available at www.uncitral.org/uncitral/en/uncitral_texts/arbitration/NYConvention.html (last accessed 30 March 2017), Article I(1). See also UNCITRAL Secretariat Guide on the Convention on the Recognition and Enforcement of Foreign Arbitral Awards (2016), available at www.uncitral.org/pdf/english/texts/arbitration/NY-conv/2016_Guide_on_the_Convention.pdf (last accessed 30 March 2017), pp. 39–40. See also *Kaverit Steel and Crane v Kone Corp.*, Alberta Court of Queen's Bench, Canada, 14 May 1991; *Compagnie de Navigation et Transports S.A. v MSC Mediterranean Shipping Company S.A.*, Federal Tribunal, Switzerland, 16 January 1995.

7. *Gas Authority of India Ltd. v SPIE-CAPAG SA and ors*, High Court of Delhi, India, 15 October 1993, Suit No. 1440; IA No. 5206; *Fred Freudensprung v Offshore Technical Services, Inc., et al.*, Court of Appeals, Fifth Circuit, United States of America, 9 August 2004, 03–20226; and *Société Bomar Oil N.V. v Entreprise tunisienne d'activités pétrolières (ETAP)*, Court of Appeal of Versailles, France, 23 January 1991, upheld by *Société Bomar Oil N.V. v Entreprise tunisienne d'activités pétrolières (ETAP)*, Court of Cassation, France, 9 November 1993, 91–15.194.

8. The New York Convention 1958, Articles IV(1)(b) and V(1)(a).

9. The New York Convention 1958, Article II. See also the UNCITRAL Model Law on International Commercial Arbitration 1985, Article 7(2).

10. The New York Convention 1958, Article 2(2).

under the New York Convention. For example, in the light of a leading case *Sphere Drake Insurance PLC v Marine Towing, Inc.*, the court reasoned that the definition of 'agreement in writing' in Article II(2) of the New York Convention should be understood as either (i) an arbitral clause in a contract; or (ii) an arbitration agreement that must be signed by the parties or contained in an exchange of letters or telegrams. Accordingly, since an arbitral clause was contained in the insurance contract, the arbitration clause in the contract should be enforced even though Marine Towing had not signed the policy.[11] The UNCITRAL Secretariat Guide on the Convention on the Recognition and Enforcement of Foreign Arbitral Awards (2016) confirms that 'where the arbitration agreement is contained in an exchange of documents, the text of Article II(2) does not, on its face, require the parties' signature on the agreement to arbitrate'.[12]

Due to the fact that the New York Convention was adopted far before the birth of the electronic communication society, the Convention did not include recognition as to the validity of arbitration agreements and awards formed via electronic communications. Online arbitration has been challenged as to whether the electronic arbitration agreements and awards are possible to meet the requirements on the written form under the New York Convention. It is commonly agreed that if the digital arbitral clauses/agreements or arbitral awards can be printed and signed, it would satisfy the written requirement. It is argued that electronic arbitration agreements and arbitral awards shall be treated as types of 'electronic contracts' in that their validity will be automatically recognised by the UN Convention on the Use of Electronic Communications in International Contracts and other national electronic contract laws. In some countries, conflict of laws may also include the determination of the validity of an arbitration agreement. In practice, it is suggested that the validity of an arbitration agreement shall be governed by the law chosen by the parties. In the absence of the parties' choice of law, it is proposed that the law of the place where the arbitration takes place or the award is made shall apply according to Article 151 of the Sixth Draft Model Law of Private International Law 2000 in China.[13] With the adoption of such rule, it may increase legal certainty. However, legal challenges still remain as to the harmonised determination of the validity of online arbitration agreements and the place of arbitration in cyberspace.

Despite the fact that there are no harmonised rules concerning the determination of valid technical measures to form an online arbitration clause or agreement, using electronic means to negotiate and generate an arbitration clause or

---

11. *Sphere Drake Insurance PLC v Marine Towing, Inc.*, 16 F.3d 666 (5th Cir. 1994).
12. UNCITRAL Secretariat Guide on the Convention on the Recognition and Enforcement of Foreign Arbitral Awards (2016), p. 56.
13. The Sixth Draft Model Law of Private International Law 2000, available at www.rucil.com.cn/admin/edit/UploadFile/200891911459766.pdf (last accessed 30 March 2017). See also Model Law of Private International Law of the People's Republic of China by Chinese Society of Private International Law, in Yearbook of Private International Law, Volume 14 (Petar Sarczvic & Paul Volken (eds.), Sellier European Law Publishers, 2001).

agreement is generally recognised across the globe. The most recent work from the UNCITRAL ODR working group even includes the proposal of a model dispute resolution clause applicable to both B2B and B2C cross-border, low-value and high-volume transactions as follows:

> Subject to the provisions of Article 1(a) of the UNCITRAL ODR Track I Rules, any dispute, controversy or claim arising hereunder and within the scope of the UNCITRAL ODR Track I Rules providing for a dispute resolution process ending in a binding arbitration, shall be settled by arbitration in accordance with the UNCITRAL ODR Track I Rules presently in force.[14]

5.1.2 The incorporation of an arbitration clause or agreement via electronic means[15]

In the absence of specific rules and law regulating the validity of arbitration agreements concluded via electronic communications, relevant rules and law concerning the validity of electronic contracts may be transplanted into the interpretation of the validity of online arbitration agreements or clauses. It is a common practice that arbitration clauses are independent and separate from the underlying contracts in order to enable arbitration proceedings relating to underlying contracts when the validity of those underlying contracts is questioned. The UK Arbitration Act recognises the principle of separability of arbitration agreements in that:

> Unless otherwise agreed by the parties, an arbitration agreement which forms or was intended to form part of another agreement (whether or not in writing) shall not be regarded as invalid, non-existent or ineffective because that other agreement is invalid, or did not come into existence or has become ineffective, and it shall for that purpose be treated as a distinct agreement.[16]

In a leading US Supreme Court case of *Buckeye Check Cashing, Inc. v Cardegna*, it was held that 'a challenge to the validity of a contract as a whole, and not specifically to the arbitration clause within it, must go to the arbitrator, not the

---

14. A/CN.9/WG.III/WP.133 – Online dispute resolution for cross-border electronic commerce transactions: draft procedural rules, United Nations Commission on International Trade Law, Working Group III (Online dispute resolution), Thirty-first session, New York, 9–13 February 2015, para. 10. See also A/CN.9/827, para. 64 (part of the second proposal). The proponents also suggested an equivalent change for Track II of the Rules, as follows: 'Where, in the event of a dispute arising hereunder and within the scope of the UNCITRAL ODR Track II Rules providing for a dispute resolution process ending in a non-binding recommendation, the parties wish to seek an amicable settlement of that dispute, the dispute shall be referred for negotiation, and in the event that negotiation fails, facilitated settlement, in accordance with the UNCITRAL ODR Track II Rules presently in force.'

15. This session partly draws upon the author's research paper: The Incorporation of Terms into Commercial Contracts: A Reassessment in the Digital Age, *Journal of Business Law* (2015) Issue 2, pp. 87–119.

16. The UK Arbitration Act 1996, s 7.

court'.[17] The court also established three propositions for determining the validity of arbitration agreements: 1) as a matter of substantive federal arbitration law, an arbitration provision is severable from the remainder of the contract; 2) unless the challenge is to the arbitration clause itself, the issue of the contract's validity is considered by the arbitrator in the first instance; and 3) this arbitration law applies in state as well as federal courts.[18]

With regard to whether an arbitration clause or agreement is validly agreed, traditionally there are three main recognised methods of incorporation of contractual terms that may be used to incorporate dispute resolution clauses such as arbitration clauses. They are: incorporation by signature; incorporation by notice/reference and incorporation by course of dealing. According to the UK Arbitration Act 1996, there is an agreement in writing '(a) if the agreement is made in writing (whether or not it is signed by the parties); (b) if the agreement is made by exchange of communications in writing, or (c) if the agreement is evidenced in writing.'[19] Although signature is not an exclusive requirement of an arbitration agreement according to the UK Arbitration Act, evidence must show that the parties have entered into an agreement to arbitration. In other words, the parties should have unambiguous awareness of their arbitration clause to agreement and consent to it in writing or by exchange of communications. In the digital age, both B2B and B2C contracts concluded by electronic means may be further challenged not only because of the requirements of assessing the reasonableness and fairness in context but also the need of examining the appropriate technical measures to give sufficient notice and consent for the incorporation. In other words, the assessment of the doctrine of the incorporation of terms in the digital age consists of three elements (the availability of terms, the provision of unambiguous consent and the content of terms) as opposed to the traditional twofold assessment (methods of incorporation and protection against unfair terms). The reassessment, thus, needs to reflect on these three elements, which is:

1) relating to the formality as to the availability of terms and reasonable awareness (i.e. the conspicuous availability of terms);
2) involving informed consent (i.e. methods of incorporation such as by signature);
3) concerning the content of terms as to the fairness and reasonableness.

It is debatable whether there are uniform rules concerning the methods and requirements of 'making contractual terms and conditions available' and 'incorporating terms and conditions into the contract' in the international legal instruments

---

17. *Buckeye Check Cashing, Inc. v Cardegna*, 126 S. Ct. 1204; 163 L. Ed. 2d 1038; 2006 U.S. LEXIS 1814 (2006). See also *Prima Paint Corp. v Flood & Conklin Manufacturing Co.*, 388 U.S. 395 (1967).

18. *Buckeye Check Cashing, Inc. v Cardegna*, 126 S. Ct. 1204; 163 L. Ed. 2d 1038; 2006 U.S. LEXIS 1814 (2006).

19. The UK Arbitration Act 1996, s 5(2).

such, as the CISG and UNIDROIT Principles.[20] Although it is suggested that 'using the CISG and UNIDROIT Principles together makes it possible to create a complex regulation of contractual relationships in the international sale of goods',[21] both instruments do not provide a specific provision regarding 'the availability of contractual terms and conditions'. It is arguable that the CISG (Article 8) provides a relevant provision regulating the manner of negotiating and incorporating terms and conditions[22] that statements made by a party and/or other conduct of a party are to be interpreted according to his intent where the other party knew or could not have been unaware what that intent was. Some other relevant provisions can also be found in the CISG and UNIDROIT Principles applicable to 'the incorporation of terms and conditions', though they are geared towards matters concerning the incorporation of standard terms and battle of forms. Moreover, the CISG provides a gap-filling procedure in its Article 7 so that it is possible that the substantive issues regarding the availability and incorporation of terms and conditions are governed by regional and national law where applicable.

In the EU, directives governing Internet-related issues provide related provisions on the availability of contractual terms such as the EC Directive on Electronic Commerce 2000 and the EC Directive on Consumer Rights 2011,[23] though there is no substantive provision in those directives regulating the incorporation of contractual terms. In contrast, the recent Proposal for a Regulation of the European Parliament and of the council on a Common European Sales Law 2011, known as 'the Proposed Common European Sales Law', suggested specific provisions such as 'pre-contractual information' (Chapter 2) for the availability of contractual terms and 'unfair contract terms' (Chapter 8) for the unfairness test for the incorporation of contractual terms.[24] The Proposed Common European Sales Law takes into consideration the new technology used in contracting and includes additional requirements of providing 'appropriate, effective and accessible technical means' for distance contracts.[25] In late 2015 the project of the

---

20. See the United Nations Convention on Contracts for the International Sale of Goods 1980 (CISG) and UNIDROIT Principles of International Commercial Contracts 2010 (UNIDROIT Principles).

21. Kotrusz, J. (2009), Gap-Filling of the CISG by the UNIDROIT Principles of International Commercial Contracts, Vol.26. No.1–2. *Uniform Law Review*, pp. 119–63, p. 145; and see also the 45th Session UNCITRAL (New York, 25 June–6 July 2012) endorsed the 2010 edition of the UNIDROIT Principles.

22. Lautenschlager, F. (2007), Current Problems Regarding the Interpretation of Statements and Party Conduct under the CISG – The Reasonable Third Person, Language Problems and Standard Terms and Conditions, Vol. 11 No.2 *Vindobona Journal of International Commercial Law & Arbitration*, pp. 259–90.

23. See the EC Directive on Electronic Commerce 2000, Article 10; and the EC Distance Selling Directive 1997 (replaced by the EC Directive on Consumer Rights (2011/83/EC) on 13 June 2014), Article 5.

24. Proposal for a Regulation of the European Parliament and of the Council on a Common European Sales Law (hereafter 'the Proposed Common European Sales Law 2011), COM/2011/0635 final – 2011/0284 (COD), Brussels 11.10.2011.

25. The Proposed Common European Sales Law 2011, Articles 10, 13, 23 and 24, available at http://eur-lex.europa.eu/LexUriServ/LexUriServ.do?uri=COM:2011:0635:FIN:EN:PDF (last accessed

proposed Common European Sales Law was divided into two proposals: Proposal for EC Directive on certain aspects concerning contracts for the supply of digital content[26] and Proposal for EC Directive on certain aspects concerning contracts for the online and other distance sales of goods.[27]

In the UK, there are no specified rules in traditional English contract law on making contractual terms available, though there are UK Regulations that implement the EC Directives concerning such matters, for instance, the Electronic Commerce (EC Directive) Regulations 2002 and the Consumer Contracts Regulations 2013.[28] The Consumer Contract Regulations 2013 supersede two previous sets of regulations, including the Consumer Protection (Distance Selling) Regulations 2000.[29] The interconnected rules on incorporating terms in English contract law are at common law, while specific rules on incorporating unfair terms in consumer contracts are also supplemented by the Unfair Contract Terms Act (UCTA) 1977 and Unfair Terms in Consumer Contracts Regulations (UTCCR) 1999.[30] UCTA applies a test of 'reasonableness' to both B2B and B2C contracts determining whether the term is fair and reasonable 'having regard to the circumstances which were, or ought reasonably to have been, known to or in the contemplation of the parties when the contract was made',[31] whereas

---

30 March 2017). On 26 February 2014 the European Parliament adopted a legislative resolution on the Proposal for a Common European Sales Law, available at www.europarl.europa.eu/oeil/popups/summary.do?id=1339866&t=e&l=en (last accessed 30 March 2017).

26. Proposal for a Directive of the European Parliament and of the Council on certain aspects concerning contracts for the supply of digital content, COM/2015/0634 final – 2015/0287 (COD).

27. Proposal for a Directive of the European Parliament and of the Council on certain aspects concerning contracts for the online and other distance sales of goods, COM/2015/0635 final – 2015/0288 (COD).

28. The Electronic Commerce (EC Directive) Regulations 2002, UK, available at www.legislation.gov.uk/uksi/2002/2013/pdfs/uksi_20022013_en.pdf (last accessed 30 March 2017); the Unfair Terms in Consumer Contracts Regulations 1999, UK, available at www.legislation.gov.uk/uksi/1999/2083/pdfs/uksi_19992083_en.pdf (last accessed 30 March 2017); and the Consumer Contracts (Information, Cancellation and Additional Charges) Regulations 2013, UK, available at www.gov.uk/government/uploads/system/uploads/attachment_data/file/265898/consumer-contracts-information-cancellation-and-additional-payments-regulations-2013.pdf (last accessed 30 March 2017).

29. The Practice Note for Consumer Contracts Regulations 2013, the Law Society, 15 May 2014, available at www.lawsociety.org.uk/advice/practice-notes/(last accessed 30 March 2017). See also the Consumer Contracts Regulations 2013, reg. 2

30. See also Unfair Terms in Consumer Contracts Regulations 1999 and Consumer Protection (Distance Selling) Regulations 2000 (placed by the EC Directive on Consumer Rights 2011 in 2014).

31. The Electronic Commerce (EC Directive) Regulations 2002, reg. 11 and Schedule 2. Schedule 2 sets out guidelines for the application of the reasonableness test that: '(a) the strength of the bargaining positions of the parties relative to each other, taking into account (among other things) alternative means by which the customer's requirements could have been met; (b) whether the customer received an inducement to agree to the term, or in accepting it had an opportunity of entering into a similar contract with other persons, but without having to accept a similar term; (c) whether the customer knew or ought reasonably to have known of the existence and extent of the term (having regard, among other things, to any custom of the trade and any previous course of dealing between the parties); (d) where the term excludes or restricts any relevant liability if some condition is not complied with, whether it was reasonable at the time of the contract to expect that compliance with that condition would be practicable; (e) whether the goods were manufactured, processed or adapted to the special order of the customer.'

UTCCR employs a test of 'fairness' based on a *non-negotiated* term that causes *a significant imbalance of the parties' rights and obligations of the parties* in B2C contracts.[32] Although there are different approaches taken by the two tests, there is something in common, namely that both tests display the necessity of drawing contracting parties' attention to unusual and significant terms affecting the proposed relationship, especially in which there is an onerous clause in the standard contract. The integrated doctrine known as 'the reasonableness and fairness test' can be employed systematically to determine whether a contractual term is fair and valid in contract law. Meanwhile, the UK Consumer Rights Act 2015 streamlines these two separate pieces of legislation into one place, which applies 'both to contracts and to notices and to both negotiated and non-negotiated terms'.[33] In parallel, the Consumer Protection (Amendment) Regulations 2014 (also known as the Consumer Protection from Unfair Trading (Amendment) Regulations 2014) have been further developed to better prevent misleading and aggressive practices.[34]

In the US, references can be found under the Uniform Commercial Code (UCC), in relevant provisions provided by the Federal Trade Commission (FTC),[35] and through the common law doctrines of unfair surprise and reasonable expectations. Section 2-302(1) of the UCC also requires the notification of clauses at the time it was made, providing that:

> [i]f the court as a matter of law finds the contractor any clause of the contract to have been unconscionable at the time it was made the court may refuse to enforce the contract, or it may enforce the remainder of the contract without the unconscionable clause, or it may so limit the application of any unconscionable clause as to avoid any unconscionable result.[36]

The 'unconscionableness' test is similar to the 'reasonableness and fairness' test in the UK in that it acknowledges the necessity of drawing contracting parties'

---

32. The Unfair Terms in Consumer Contracts Regulations (UTCCR) 1999, regs 5 and 6. The UTCCR (reg. 5(1)) defines unfair terms as 'a contractual term which has not been individually negotiated shall be regarded as unfair if, contrary to the requirement of good faith, it causes a significant imbalance in the parties' rights and obligations arising under the contract, to the detriment of the consumer.' See also the EC Directive 93/13/EEC of 5 April 1993 on unfair terms in consumer contracts (OJ 1993 L 95), Article 3.

33. The UK Consumer Rights Act 2015, available at www.legislation.gov.uk/ukpga/2015/15/contents/enacted (last accessed 30 March 2017). See also The Consumer Rights Bill: Statement on Policy Reform and Responses to Pre-Legislative Scrutiny, January 2014, available at www.gov.uk/government/uploads/system/uploads/attachment_data/file/274912/bis-14-566-consumer-rights-bill-statement-on-policy-reform-and-responses-to-pre-legislative-scrutiny.pdf (last accessed 30 March 2017), see Annex H. Unfair Terms, p. 59.

34. The Consumer Protection (Amendment) Regulations 2014, available at www.legislation.gov.uk/uksi/2014/870/made (last accessed 30 March 2017); see also Misleading and aggressive commercial practices – The Draft Consumer Protection from Unfair Trading (Amendment) Regulations 2013, August 2013, available at www.gov.uk/government/publications/misleading-and-aggressive-commercial-practices-the-draft-consumer-protection-from-unfair-trading-amendment-regulations-2013 (last accessed 30 March 2017).

35. Uniform Commercial Code (UCC), Section 2-207.

36. UCC, Section 2-302(1).

attention to terms affecting their rights and obligations at the time the contract was made.

In China, the Contract Law of the People's Republic of China 1999 provides explicit requirements for the valid form of incorporating contractual terms in particular standard terms,[37] whilst the Law of the People's Republic of China on Protection of Consumer Rights and Interests 1993 further prohibits business operators 'through format contracts, notices, announcements and entrance hall bulletins' from imposing unfair or unreasonable rules on consumers, and reducing or escaping their civil liability for their infringement of the legitimate rights and interests of consumers.[38] On 25 October 2013 the Law of the People's Republic of China on the Protection of Consumer Rights and Interests (hereafter 'China Consumer Protection Law') was amended for the second time in accordance with the Decision on Amending the Law of the People's Republic of China on the Protection of Consumer Rights and Interests adopted at the 5th Session of the Standing Committee of the Twelfth National People's Congress. Its Article 26 amends the old Article 24, inserting an additional requirement that business operators should draw consumers' attention to significant terms in the standard contract, which may affect the significant relationship in the parties' rights and obligation, by conspicuous means.[39] This amendment brings a consistent standard to the protection of unfair terms in consumer contracts as that in the EU, UK and US. The advancement of this provision lies in the requirement of a specific notification standard – 'by conspicuous means' – which has been employed to determine the validity of terms in common law cases.[40] This is similar to Lord Denning's red hand rule in the UK and the requirement for disclaimers of certain implied warranties to be 'conspicuous' under the UCC in the US.[41] Most recently the Ministry of Commerce also adopted the Regulations of Online Signing Process

---

37. Contract Law of the People's Republic of China (adopted by the National People's Congress on 15 March 1999, and promulgated by the Presidential Order No. 15) (hereafter 'China Contract Law') 1999, see Articles 36–41. Article 39 of China Contract Law provides a provision on 'standard terms' as:

> Where a contract is concluded by way of standard terms, the party supplying the standard terms shall abide by the principle of fairness in prescribing the rights and obligations of the parties and shall, in a reasonable manner, call the other party's attention to the provision(s) whereby such party's liabilities are excluded or limited, and shall explain such provision(s) upon request by the other party.

38. Law of the People's Republic of China on Protection of Consumer Rights and Interests 1993, Article 24.

39. Law of the People's Republic of China on Protection of Consumer Rights and Interests (2013 amendment), Article 24.

40. See for example *Specht v Netscape* 306 F.3d 17 (2d Cir. 2002), para. 20.

41. See *J Spurling Ltd v Bradshaw* [1956] EWCA Civ 3, as Lord Denning explained 'the more unreasonable a clause is, the greater the notice which must be given of it. Some clauses I have seen would need to be printed in red ink on the face of the document with a red hand pointing to it before the notice could be held to be sufficient'; and UCC, Article 2–316(2).

of Electronic Contract, which promotes the integrity and unchanged reproduction of an electronic contract.[42]

With regard to technological measures of agreeing an arbitration clause or agreement via electronic communications, there is a variety of electronic means which enable terms and conditions including an arbitration clause to be notified and incorporated into a contract, though their appropriateness and legal effects are debatable. For example, terms and conditions may be displayed on a smartphone screen when users click on a digital product such as e-books, games or networking software; and deemed to be incorporated when users click the 'install' or 'download' button. With the invention of Google Glass technology embedded with Google Wallet, a device can be worn by an individual and used to make transactions.[43] With the possible future civilian use of so-called 'beaming' technology, a robot can physically represent an individual or legal entity to negotiate and conclude contracts with other parties in another place or country.[44] The possibility of employing the intelligent and adaptive system of service-oriented computing could also provide intelligence and reasoning capabilities to give automated support to the incorporation of terms and conditions in automated transactions without direct human intervention. In other words, the deployment of service-oriented computing in automated transaction systems would allow contracting parties to form real-time contracts without any human interaction. Due to ever-changing technology and its impact on commercial practice, today, more than ever before, it prompts us to consider the need to adopt consistent and fair international standards of 'making terms and conditions available online' and 'incorporating them into the electronic agreement' taking into account the features of electronic communications and the nature and frequency of cross-border transactions. A set of mature and effective international legislation, regional and national instruments, or consistent judicial interpretation, may help filling a gap among traditional international instruments,[45] and coping with the increasing challenges that new technologies place upon the assessment of the fairness and reasonableness to the availability and incorporation of contractual terms. In other words, the reasonableness and fairness test in the information age extends to the assessment of the electronic availability of terms in a digital form and the examination of incorporation by electronic means. The assessment of protection against unfair terms under the reasonableness and fairness test remains the same

---

42. The Regulations of Online Signing Process of Electronic Contract (come to enforce 1 December 2013), MOFCOM Announcement of No.41 of 2013 by Ministry of Commerce of the People's Republic of China, Articles 5.1(5) and 8.

43. Google Wallet is said to be landing on Google Glass, published on 6 May 2014, available at www.cnet.com/uk/news/google-is-said-to-be-tacking-google-wallet-onto-google-glass/ (last accessed 30 March 2017). Please note this test product discontinued on 19 January 2015, available at https://techcrunch.com/2015/01/19/today-is-the-last-day-to-buy-google-glass/ (last accessed 30 March 2017).

44. Robot avatar beaming put to the test, BBC News, 10 May 2012, available at www.bbc.co.uk/news/technology-18017745 (last accessed 30 March 2017).

45. See the United Nations Convention on Contracts for the International Sale of Goods (CISG) 1980, Article 7.

in electronic transactions as that of paper-based transactions in substance, though further interpretation is required, taking into account the appropriateness of the technical measures for incorporation.

5.2 Online consumer arbitration agreements

5.2.1 Private online consumer arbitration agreements

Where arbitration is offered for consumer contracts, a major legal barrier is whether the arbitration agreement is valid or effective as the law of the country of consumer protection may establish exclusive jurisdiction to the court in the country of the consumer's domicile, or the arbitration agreement may be deemed to be unconscionable or an unfair term in the particular context.[46] Countries may restrict the enforceability of a pre-dispute arbitration agreement against a consumer. In the EU, the EC Directive on Consumer ADR confirms that:

> Member States shall ensure that an agreement between a consumer and a trader to submit complaints to an ADR entity is not binding on the consumer if it was concluded before the dispute has materialised and if it has the effect of depriving the consumer of his right to bring an action before the courts for the settlement of the dispute.[47]

It further clarifies that the ADR solution/settlement may be binding on the parties only if parties were informed of its binding nature in advance and specifically accepted this.[48] The Court of Justice of the European Union (CJEU) also ruled on several occasions that consumers would not be bound by a pre-dispute arbitration clause in a contract concluded between sellers/suppliers and consumers, if consumers were unaware of such clause.[49] In the UK, according to the Arbitration Act, an arbitration agreement concluded with a consumer is considered to be unfair and thus unenforceable,[50] where there are low value claims below £5,000.[51] It means that in England, if the amount in dispute does not exceed £5,000, an arbitration clause with consumers is non-binding.

---

46. Herrmann, G (2001), Some Legal E-flections on Online Arbitration, in Briner, R., Fortier, L., Berger, K. and Bredow, J. (eds.), *Law of International Business and Dispute Settlement in the 21st Century* (Cologne: Carl Heymanns Verlag KG), pp. 267–76, p. 268.
47. Directive 2013/11/EU of the European Parliament and of the Council of 21 May 2013 on alternative dispute resolution for consumer disputes and amending Regulation (EC) No 2006/2004 and Directive 2009/22/EC (Directive on consumer ADR), OJ L 165, 18.6.2013, pp. 63–79, Article 10(1).
48. EC Directive on Consumer ADR 2013, Article 10(2).
49. Case C-168/05, *Elisa María Mostaza Claro v Centro Móvil Milenium SL*, Judgment of the Court (First Chamber) 26 October 2006; and C-40/08 *Asturcom Telecomunicaciones SL v Cristina Rodríguez Nogueira*, Judgment of the Court (First Chamber) of 6 October 2009.
50. The UK Arbitration Act 1996, s 91(1).
51. Unfair Arbitration Agreements (Specified Amounts) Order 1999 (SI 1999/2167). See also Practice Guideline 17: Guidelines for Arbitrators dealing with cases involving consumers and parties with significant differences of resources, by Charter Institute of Arbitrators (CIArb), 2011.

In the past, there was a UK Consumer Agreements Act 1988. Although this Act is repealed, it provides some reference as to how to determine valid consumer agreements: where a person enters into a contract as a consumer, an agreement that future differences arising between parties to the contract are to be referred to arbitration cannot be enforced against him in respect of any cause of action so arising to which this section applies except (a) with his written consent signified after the differences in question have arisen; or (b) where he has submitted to arbitration in pursuance of the agreement, whether in respect of those or any other differences; or (c) where the court makes an order in respect of that cause of action.[52] In the case of *Richard Zellner v Phillip Alexander Securities and Futures Ltd*,[53] the German Court and the English (Appeal) Court both assessed the validity of the arbitration agreement and held that the arbitration agreement was invalid as it was an unfair term towards the consumer. This position is affirmed by the Consumer Rights Act 2015 (Schedule 2, paragraph 20(a)) – consumer contract terms may be regarded as unfair when a term which has the object or effect of excluding or hindering the consumer's right to take legal action or exercise any other legal remedy, in particular by requiring the consumer to take disputes exclusively to arbitration not covered by legal provisions.[54] In the leading UK case of *Mylcrist Builders Limited v Mrs G Buck*, the judge invalidated an arbitration clause, pointing out that for consumer transactions the arbitration clause and its effect need to be more fully, clearly and prominently set out than through just a box signed by Mrs Buck drawing her attention to all contractual terms as the impact of the arbitration clause would not be apparent to a layperson.[55]

Some countries may have a different view towards the validity of consumer arbitration clauses and agreements. In the US, both the Federal Arbitration Act (FAA) 1925 and the courts are in favour of enforcing mandatory arbitration agreements.[56] It is arguable that an arbitration clause with consumers could be enforceable as sec. 2 of the FAA is an open clause providing that a written provision in any maritime transaction or a contract evidencing a transaction involving commerce to settle by arbitration shall be valid, irrevocable, and enforceable. It will be up to the judge to determine the scope of 'involving commerce'. Sometimes, a pre-dispute arbitration agreement can be valid but unenforceable. For example, in the case of *Allied-Bruce Terminix Cos. v Dobson*,[57] the Court concluded that the phrase 'involving commerce' is broad and was intended as the functional equivalent of 'affecting commerce'. Sometimes, the courts also

---

52. UK Consumer Arbitration Agreements Act 1988 (repealed 31 January 1997), s 1(1), available at www.legislation.gov.uk/ukpga/1988/21/pdfs/ukpga_19880021_en.pdf (last accessed 30 March 2017).
53. *Zellner v Phillip Alexander Securities and Futures Ltd,* Landgericht Krefeld Case 6 O 186/95, Judgment of 29 April 1996 [1997] ILPr 716; [1997] ILPr 730 (QB) 736–8.
54. Consumer Rights Act 2015 (Schedule 2, Session 20(a)), available at www.legislation.gov.uk/ukpga/2015/15/pdfs/ukpga_20150015_en.pdf (last accessed 30 March 2017).
55. *Mylcrist Builders Limited v Mrs G Buck* [2008] EWHC 2172 (TCC).
56. See *Moses H. Cone Memorial Hospital v Mercury Construction Corp*, 460 U.S. 1 (1983).
57. *Allied-Bruce Terminix Cos. v Dobson*, 513 U.S. 265, 273 (1995).

intend to protect consumers. In the case of *Brower v Gateway 2000, Inc*, the New York Appellate Court held that there was an arbitration agreement to the consumer dispute between the parties according to the Federal Arbitration Act; however, the arbitrator chosen was not fair to the consumer and thus asked the parties to find the appropriate arbitrator.[58]

With regard to pre-dispute arbitration clauses or agreements, it appears to be a common, but not a universal, feature of consumer financial contracts with pre-dispute arbitration clauses.[59] It is suggested that to establish a binding pre-dispute mandatory arbitration provision in a consumer transaction, it is only necessary to show that the agreement exists in writing, and that the consumer apparently has consented to the agreement. The agreement will be presumed valid and enforceable unless the consumer establishes that it is invalid because of a traditional contract defence.[60] It is observed that in practice 'imposition of mandatory arbitration generally precludes the consumer's freedom to choose to litigate in a class action and eliminates any favourable precedent or law reform that could arise through litigation'.[61] Class action means that one or more plaintiffs may file suit on behalf of similarly situated individuals.[62] If no class provision is allowed in a consumer arbitration clause, it means that consumer organisations cannot bring claims on behalf of consumers. In 2011 in a US leading case of *AT&T Mobility LLC v Concepcion*,[63] the Supreme Court clarified that the Federal Arbitration Act of 1925 (FAA) would have prohibited the enforcement of a consumer arbitration clause with a 'no class action' provision.

As consumers rarely, if ever, choose arbitration, it is common that pre-dispute arbitration is imposed upon the consumer without any choice by a contract of adhesion.[64] Moreover, informal rules and consumer arbitral decisions often favour the business organisation, due in large part to its significant role as a 'repeat-player'.[65] In 2009, the Arbitration Fairness Act of 2009 (AFA) amended the FAA and invalidated pre-dispute agreements to arbitrate 'franchise,' 'consumer', 'employment' or 'civil rights' disputes,[66] which prevent the use of pre-dispute mandatory arbitration clauses. Although the AFA updated the provisions for

---

58. *Brower v Gateway 2000, Inc.*, 676 N.Y.S. 2d 569, 572 (1998).
59. Arbitration Study Report to Congress, pursuant to Dodd–Frank Wall Street Reform and Consumer Protection Act § 1028(a), Consumer Financial Protection Bureau, March 2015, p. 4.
60. Alderman, R. M. (2001), Pre-dispute mandatory arbitration in consumer contracts: a call for reform, *Houston law review*, Volume 38, Issue 4, pp. 1237–68, p. 1246.
61. Alderman, R. M. (2001), Pre-dispute mandatory arbitration in consumer contracts: a call for reform, *Houston law review*, Volume 38, Issue 4, pp. 1237–68, pp. 1240–2.
62. Arbitration Study Report to Congress, pursuant to Dodd–Frank Wall Street Reform and Consumer Protection Act § 1028(a), Consumer Financial Protection Bureau, March 2015, p. 3.
63. *AT&T Mobility LLC v Concepcion*, 131 S. Ct. 1740 (2011).
64. Alderman, R. M. (2001), Pre-dispute mandatory arbitration in consumer contracts: a call for reform, *Houston law review*, Volume 38, Issue 4, pp. 1237–68, pp. 1240–2.
65. Alderman, R. M. (2001), Pre-dispute mandatory arbitration in consumer contracts: a call for reform, *Houston law review*, Volume 38, Issue 4, pp. 1237–68, pp. 1240–2.
66. Section 402 of the Arbitration Fairness Act of 2009, available at www.govtrack.us/congress/billtext.xpd?bill=s111-931 (last accessed 30 March 2017).

protecting consumers, it does not propose new rules for arbitration agreements or proceedings that are formed over the Internet.

With regard to pre-dispute arbitration agreements formed via electronic communications, it should be understood that no online pre-dispute arbitration agreement for B2C/consumer disputes shall be valid or enforceable under the AFA. It is common that in a B2C e-commerce situation sellers or suppliers often include an arbitration clause in a standard form contract for future consumer disputes. It is unfair that consumers are given no opportunity to negotiate any arbitration clauses. Once consumers click the 'I agree' button, the contract is formed. With the amendment of the rule on the pre-dispute arbitration agreement, such electronic pre-dispute arbitration agreement shall be invalid. If parties form an electronic arbitration agreement for consumer disputes after the disputes arise, such electronic arbitration agreements shall be assented to by both parties in order to be valid. That is, if the interpretation of 'written' arbitration agreements under AFA is to be in line with the position in the Electronic Signatures in Global and National Act (E-SIGN), an electronic consumer arbitration agreement shall be deemed as valid and enforceable if parties sign and consent to it.

As it stands, a realistic assessment of the reasonableness and fairness of the notice of arbitration clauses/agreements by electronic means is required in order to determine whether consumers are conscionable about those pre-dispute arbitration clauses and have made their informed decision of agreeing to them. In the case of *Brower v Gateway 2000*, a consumer purchased software with a dispute resolution clause in the general conditions, which was imposed on the consumer to submit disputes to the ICC. The court decided that the ICC arbitration clause was unconscionable in consumer contracts and that the arbitration could not be imposed on the buyer.[67] In a US leading case of *Specht v Netscape Communications Corp.*,[68] the court ruled that the end-user licence agreement for the SmartDownload software was not binding on the plaintiffs and thus denied to compel arbitration for the plaintiff's breach of the licence agreement, because Netscape's SmartDownload (Shrinkwrap agreement) allows a user to download and use the software without taking any action that plainly manifests assent to the terms of the associated licence or indicates an understanding that a contract is being formed. As illustrated in *Specht v Netscape*, a realistic assessment of the reasonableness and fairness of the notice of terms online should be based on two principal elements, namely, reasonably conspicuous notice and manifested unambiguous consent.[69] In *Specht*, it concerned whether the arbitration clause was incorporated in the SmartDownload licence terms that the user plaintiffs had reasonable notice of and manifested assent to the SmartDownload Licence

---

67. *Brower v Gateway 2000*, 246 A.2d 246 (N.Y.App. 1998).
68. *Specht v Netscape Communications Corp*, 150 F.Supp.2d 585 (SDNY 2001), aff'd, 306 F.3d 17 (2d Cir. 2002).
69. *Specht v Netscape Communications Corporation* 306 F.3d 17 (2d Cir. 2002).

Agreement.[70] The court emphasised that: 'Reasonably conspicuous notice of the existence of contract terms and unambiguous manifestation of assent to those terms by consumers are essential if electronic bargaining is to have integrity and credibility.'[71] Subsequently there were various concerns over informed consent: 1) no clear expression in a visible place indicating 'Please review and agree to the terms of the Netscape SmartDownload software license agreement', but an invitation to click a hyperlink for more information; 2) licence terms on the 'SmartDownload Communicator' webpage was located in text that 'would have become visible to plaintiffs only if they had scrolled down to the next screen'; and 3) a website operated by ZDNet offered only a hypertext link to 'more information' about SmartDownload without a clear reference to the licence agreement. It was concluded that Netscape's webpage, unlike typical examples of clickwrap, neither adequately alerted users to the existence of SmartDownload's licence terms nor required users unambiguously to manifest assent to those terms as a condition of downloading the product. Thus, the court affirmed that the user plaintiffs had not entered into the SmartDownload licence agreement.[72] This case asserts that the terms in question must be 'readily identifiable or sufficiently visible' to the users of the website and should be placed in a position on the webpage that a user could not miss them for any clickwrap, shrinkwrap or browsewrap agreements.

With regard to pre-dispute consumer arbitration clauses or agreements that are displayed on a website, their validity is debatable. This can be learnt from previous experience concerning the validity of contractual terms and conditions displayed on an online marketplace. It is suggested that an online PDF file containing terms and conditions that are displayed on a website may amount to an actual awareness of information for users, whereas information or a statement on a website may not be sufficient to be treated as a term. For example, the English case of *Gary Patchett v Swimming Pool and Allied Trades Association Limited (SPATA)* concerns the validity of details of installers from a drop down list on SPATA (a company)'s website to build a swimming pool in their garden.[73] The SPATA website stated that members were fully vetted (with checks on their financial record and experience and an inspection of their work) and that they benefited from a bond and warranty scheme known as SPATASHIELD. Also SPATA's website included a reference to and encouraged people to obtain a copy of an information pack. It turned out that the chosen builder in the drop down list on the website was not a full member and therefore had not been vetted and did not benefit from the SPATASHEILD scheme. The claimant claimed that he relied on the statements on the website as he did not check the information

---

70. *Specht v Netscape Communications Corporation* 306 F.3d 17 (2d Cir. 2002).
71. *Specht v Netscape Communications Corporation* 306 F.3d 17 (2d Cir. 2002), para. 20.
72. *Specht*, 150 F.Supp.2d (S.D.N.Y. 2001) at 595–6.
73. *Gary Patchett v Swimming Pool and Allied Trades Association Limited (SPATA)* [2009] EWCA Civ 717.

pack. The Court of Appeal held that it was reasonable that a customer would be expected to look at the website as a whole and obtain the relevant information pack; therefore, the SPATA was not liable for the error on the website as all information was correctly recorded in an information pack confirming the terms of cover.[74] In other words, SPATA had performed duties to inform as 'the website should not be taken as inviting reliance without further enquiry, that is without applying for and reading the information pack referred to in paragraph 8 of the website',[75] whereas 'the appellants had been grossly negligent in failing to make enquiries as to the availability of SPATASHIELD insurance'.[76] This is identical to a situation when customers purchase travel insurance on a website. It is sensible that customers are reasonably expected to download the PDF files of 'the fact sheet' and 'terms and conditions' and read them before they complete the purchase of insurance.

In the case of *Paola Briceño v Sprint Spectrum, L.P.*, it was confirmed that

> Sprint printed a 'Notice of Changes' on the front of the June 16, 2003 invoice that it mailed to Briceño. This notice informed her that amendments to the original Terms and Conditions were posted on Sprint's website. Briceño stated that she never read any of the original or amended Terms and Conditions, either on the internet or in hard-copy, because it was 'not important' to her. She also stated that she saw the 'Terms and Conditions of Service' internet link, but did not care to click it'[77]

The court held that a customer would be bound to the amended terms and conditions if a customer was properly informed of them, though the customer did not read them. In particular there was no evidence that Sprint concealed or attempted to conceal the aforementioned original or amended terms and conditions.[78] Thus, proper notice of the modified terms is so important that it is required for consent to be effective.[79]

In order to further protect consumers' rights online, the consumer must receive written confirmation or confirmation in another durable medium available. In the EU, the judge in the recent ECJ case of *Content Services Ltd. v Bundesarbeitskammer* provided an interpretation on whether information (such as terms and conditions) that is available via a hyperlink on a website should be effective and enforceable.[80] This is in sharp contrast to the recognition of the effectiveness

---

74. *Gary Patchett v Swimming Pool and Allied Trades Association Limited (SPATA)* [2009] EWCA Civ 717.
75. *Gary Patchett v Swimming Pool and Allied Trades Association Limited (SPATA)* [2009] EWCA Civ 717, para. 51.
76. *Gary Patchett v Swimming Pool and Allied Trades Association Limited (SPATA)* [2009] EWCA Civ 717, para. 58.
77. *Paola Briceño v Sprint Spectrum L.P.*, 911 So.2d 176, 177–80 (Fla. Ct. App. 2005), in the District Court of Appeal of Florida, Third District.
78. 911 So.2d 176, 177–80 (Fla. Ct. App. 2005), p. 8.
79. Casady, B. (2009), Electronic Pitfalls: The Online Modification of Ongoing Consumer Service Agreements, 5 *Shidler Journal of Law, Commerce and Technology*, 12.
80. ECJ Case C 49/11, *Content Services Ltd. v Bundesarbeitskammer*, 5 July 2012.

of clicking a hyperlink to terms as implied in *Ryanair v Billigfluege.de*[81] and *Specht v Netscape*.[82] On 5 July 2012, in the *Content Services* case, the European Court of Justice ruled that

> Article 5(1) of Directive 97/7/EC of the European Parliament and of the Council of 20 May 1997 on the protection of consumers in respect of distance contracts (now the EC Directive on Consumer Rights, Articles 2(10), 7 and 8[83]) must be interpreted as meaning that a business practice consisting of making the information referred to in that provision accessible to the consumer *only via a hyperlink on a website* of the undertaking concerned does not meet the requirements of that provision, since that information is neither 'given' by that undertaking nor 'received' by the consumer, within the meaning of that provision, and *a website* such as that at issue in the main proceedings *cannot be regarded as a 'durable medium'* within the meaning of Article 5(1).[84]

It is noteworthy that the definition of 'durable medium' is now given by Article 2(10) of the new EC Directive on Consumer Rights: 'any instrument which enables the consumer or the trader to store information addressed personally to him in a way *accessible for future reference* for a period of time adequate for the purposes of the information and which allows the *unchanged reproduction* of the information stored.'[85] (Emphasis added)

It was evidenced that a hyperlink itself did not determine the validity of the terms and conditions, but the problem was that a website itself referred to by a hyperlink could not be deemed as a 'durable medium'. This is because information on a website (i.e. the content of a webpage) can be altered constantly. If a hyperlink leads to a PDF document which can be stored, accessed and reproduced, such PDF document/file can be transferred to a 'durable medium' and thus should meet the requirements.[86] Or if the technology is developed for a website to ensure that information, can be stored, accessed and reproduced on that website by the consumer during an adequate period, this can then meet the requirements of 'a durable medium'.[87]

In response to the emergence of new technologies in the future, it is important to develop a set of technologically neutral principles/rules on the determination of how appropriate and feasible terms were brought to the contracting party's

---

81. *Ryanair v Billigfluege.de* [2010] IEHC 47, available at www.bailii.org/ie/cases/IEHC/2010/H47.html (last accessed 30 March 2017).

82. *Specht v Netscape Communications Corporation* 306 F.3d 17 (2d Cir. 2002).

83. Directive 2011/83/EU of the European Parliament and of the Council of 25 October 2011 on consumer rights, amending Council Directive 93/13/EEC and Directive 1999/44/EC of the European Parliament and of the Council and repealing Council Directive 85/577/EEC and Directive 97/7/EC of the European Parliament and of the Council Text with EEA relevance, Official Journal L 304, 22/11/2011 P. 0064–0088.

84. ECJ Case C-49/11, *Content Services Ltd. v Bundesarbeitskammer*, 5 July 2012.

85. EC Directive on Consumer Rights 2011, Article 2(10).

86. Wang, F. (2013), Hyperlinking: Debate on Contract, IP and Database Regulation, *Intellectual Property Forum* (a quarterly journal published by the Intellectual Property Society of Australia and New Zealand Inc), Issue 93, pp. 85–9.

87. CJEU Case C-49/11, para. 48. See also the Consumer Contracts Regulations (UK) 2013, reg. 5.

attention and when exactly terms are incorporated into the contract. According to the observations provided above, principles to be considered include 'the parties' intention', 'contemporaneous inclusion', 'reasonable and adequate notice' and 'accessible in a durable medium for future reference'.

5.2.2 Public/statutory small claims arbitration

It is suggested that 'arbitration often is not as prompt or as inexpensive as alternative courts, especially small claims courts'.[88] In the US, in practice arbitration may not be the process desired for small-value and straightforward consumer disputes that require speedy settlement,[89] although it may remain open as an option subject to national consumer protection law and arbitration law. In view of that, many arbitration clauses may contain small claims court 'carve-outs', generally enabling either the consumer (or the company) to use small claims courts, rather than arbitration, for claims resolution.[90]

There is also similar practice in other regions and countries. In the EU, the Small Claims Procedure was adopted in 2007 to improve and simplify procedures in civil and commercial matters between all member states (except for Denmark) where the value of a claim did not exceed €2,000.[91] In December 2015, the Regulation (EU) amending the European Small Claims Procedure increased the threshold for a small claim from €2,000 to €5,000.[92] In recent years, the European e-Justice portal has also provided a simple online filing system for the European Small Claims Procedure including four standard web-based small claim forms for users to file and manage their cases, which make easy access to the small claims process. In the UK, there is a distinction between private arbitration (such as ad hoc or institutional arbitration) and public/statutory arbitration (such as a small claims arbitration by courts and an ombudsman procedure).[93] It

---

88. Alderman, R. M. (2001), Pre-dispute mandatory arbitration in consumer contracts: a call for reform, *Houston law review*, Volume 38, Issue 4, pp. 1237–68, pp. 1240–2.
89. Philippe, M. (2014), ODR Redress System for Consumer Disputes Clarifications, UNCITRAL Works & EU Regulation on ODR, *International Journal of Online Dispute Resolution*, Volume 1, Issue 1, pp. 57–69, p. 61.
90. Arbitration Study Report to Congress, pursuant to Dodd–Frank Wall Street Reform and Consumer Protection Act § 1028(a), Consumer Financial Protection Bureau, March 2015, available at http://files.consumerfinance.gov/f/201503_cfpb_arbitration-study-report-to-congress-2015.pdf (last accessed 30 March 2017), pp. 8 and 10.
91. European Small Claims, available at https://e-justice.europa.eu/content_small_claims_forms-177-en.do (last accessed 30 March 2017). See also Regulation (EC) No 861/2007 of the European Parliament and of the Council of 11 July 2007 establishing a European Small Claims Procedure, OJ L 199, 31.7.2007, pp. 1–22.
92. Regulation (EU) 2015/2421 of the European Parliament and of the Council of 16 December 2015 amending Regulation (EC) No 861/2007 establishing a European Small Claims Procedure and Regulation (EC) No 1896/2006 creating a European order for payment procedure, OJ L 341, 24.12.2015, p. 1–13, Recital (4) and Article 2(1).
93. *Landgericht Krefeld* Case 6 O 186/95. Judgment of 29 April 1996 [1997] ILPr 716; *Picardi v Cuniberti* [2002] EWHC 2923 (QB), para. 102; Heifer paras. 231-2 and *Mylcrist Builders Ltd v Mrs G Buck* [2008] EWHC 2172 (TCC), para. 54; see also Hörnle, J. and Cortes, P. (2014), Legal Issues

is suggested that where there is a public/statutory arbitration scheme, the unfair terms provision under the Consumer Rights Act 2015 shall not apply. This means that statutory small claims arbitration cannot be considered to be unfair and invalid.[94] Moreover, there is a small claim track in courts for any claim that has a financial value of not more than £10,000.[95] In 2014 an online money claim portal was also established for both business and consumers to claim for a fixed sum under £100,000;[96] however the purpose of this portal is different from other small claims court systems in the US and EU because it can only be used after following the Practice Direction for 'pre-action conduct' including the use of ADR to resolve disputes.[97]

5.3 Online commercial arbitration agreements

Commercial arbitration clauses or agreements refer to parties agreeing to go to arbitration when their disputes arise with regard to their B2B commercial contracts. Commercial arbitration is favoured by merchants to maintain a long-term business relationship as it may consistently provide early resolution and 'forestall mercantile strife which might otherwise imperil the marketplace'.[98] There are two categories for the determination of a valid international commercial arbitration agreement: one is formal validity and the other is substantive validity.[99] The formal validity refers to the requirement of 'writing', which is specified by the New York Convention 1958.[100] The substantive validity relates to various factors including but not limited to unconscionability and duress; fraudulent inducement or fraud; impossibility, frustration and repudiation; illegality; lack of capacity and waiver of right to arbitrate.

One of the most crucial issues concerning the formal and substantive validity of international commercial arbitration agreements is the determination of the applicable law of an arbitration agreement. In international commercial

---

in Online Dispute Resolution, Working Paper for the UK Civil Justice Council's ODR Advisory Group, available at www.judiciary.gov.uk/wp-content/uploads/2015/02/Legal-Issues-Hornle.pdf (last accessed 30 March 2017).

94. Cortes, P. (2016), The consumer Arbitration Conundrum: A Matter of Statutory Interpretation or Time for Reform?, Corte, P. (ed.), *The New Regulatory Framework for Consumer Dispute Resolution* (Oxford: Oxford University Press, 2016), pp. 65–78, p. 69.

95. The Small Claims Track, available at www.justice.gov.uk/courts/procedure-rules/civil/rules/part27 (last accessed 30 March 2017).

96. Make a money claim online, available at www.gov.uk/make-money-claim-online#before-you-start (last accessed 30 March 2017).

97. Money Claim Online (MCOL) – User Guide for Claimants, 7 February 2017, available at www.gov.uk/government/uploads/system/uploads/attachment_data/file/520203/money-claim-online-user-guide.pdf (last accessed 30 March 2017).

98. Furnish, D.B. (1979) Commercial Arbitration Agreements and the Uniform Commercial Code, 67 California Law Review, Volume 67, Issue 2, pp. 317–49, p. 320, available at: http://scholarship.law.berkeley.edu/californialawreview/vol67/iss2/3 (last accessed 30 March 2017).

99. Born, G. (2011), International Arbitration: Cases and Materials (New York: Aspen Publishers, 2011), Chapter 2.

100. The New York Convention 1958, Article II.

arbitration, it is possible that different systems of law may govern the substantive contract, the arbitration agreement, the individual reference and the arbitral proceedings.[101] It is suggested that there are four alternatives on the law applicable to an arbitration agreement: a) law for the arbitration agreement chosen by parties expressly and impliedly; b) law for the seat of arbitration; c) law for the underlying/substantive contract; and d) law where judicial enforcement of the agreement is sought.[102] In the absence of the chosen law for an arbitration agreement, applicable choice-of-law standards (i.e. most significant relationship and closest connection standards) have been employed to determine the applicable law for the arbitration agreement.[103] It is evidenced that the law of the country in the seat of arbitration has often been considered as its closest and most real connection to the arbitration agreement. For example, in the leading international case of *Sulamerica CIA Nacional de Seguros SA and others v Enesa Engenharia SA and others*, the judge held that the proper law of the arbitration agreement in this case was English law, notwithstanding the express choice of Brazilian law as the law governing the policies and the obvious connection of the policy to Brazil.[104] The judge also pointed out that the choice of the seat of the arbitration determines the curial law and the supervising jurisdiction of the courts of the country where the seat is located, in this case England.[105] Accordingly, the law with which the agreement to arbitrate had its closest and most real connection was the law of England.[106] Although in *Sulamerica CIA Nacional de Seguros SA and others v Enesa Engenharia SA and others*, the seat of the arbitration is used to determine the law governing the agreement to arbitrate according to various factors in the case, the judge also acknowledged that

> an express choice of law governing the substantive contract is a strong indication of the parties' intention in relation to the agreement to arbitrate. A search for an implied choice of proper law to govern the arbitration agreement is therefore likely to lead to the conclusion that the parties intended the arbitration agreement to be governed by the same system of law as the substantive contract, unless there are other factors present which point to a different conclusion.[107]

---

101. *Black Clawson International Ltd v Papierwerke Waldhof-Aschaffenburg AG* [1982] 2 Lloyd's Rep. 446; see also *Channel Tunnel Group Ltd v Balfour Beatty Construction Ltd* [1993] AC 334.
102. Born, G., International Arbitration: Cases and Materials (New York: Aspen Publishers, 2011), pp. 234–5.
103. See Restatement (Second) Conflict of Law §187, 188 and 218.
104. *Sulamerica CIA Nacional de Seguros SA and others v Enesa Engenharia SA and others* [2012] EWCA Civ 638 (16 May 2012), available at www.bailii.org/ew/cases/EWCA/Civ/2012/638.html (last accessed 30 March 2017), para. 8.
105. *Sulamerica CIA Nacional de Seguros SA and others v Enesa Engenharia SA and others* [2012] EWCA Civ 638 (16 May 2012), available at www.bailii.org/ew/cases/EWCA/Civ/2012/638.html (last accessed 30 March 2017), para. 8.
106. *Sulamerica CIA Nacional de Seguros SA and others v Enesa Engenharia SA and others* [2012] EWCA Civ 638 (16 May 2012), available at www.bailii.org/ew/cases/EWCA/Civ/2012/638.html (last accessed 30 March 2017), para. 8.
107. *Sulamerica CIA Nacional de Seguros SA and others v Enesa Engenharia SA and others* [2012] EWCA Civ 638 (16 May 2012), para. 26; see also *XL Insurance v Owens Corning* [2000] 2 Lloyd's Rep. 500.

In other words, in this case there was a general connection between the law applicable to the policy and the law applicable to the arbitration clause so that an express choice of substantive law would amount to an implied choice of the law of the arbitration clause, but on the facts there was a closer connection between the seat of the arbitration and the law applicable to the arbitration clause.[108]

The fact that international commercial arbitration clauses or agreements are included in standard form of contracts (it is also known as contracts of adhesion) does not necessarily render such clauses or agreement unenforceable. If parties are conscionable about such clauses in the standard form of contracts, such clauses shall be enforceable.[109] In the information society, when international commercial arbitration clauses and agreements are formed via electronic communications, the awareness test of parties entering into an arbitration agreement needs to be employed. The 'awareness' test is known as the 'reasonably sufficient notice' test. That is, the party seeking to rely on the term is required to give reasonably sufficient notice to the other contracting party regarding the term. However, actual knowledge of the content of the relevant term is not essential. It is suggested that 'since in the previous contracts a party may have bound himself by terms which he has not read and of which therefore he has no actual knowledge, these terms can surely be incorporated without actual knowledge into a subsequent contract by course of dealing'.[110] In other words, if a term is reasonably brought to the other party's attention, it satisfies the awareness test regardless of whether the other party reads the term as evidenced in traditional ticket cases, though 'reasonable notice' is particularly required for cases involving an automated ticket machine.[111] For example, the recent English case of *Allen Fabrications Limited v ASD Limited* concerned contractual documents that made no reference to either party's standard terms.[112] In the *Allen* case, there had been over 250 transactions between the parties, which, in each case, involved the sending to the plaintiff of an advice note and an invoice; but both parties had their own set of standard terms.[113] The reasoning in the judgment of the *Allen* case relied on the 'reasonably sufficient notice' test established in the automated ticket machine case, *Thornton*.[114] It was suggested that the assessment of fairness and reasonableness should consist of four elements when the case or situation

---

108. Merkin, R. (2012), International: Arbitration governed by seat of arbitration, *Mondaq business briefing*, 16 June.

109. *Coleman v Prudential-Bache Securities, Inc.*, 802 F.2d 1350, 1352 (llth Cir. 1986).

110. Evans, M. (1964), Incorporation of Exemption Clauses in a Contract – Course of Dealing, Vol.27, No.3, *Modern Law Review*, pp. 354–6, p. 356.

111. *Thornton v Shoe Lane Parking Ltd* [1971] 2 QB 163. In *Thornton* case, Sir Gordon Willmer considered the nature of the case taking into account particular conditions, and asserted that 'at least it seems to me that any attempt to introduce conditions after the irrevocable step has been taken of causing the machine to operate must be doomed to failure.'

112. *Allen Fabrications Limited v ASD Limited* [2012] EWHC 2213 (TCC), para. 17.

113. [2012] EWHC 2213 (TCC), para. 13.

114. *Thornton v Shoe Lane Parking Ltd* [1971] 2 QB 163; and see also *Allen Fabrications Limited v ASD Limited* [2012] EWHC 2213 (TCC).

was fact-sensitive: '(a) the nature of the clause (b) what actual steps were taken to draw it to the other party's attention (c) the character of the parties and (d) their particular dealings'.[115] Subsequently, it was held that the exclusion clause was incorporated by express acceptance (under the credit facility application) or by a course of dealing and the seller only needed to satisfy the normal 'notice' test for incorporation as the clause was found to be reasonable.[116]

In electronic communications, there are technological and legal challenges to the appropriateness of making terms available in a digital form. In other words, there is debate over what legal and technological measures are appropriated for reasonable notification. There are various ways of exhibiting arbitration clauses online such as including it in a PDF file online or displaying it on a website. The clause may also be presented via a hyperlink that directs parties to an arbitration clause by clicking a link. There are concerns over whether an arbitration clause displayed via a hyperlink is valid. Occasionally, there may be a conflict between written agreements and online agreements (displayed on a webpage or via a hyperlink) regarding the same transaction. For example, in the US, in the case of *Fadal Machining Centers LLC v Compumachine Inc*, the terms and conditions on Fadal's website provided that within six months after any act or omission in controversy, claims or disputes 'arising out of or related to this agreement, or the breach thereof' shall exclusively be submitted to arbitration in Los Angeles, California under the Commercial Arbitration Rules of the American Arbitration Association (AAA).[117] However, the distributorship agreement in writing had a contradictory clause designating the US District Court for the Central District of California as the forum to resolve disputes. In this case, the Ninth Circuit (US Court of Appeals) upheld a district court's enforcement of an arbitration clause included in a manufacturer's online terms and conditions regardless of a conflicting distributorship agreement, as the written agreement provided that Fadal would unilaterally establish 'the terms of sale . . . from time to time'.[118]

Terms may also be incorporated into a contract by reference via email communications and their attachments. This is intertwined with the incorporation by electronic signature as discussed earlier. According to the previous analysis concerning the US case of *Golden Valley Grape Juice and Wine, LLC v Centrisys Corporation et al*, the offer was made by email providing the sale quotes, which was an adequate office pursuant to the CISG. Displaying three other attachments in the same email would meet the criteria of 'reasonably sufficient notice' to additional terms. Thus, the general conditions were not attached to

---

115. [2012] EWHC 2213 (TCC), para. 61.
116. [2012] EWHC 2213 (TCC), paras. 13, 30, 64 and 66.
117. Memorandum for: *Fadal Machining Centers LLC v Compumachine, Inc* No.10–55719 (9th Cir. 15 December 2011).
118. Memorandum for: *Fadal Machining Centers LLC v Compumachine, Inc* No.10–55719 (9th Cir. 15 December 2011), p. 3.

just any correspondence but were provided *contemporaneously* with the sales quotes and, thus, were part of the contract.[119]

It is also advisable that a notice/reference on a website must be *reasonable* and *adequate* for the terms to be effectively incorporated. For instance, in the US, in the case of *Manasher v NECC Telecom*, the court held that an arbitration clause found in the defendant's online terms and condition was not incorporated into the contract terms by reference, because an arbitration clause added in an amended terms and conditions was unconscionable – the online terms were placed and referenced in the fifth statement of the second page of the defendant's invoice and in ambiguous language.[120]

---

119. *Golden Valley Grape Juice and Wine, LLC v Centrisys Corporation et al*, Case No. CV F 09–1424 LJO GSA, 21 January 2010 (the United States District Court of the Eastern District of California). In this case, although a forum selection clause was included in the General Conditions and should in theory be considered as part of the contract, the wording was too broadly expressed and thus invoked.

120. *Manasher v NECC Telecom*, No. 06–10749, 2007 WL 2713845 (E.D. Mich. 2007).

CHAPTER 6

The enforcement of online arbitral awards

6.1 Legal framework for online arbitral awards

Arbitral awards are made at the final step in the arbitration proceedings, which 'shall include not only awards made by arbitrators appointed for each case but also those made by permanent arbitral bodies to which the parties have submitted'.[1] There is no express definition of arbitral awards in international and national arbitration legislation. The majority of institutional arbitration rules and national law provide similar basic requirements as to the format and issuance of arbitral awards and the reasoning of the awards, though the requirement as to the standard of reasoning may vary. The New York Convention on the Recognition and Enforcement of Foreign Arbitral Law also implies the form requirement of arbitral awards that the party applying for recognition and enforcement shall, at the time of the application, supply 'the duly authenticated original award or a duly certified copy'.[2] Such arbitral awards shall be binding and enforceable in each contracting State subject to the grounds for refusal of enforcement in its Article V.[3]

With the deployment of ODR systems, there may be additional legal requirements regarding the format and issuance of online arbitral awards compared with traditional arbitral awards. The most recent UNCITRAL Draft ODR Procedural Rules (Track I) provides arbitration procedures leading to final and binding arbitral awards. According to Article 7(3) and (4) of the UNCITRAL Draft ODR Procedural Rules, online arbitral awards shall be in writing and recorded on the ODR platform:

> (3) The neutral shall evaluate the dispute based on the information submitted by the parties [, and having regard to the terms of the agreement,] and shall render an award. The ODR administrator shall communicate the award to the parties and the award shall be *recorded on the ODR platform.* (4) The award shall be made *in*

---

1. 1958 Convention on the Recognition and Enforcement of Foreign Arbitral Awards – the 'New York' Convention, available at www.uncitral.org/pdf/english/texts/arbitration/NY-conv/XXII_1_e.pdf (last accessed 30 March 2017), Article I(2).
2. The New York Convention 1958, Article IV(1)(a).
3. The New York Convention 1958, Article V.

writing and *signed* by the neutral, and shall indicate the date on which it was made and the place of arbitration.[4] (emphasis added)

With regard to the 'writing' requirement for an online arbitral award, it further specifies that:

> (a) The award to be in writing shall be met where the information contained in the award is accessible so as to be usable for subsequent reference; and (b) The award to be signed shall be met where data is used to identify the neutral and to indicate his or her approval of the information contained in the award.[5]

Online arbitral awards share the same effect as traditional awards in that valid arbitral awards are final and binding on the parties.[6] Traditionally, physical originals of the signed award would be delivered by courier to the parties, their representatives and arbitral institution so that the delivery acknowledgment could be produced as evidence in setting aside and/or enforcement proceedings. In current practice, most arbitration rules still require a physical original of awards.[7] Sometimes where electronic communication is allowed, hard copy originals shall still be delivered.[8] The adoption of the UNCITRAL Draft ODR Procedural Rules may bridge such differences in practice in different countries and promote the efficiency and legal certainty of delivering arbitral awards by electronic means.

In addition, UNCITRAL Draft ODR Procedural Rules also require reasoning for arbitral awards in that 'the award shall state brief grounds upon which it is based',[9] though the level of reasoning only needs to be short and concise but takes into consideration any relevant facts and circumstances and any usage of trade applicable to the transaction in accordance with the terms of the contract.[10] This proposed requirement of online reasoned awards seems be more simple, compared with a traditional explanation of a reasoned award provided by an English leading case *Bremer Handelsgesellschaft mbH v Westzucker GmbH* that:

> All that is necessary is that the arbitrators should set out what, on their view of the evidence, did or did not happen and should explain succinctly why, in the light of

---

4. A/CN.9/WG.III/WP.133 – Online dispute resolution for cross-border electronic commerce transactions: draft procedural rules, United Nations Commission on International Trade Law, Working Group III (Online dispute resolution), Thirty-first session, New York, 9–13 February 2015 (hereafter 'UNCITRAL Draft ODR Procedural Rules 2014'), Article 7(3) and (4).

5. UNCITRAL Draft ODR Procedural Rules 2014 (A/CN.9/WG.III/WP.133), Article 7(4) bis.

6. UNCITRAL Draft ODR Procedural Rules 2014 (A/CN.9/WG.III/WP.133), Article 7(7). It provides that 'the award shall be final and binding on the parties. The parties shall carry out the award without delay'.

7. Drafting Arbitral Awards, Part I – General, International Arbitration Practice Guideline 2016, Chartered Institute of Arbitrators, available at www.ciarb.org/guidelines-and-ethics/guidelines/practice-guidelines-protocols-and-rules (last accessed 30 March 2017), p. 6.

8. Fry, J., Greenberg, S and Mazza, F. (2012), The Secretariat's Guide to ICC Arbitration, ICC Publication 729, p. 341. It advises that under the ICC Rules, an electronic transmission of the award does not constitute official notification of an award and official notification is deemed to occur when a party receives the original signed award.

9. UNCITRAL Draft ODR Procedural Rules 2014 (A/CN.9/WG.III/WP.133), Article 7(5).

10. UNCITRAL Draft ODR Procedural Rules 2014 (A/CN.9/WG.III/WP.133), Article 7(8).

what happened, they have reached their decision and what that decision is. This is all that is meant by a 'reasoned award'.[11]

It is possible that the reason that the grounds of an online award is advised to be brief is to match the vision or purposes of using online arbitration, which intends to give faster, cheaper and more efficient service than traditional arbitration. A brief reasoned award may also have the benefit of helping ordinary parties to understand the content/context of an award. However, a fast, less-costly and efficient online arbitration process does not mean that the quality and level of standard needs to be compromised; in fact, with the deployment of computer algorithms assisting making the award decision, a detailed and well-structured reasoned award may be provided in a short span of time. According to the UNCITRAL Draft ODR Procedural Rules, online arbitral awards should also be made in a timely fashion within ten calendar days from a specified point in proceedings.[12] There is no explanation as to what 'from a specified point in proceedings' actually refers to. It may be understood as from a point that an arbitral award can be concluded in proceedings or from the point that post-hearing submissions (e.g. revising and confirming solutions) are completed.

It appears that UNCITRAL Draft ODR Procedural Rules have not mentioned the possibility of consent awards during online arbitration. Consent awards refer to a settlement negotiated by the parties during arbitral proceedings that have the same effect as arbitral awards. For example, Article 30 of the UNCITRAL Model Law on International Commercial Arbitration provides that:

> (1) If, during arbitral proceedings, the parties settle the dispute, the arbitral tribunal shall terminate the proceedings and, if requested by the parties and not objected to by the arbitral tribunal, record the settlement in the form of an arbitral award on agreed terms.
>
> (2) An award on agreed terms . . . and shall state that it is an award. Such an award has the same status and effect as any other award on the merits of the case.

It means that when parties reach their own agreement/settlement during arbitral proceedings, parties can dismiss the arbitration and record the terms of the settlement agreement. It is suggested that a consent award, which records some or all of the terms of the settlement in particular with a payment obligation, may provide a greater degree of certainty and enforceability than a simple settlement agreement.[13] The design of ODR systems shall provide an option to allow parties to reach any agreement at any point during arbitral proceedings and generate an

---

11. *Bremer Handelsgesellschaft mbH v Westzucker GmbH* [1981] 2 Lloyd's Rep 130 at 132–3.
12. UNCITRAL Draft ODR Procedural Rules 2014 (A/CN.9/WG.III/WP.133), Article 7(6). It provides that 'The award shall be rendered promptly, preferably within ten calendar days [from a specified point in proceedings].' 6. bis. continues 'an award may be made public with the consent of all parties or where and to the extent disclosure is required of a party by legal duty, to protect or pursue a legal right or in relation to legal proceedings before a court or other competent authority'.
13. Born, G. (2011), International Arbitration: Cases and Materials (New York: Aspen Publishers, 2011), p. 1011.

automated record of evidential materials and discussion to the point that parties dismiss the arbitration for reference. The parties' settlement agreement shall be signed by both parties and recorded on the ODR platform.

6.2 Jurisdiction and applicable law concerning online arbitral awards

In international commercial arbitration, there are three critical factors that determine whether an international arbitration convention or rules shall apply to ascertain the validity of the arbitration agreement and to enforce an arbitral award. They are: the nature of subject matters (e.g. commercial or defined legal relationship); the jurisdiction of the awards ('foreign' or 'non-domestic'); and the status or effect of the awards ('binding' or 'final'). An arbitration shall be considered as 'international' or 'foreign' in the light of a place of business test. That is, if 'the parties to an arbitration agreement have, at the time of the conclusion of that agreement, their places of business in different states'.[14] Parties may also expressly agree that the subject matter of the arbitration agreement relates to more than one country.[15] An arbitration will still be international despite both parties having their places of business in the same state, if the legal seat/place of arbitration, any place where a substantial part of the obligations of commercial relationship is to be performed, or the place with which the subject-matter of the dispute is most closely connected, is situated outside the state in which parties have their places of business.[16] For example, in *Fung Sang Trading Ltd. v Kai Sun Sea Products and Food Co. Ltd*[17] two parties from Hong Kong entered into a FOB contract on sale of goods with delivery of goods outside Hong Kong (delivery of the goods was in Dalian, China). It was held that it is possible for two Hong Kong parties to enter into a contract in Hong Kong under Hong Kong law and still find themselves in an international arbitration if substantial performance of the obligations of the commercial relationship is outside Hong Kong.[18] *Heung & Associates, Architects & Engineers v Pacific Enterprises (Holdings) Company Limited*[19] concerned two parties from Hong Kong who disputed over professional fees due for the design of a project in Dongshan Island, China. It was held that the arbitration agreement was with an 'international' character as the subject matter of the dispute was most closely connected to the project in

---

14. UNCITRAL Model Law on International Commercial Arbitration 1985, Article 1(3)(a).
15. UNCITRAL Model Law on International Commercial Arbitration 1985, Article 1(3)(c).
16. UNCITRAL Model Law on International Commercial Arbitration 1985, Article 1(3)(b).
17. *Fung Sang Trading Ltd. v Kai Sun Sea Products and Food Co. Ltd.* [1991] 2 HKC 526.
18. [1991] 2 HKC 526 at 527.
19. *Heung & Associates, Architects & Engineers v Pacific Enterprises (Holdings) Company Ltd.* (May 4, 1995) Hong Kong/High Court of Hong Kong, available at http://interarb.com/clout/clout108.htm (last accessed 30 March 2017).

Dongshan, China, and that a substantial part of the defendant's duties related to the entire design and supervision of that project.[20]

Arbitral awards arising out of an international arbitration may also be deemed as 'international' or 'foreign' arbitral awards. According to the New York Convention, the recognition and enforcement of arbitral awards made in the territory of a state other than the state where the recognition and enforcement of such awards are sought, shall be considered as foreign and non-domestic awards.[21] It means that arbitral awards made outside the judicial enforcement forum are 'foreign'.[22] For example, the US leading case of *Bergesen v Joseph Muller Corp.*[23] concerned whether the New York Convention was applicable to an award arising from an arbitration held by AAA in New York between two foreign entities – Norwegian and Swiss companies for the transportation of chemicals from the United States to Europe. The Court interpreted 'non-domestic' in §202 of the Federal Arbitration Act (FAA) so that if a US arbitration involves only US citizens, the Convention may be applicable, but only if the parties' relationship involves property located abroad, envisages performance or enforcement aboard, or has some other reasonable relation with one or more foreign states. The Court pointed out that the New York Convention shall also apply to awards made in a country other than the state where enforcement was sought as well as to awards not considered domestic in that state.[24] This is in accordance with Article I(3) of the New York Convention that 'it also applies to all awards not considered as domestic in the state of enforcement, whether or not any of such awards may have been rendered in the territory of that state'.[25] The court held that the arbitral award was not domestic, and thus was enforceable in the United States, due to the fact that

> awards 'not considered as domestic' denotes awards which are subject to the Convention not because made abroad, but because made within the legal framework of another country, e.g., pronounced in accordance with foreign law or involving parties domiciled or having their principal place of business outside the enforcing jurisdiction.[26]

In accordance with the *Bergesen* case, in *Yusuf Ahmed Alghanim & Sons, WLL v Toys "R" Us, Inc.*,[27] the court held that

> the Convention's applicability in this case is clear. The dispute giving rise to this appeal involved two non-domestic parties and one US corporation, and principally involved conduct and contract performance in the Middle East. Thus, we consider

---

20. *Heung & Associates, Architects & Engineers v Pacific Enterprises (Holdings) Company Ltd.* (4 May 1995) Hong Kong/High Court of Hong Kong.
21. The New York Convention 1958, Article I.
22. Born, G., International Arbitration: Cases and Materials (New York: Aspen Publishers, 2011), p. 1019.
23. *Bergesen v Joseph Muller Corp.*, 710 F.2d 928 (1983).
24. *Bergesen v Joseph Muller Corp.*, 710 F.2d 928 (1983), 931.
25. The New York Convention 1958, Article I(3).
26. *Bergesen v Joseph Muller Corp.*, 710 F.2d 928 (1983), 932.
27. *Yusuf Ahmed Alghanim & Sons, WLL v Toys 'R' Us, Inc.*, 126 F.3d 15 (2d Cir. 1997).

the arbitral award leading to this action a non-domestic award and thus within the scope of the Convention.[28]

Accordingly, this means that the New York Convention covers delocalisation of arbitration as the Convention does not limit its field of application to awards governed by national laws. Thus, an award generally can be enforced in a state that has ratified the Convention. The fact that the award is rendered in some countries does not necessarily mean that it is a domestic award, as the nationality of an arbitral award might depend on the law governing the arbitral procedure. Thus, the application of foreign rules or non-national substantive laws to the subject matter of the dispute could make an award 'international', 'foreign' or 'non-domestic'. 'International', 'foreign' and 'non-domestic' awards are presumptively entitled to recognition under Article III of the New York Convention and can be denied recognition and enforcement only on grounds specified in Article V of the New York Convention.[29]

The success of ODR practice relies on resolving the legal uncertainty of online international arbitral awards, as it is difficult to determine the legal place of arbitration or arbitral proceedings. In other words, it is debatable as to whether an online arbitral award shall be considered to be 'domestic' or 'foreign'. This could in turn lead to a so-called 'floating arbitration', 'delocalisation of arbitration' or 'floating award'. Delocalised arbitration means that it is floating on the surface of legal systems of different countries, not attaching itself to any municipal legal order.[30] Delocalised arbitration is detached from the procedural rules and the substantive law of the place of arbitration; the procedural rules of any specific national law; and the national substantive law of any specific jurisdiction.[31] However, parties should incorporate a delocalised arbitration clause in their agreement so that the award could be eligible for enforcement.[32]

Currently, there are no uniform ODR rules with regard to online arbitral awards at the international level. It may be helpful to establish harmonised best practices or a set of special rules concerning the recognition of online international arbitral awards both procedurally and substantively. It was suggested that the application of transnational substantive rules through denationalised online arbitration would be the pinnacle of autonomy of e-business and online arbitration.[33]

---

28. *Yusuf Ahmed Alghanim & Sons, WLL v Toys 'R' Us, Inc.*, 126 F.3d 15 (2d Cir. 1997), 19.
29. Born, G., International Arbitration: Cases and Materials (New York: Aspen Publishers, 2011), p. 1024.
30. Janićijević, D. (2005), Delocalization of International Commercial Arbitration, *Law and Politics* Volume 3 No.1, pp. 63–71, available at http://facta.junis.ni.ac.rs/lap/lap2005/lap2005-07.pdf (last accessed 30 March 2017), p. 63.
31. Janićijević, D. (2005), Delocalization of International Commercial Arbitration, *Law and Politics* Volume 3 No.1, pp. 63–71, available at http://facta.junis.ni.ac.rs/lap/lap2005/lap2005-07.pdf (last accessed 30 March 2017), p. 64.
32. *Beaufort Developments (NI) Ltd. v Gilbert-Ash N.I. Ltd.* [1998] 2 WLR 860 (Eng.).
33. Patrikios, A. (2006–7), Resolution of Cross-Border E-business Disputes by Arbitration Tribunals on the Basis of Transnational Substantive Rules of Law and E-business Usages: The Emergence of the Lex Informatica, *University of Toledo Review,* Volume 38, pp. 271–306, p. 282.

In absence of relevant rules concerning online international arbitral awards, as discussed in Chapter 4 above on the selection of the seat of online arbitration, the pre-selection of the legal seat of online arbitration is of paramount importance. Ideally parties should agree on the place or seat of arbitration in the arbitration agreement before arbitral proceedings. If there is no agreement on the seat of arbitration between parties, the arbitral tribunal or arbitral institution has the power to determine the place of arbitration at the beginning of the arbitral proceedings. Some arbitration institutional rules may also contain a default place of arbitration, applicable where the parties have not chosen one.[34] There are legal and other consequences of the place of arbitration, because arbitral awards are usually considered to be made at the legal seat of the arbitration, either as indicated in the arbitration agreement or subsequently by the arbitral institution or tribunal. For example, the UK Arbitration Act 1996 provides that

> unless otherwise agreed by the parties, where the seat of the arbitration is in England and Wales or Northern Ireland, any award in the proceedings shall be treated as made there, regardless of where it was signed, despatched or delivered to any of the parties.[35]

Due to the fact that the legal seat of arbitration often determines the applicable arbitration law, which may have various impacts on subsequent matters, the legal seat of arbitration has to be carefully chosen. Such matters include but are not limited to

> the requirements relating to the appointment and challenge of arbitrators, whether and on what grounds a party can seek judicial review or setting aside of an arbitral award, which court is competent with respect to the arbitral proceedings, as well as the conditions for recognition and enforcement of an arbitral award in other jurisdictions.[36]

In other words, the place of arbitration or seat of arbitration is usually used to ascertain the application of the country's arbitration law and later the country of origin for enforcement purposes.

In ODR systems, parties' pre-agreement on the legal seat of arbitration is of paramount importance. In absence of such choice, it is problematic to determine the legal seat of arbitration in cyberspace due to the fact that arbitral proceedings in cyberspace have no physical location. Under these circumstances, the determination of the legal seat of arbitration may rely on the connection between various factors such as the arbitral institutional rules chosen by the parties, the business location of chairman of arbitration and applicable law for arbitral proceedings and for the substance of disputes or subject matters. However, it is not necessary that all these factors exist, because parties may not choose any applicable law or arbitral tribunals. It is also suggested that if there is no agreement on the legal

---

34. UNCITRAL Notes on Organizing Arbitral Proceedings (2016), pp. 11–12, para. 27.
35. UK Arbitration Act 1996, s 53.
36. UNCITRAL Notes on Organizing Arbitral Proceedings (2016), pp. 11–12, para. 28.

seat of arbitration, the legal seat of arbitration in cyberspace shall be determined by the domicile of the chairman of the arbitral tribunal, the location of the main server or the place of business of the dispute resolution provider.[37] It appears that 'the domicile of the chairman of the arbitral tribunal' or 'the place of business of the chairman of arbitration' may be a more close, appropriate and effective connecting factor in determining the location of arbitral proceedings than 'the location of the main server or the place of business of the dispute resolution provider'. The latter contradicts the underlying logic of the determination of the location of the party in cyberspace under Article 6 of the UN Convention of the Use of Electronic Communications in International Contracts. The underlying logic of the determination of the location of the parties in cyberspace may be transplanted as the determination of the legal location of arbitration. According to the UN Convention, a party's place of business is presumed to be the location indicated by that party, unless another party demonstrates that the party making the indication does not have a place of business at that location.[38] If a party has not indicated a place of business and has more than one place of business, the place of business is that which has the closest relationship to the relevant contract, having regard to the circumstances known to or contemplated by the parties at any time before or at the conclusion of the contract.[39] If a natural person does not have a place of business, the person's habitual residence may be considered as the place of business.[40] A location is not a place of business merely because that is: (a) where equipment and technology supporting an information system used by a party in connection with the formation of a contract are located; or (b) where the information system may be accessed by other parties.[41] The sole fact that a party makes use of a domain name or electronic mail address connected to a specific country does not create a presumption that its place of business is located in that country.[42] Accordingly, where the technological equipment of ODR systems is located shall not be used as a close connecting factor to determine the legal location of arbitration. Domain names or electronic mail addresses connected to a specific country for ODR systems and ODR administration shall also not be considered as appropriate linking factors for the determination of the legal seat of arbitration.

---

37. Herrmann, G. (2001), Some Legal E-flections on Online Arbitration, in Briner, R., Fortier, L., Berger, K. and Bredow, J. (eds.), *Law of International Business and Dispute Settlement in the 21st Century* (Cologne: Carl Heymanns Verlag KG), pp. 267–76, p. 273.
38. UN Convention on the Use of Electronic Communications in International Contracts 2005, Article 6(1).
39. UN Convention on the Use of Electronic Communications in International Contracts 2005, Article 6(2).
40. UN Convention on the Use of Electronic Communications in International Contracts 2005, Article 6(3).
41. UN Convention on the Use of Electronic Communications in International Contracts 2005, Article 6(4).
42. UN Convention on the Use of Electronic Communications in International Contracts 2005, Article 6(5).

With regard to applicable law for arbitration, there are various applicable laws for different matters in arbitration, such as the applicable law to the substance of the parties' dispute; applicable law to the arbitration agreement; applicable procedural law to the arbitral proceedings; and applicable choice-of-law rules in international arbitration. Similar to the selection of the seat of arbitration, parties may agree on a set of applicable laws on various matters, though such choice shall not infringe the mandatory rule or public policy of the country. Within the scope of application of party autonomy, arbitral tribunals do not have the power to disregard the parties' instructions, because excess of power and procedural irregularity are both grounds for setting aside or refusing to enforce an arbitral award,[43] according to Article 34(2)(a)(iii) and 34(2)(a)(iv) of the UNCITRAL Model Law on International Commercial Arbitration and Article V(1)(c) and (1)(d) of the New York Convention. Beyond the party autonomy's scope of application, the parties' instructions do not have effect and do not limit the arbitral tribunal's power to determine the applicable law.[44] Under these circumstances, the arbitral tribunal may determine the private international law (i.e. Brussels I Regulation Recast and Rome I Regulation in the EU), and then the chosen rule/regulation of private international law will direct the appropriate jurisdiction and substantive applicable law. It is suggested that the parties shall choose the system of private international law that the arbitral tribunal shall use in order to avoid ambiguous application and to create legal certainty, as in the absence of any reference to a private international law, there is no indication that the tribunal will definitely apply a conflict rule to identify the proper law.[45] Meanwhile, if the arbitral tribunal decides to apply a conflict rule, it will face the same challenges of the determination of applicable law of electronic contracts as that in court litigation. With regard to choice of arbitral procedure, in practice, the procedure of arbitration shall be governed by the procedural rules agreed upon by the parties, which shall not be contrary to the mandatory provisions of the law of the place where the arbitration takes place or the award is made. In the absence of the agreement, procedural rules determined by the arbitral tribunal shall apply.

6.3 Challenge of online arbitral awards

The purpose of challenging an arbitral award is to have it corrected in some way or more often have it annulled or set aside in whole or in part.[46] There are two main ways of challenging arbitral awards: one is internal challenge via arbitral

---

43. Moss, G. C. (2008), Arbitration and Private International Law, *International Arbitration Law Review* (2008) Volume 11, Issue 4, pp. 153–64, p. 163.
44. Moss, G. C. (2008), Arbitration and Private International Law, *International Arbitration Law Review* (2008) Volume 11, Issue 4, pp. 153–64, p. 163.
45. Moss, G. C. (2008), Arbitration and Private International Law, *International Arbitration Law Review* (2008) Volume 11, Issue 4, pp. 153–64, p. 163.
46. Redfern, A., Hunter, M., Blackaby, N. and Partasides, C. (2015), Redfern and Hunter on International Arbitration (Oxford: Oxford University Press, 6th edition, 2015), p. 570.

institutions/tribunals; and the other is recourse to the courts. Article 34(2) of the UNCITRAL Model Law on International Commercial Arbitration provides grounds for application for challenging an arbitral award, in which an arbitral award may be set aside by the court only if:

> (a) the party making the application furnishes proof that: (i) a party to the arbitration agreement was under some *incapacity*; or the said *agreement is not valid* under the law to which the parties have subjected it or, failing any indication thereon, under the law of this State; or (ii) the party making the application was *not given proper notice* of the appointment of an arbitrator or of the arbitral proceedings or was otherwise unable to present his case; or (iii) the award deals with a dispute *not contemplated by* or *not falling within the terms* of the submission to arbitration, or contains decisions on matters *beyond the scope* of the submission to arbitration, provided that, if the decisions on matters submitted to arbitration can be separated from those not so submitted, only that part of the award which contains decisions on matters not submitted to arbitration may be set aside; or (iv) *the composition of the arbitral tribunal or the arbitral procedure* was not in accordance with the agreement of the parties, unless such agreement was in conflict with a provision of this Law from which the parties cannot derogate, or, failing such agreement, was not in accordance with this Law; or
>
> (b) the court finds that: (i) the *subject-matter* of the dispute is not capable of settlement by arbitration under the law of this State; or (ii) the award is in conflict with the *public policy* of this State. (edited and emphasis added)

The provision of the annulment of an arbitral award under the UNCITRAL Model Law on International Commercial Arbitration has a close link with Article V(1)(e) of the New York Convention. It is suggested that where a challenge to the validity or effect of an arbitral award is made, it shall be addressed to the designated competent court of the legal seat of arbitration.[47] That is, if the arbitral award is made in state A, only the courts in state A have jurisdiction to annul such award, though courts in State A and other nations may all have power to confirm, recognise and enforce the award.[48] For example, in *PT Garuda Indonesia v Birgen Air*,[49] the Singapore courts have no jurisdiction to annual the arbitral award as the legal seat of arbitration was not in Singapore where the hearings took place; but Jakarta, Indonesia was agreed as the legal seat of arbitration in the arbitration agreement.[50]

In ODR systems, after the online arbitral award is made, parties may also be given an opportunity to request the neutral/arbitrator to correct any error in computation, any clerical or typographical error, or any error or omission of a similar nature, within five calendar days, and action shall be made and recorded

---

47. Redfern, A., Hunter, M., Blackaby, N. and Partasides, C. (2015), Redfern and Hunter on International Arbitration (Oxford: Oxford University Press, 6th edition, 2015), p. 577.
48. Born, G. (2011), International Arbitration: Cases and Materials (New York: Aspen Publishers, 2011), p. 1032.
49. [2002] 1 SLR 393.
50. *PT Garuda Indonesia v Birgen Air* [2002] 1 SLR 393, 411–12.

on the ODR platform within two calendar days if approved.[51] Moreover, the UNCITRAL Draft ODR Procedural Rules propose an internal review mechanism for parties to request annulment of the arbitral award within ten calendar days of the communication of the award by application to the ODR administrator if (a) the place of arbitration unfairly prejudiced that party; or (b) there has been a serious departure from a fundamental rule of procedure prejudicing that party's right to due process.[52] Upon parties' request, the ODR administrator shall appoint a neutral unaffiliated with the ODR proceedings the subject of the request to assess the request within five calendar days, and notify the parties of such appointment. The decision should be made within seven calendar days of the new neutral's appointment. If the award is annulled, the parties will be given an option to start the whole proceeding again appointing a new neutral.[53]

6.4 Recognition and enforcement of online arbitral awards

It is recognised that one of the great achievements of the New York Convention is the establishment of a harmonised and simplified international regime for the cross-border enforcement of arbitral awards.[54] Article III of the New York Convention establishes that each contracting state shall recognise arbitral awards as binding and enforce them in accordance with the rules of procedure of the territory where the award is relied upon, whilst Article V provides grounds for refusal of recognition and enforcement of an arbitral award.

There are seven grounds for refusal of recognition and enforcement of an arbitral award according to Article V of the New York Convention. Article V(1) lists five grounds for refusal that must be raised 'at the request of the party against whom [the award] is invoked', whilst Article V(2) lists two grounds on which a court may refuse enforcement of its own motion.[55] The grounds for refusal under Article V do not include an erroneous decision in law or in fact by the

---

51. UNCITRAL Draft ODR Procedural Rules 2014 (A/CN.9/WG.III/WP.133), Article 7 bis Correction of award. It provides 'within [five (5)] calendar days [after the receipt of the award], a party, with notice to the other party, may request the neutral to correct in the award any error in computation, any clerical or typographical error, [or any error or omission of a similar nature]. If the neutral considers that the request is justified, he or she shall make the correction [including a brief statement of reasons therefor] within [two (2)] calendar days of receipt of the request. Such corrections [shall be recorded on the ODR platform and] shall form part of the award. [The neutral may within [five (5)] calendar days after the communication of the award make such corrections on its own initiative.]]'

52. UNCITRAL Draft ODR Procedural Rules 2014 (A/CN.9/WG.III/WP.133), draft article 7 (ter) Internal review mechanism.

53. UNCITRAL Draft ODR Procedural Rules 2014 (A/CN.9/WG.III/WP.133), draft article 7 (ter) Internal review mechanism.

54. Hill, J. (2016), The Exercise of Judicial Discretion in Relation to Applications to Enforce Arbitral Awards under the New York Convention 1958, *Oxford Journal of Legal Studies,* Volume 36 Issue 2, pp. 304–33, p. 304.

55. UNCITRAL Secretariat Guide on the Convention on the Recognition and Enforcement of Foreign Arbitral Awards (New York, 1958), 2016 Edition, available at www.uncitral.org/pdf/english/texts/arbitration/NY-conv/2016_Guide_on_the_Convention.pdf (last accessed 30 March 2017), p. 124.

arbitral tribunal.[56] Courts have consistently recognised that 'the party opposing recognition and enforcement has the burden of raising and proving the grounds for non-enforcement under article V (1)'.[57] Article V(1) of the Convention provides that recognition and enforcement of the award may be refused, at the request of the party against whom it is invoked, only if that party furnishes to the competent authority where the recognition and enforcement is sought, proof that:

> (a) first ground: The parties to the agreement referred to in article II were, under the law applicable to them, under some incapacity, or the said agreement is not valid under the law to which the parties have subjected it or, failing any indication thereon, under the law of the country where the award was made. (edited)

There are two subject matters governed by Article V(1)(a): one is incapacity of parties and the other is the validity of an arbitration agreement.[58] It is suggested that Article V(1)(a) of the New York Convention also contains choice-of-law rules for determining the applicable law for the validity of the arbitration agreement.[59] In practice, it is not common that parties choose a specific applicable law to govern the arbitration agreement. Parties usually choose an application law to govern the arbitration procedure or arbitral proceedings, which may implicitly become a chosen law for the determination of the validity of the arbitration agreement.[60] There are also cases where the law applicable to the substance of parties' contract also governs the validity of the arbitration agreement.[61] The principle of separability is often adopted by courts to determine the validity of the arbitration; for example, in *China Minmetals Materials Import and Exp. Co. v Chi Mei Corp.*, a forged main contract did not simply render the arbitration clause void.[62] In ODR systems, in order to avoid refusal of recognition and enforcement of an

---

56. UNCITRAL Secretariat Guide on the Convention on the Recognition and Enforcement of Foreign Arbitral Awards (New York, 1958), 2016 Edition, p. 126.

57. UNCITRAL Secretariat Guide on the Convention on the Recognition and Enforcement of Foreign Arbitral Awards (New York, 1958), 2016 Edition, p. 129; *Dutch Shipowner v German Cattle and Meat Dealer, Bundesgerichtshof*, Germany, 1 February 2001, XXIX Y.B. Com. Arb. 700 (2004); *Trans World Film SpA v Film Polski Import and Export of Films, Corte di Cassazione*, Italy, 22 February 1992, XVIII Y.B. Com. Arb. 433 (1993); *Europcar Italia SpA v Maiellano Tours Inc.*, Court of Appeals, Second Circuit, United States of America, 2 September 1998, 97–7224, XXIV Y.B. Com. Arb. 860 (1999); *Encyclopedia Universalis S.A. v Encyclopedia Britannica Inc.*, Court of Appeals, Second Circuit, United States of America, 31 March 2005, 04–0288-cv, XXX Y.B. Com. Arb. 1136 (2005).

58. See Chapter 5 on the discussion concerning the validity of an arbitration agreement.

59. Born, G. (2011), International Arbitration: Cases and Materials (New York: Aspen Publishers, 2011), p. 1049.

60. UNCITRAL Secretariat Guide on the Convention on the Recognition and Enforcement of Foreign Arbitral Awards (New York, 1958), 2016 Edition, p. 142. *Telenor Mobile Communications AS v Storm LLC*, District Court, Southern District of New York, United States of America, 2 November 2007, 524 F. Supp. 2d 332.

61. *Egyptian Company for Concrete & Hashem Ali Maher v STC Finance & Ismail Ibrahim Mahmoud Thabet & Sabishi Trading and Contracting Company*, Court of Cassation, Egypt, 27 March 1996, 2660/59. See also *Stena RoRo AB v OAO Baltiysky Zavod*, Highest Arbitrazh Court, Russian Federation, 13 September 2011, A56–60007/2008; *Ltd. 'R.L.' v JSC 'Z. Factory'*, Supreme Court, Georgia, 2 April 2004, a-204-sh-43–03.

62. *China Minmetals Materials Import and Exp. Co. v Chi Mei Corp.* 334 F.3d 274 (3d Cir. 2003).

online arbitral award on the ground of the invalidity of arbitration agreements, it is crucial for all parties to sign the arbitration agreement and for the ODR system to generate a time stamp, electronic seal and authentication certificate[63] to certify parties' signed arbitration agreement. In intelligent/advanced ODR systems, arbitrators may not be natural persons, which may challenge the validity of appointment of arbitrators in the arbitration agreement subject to applicable law.

> (b) second ground: The party against whom the award is invoked was not given proper notice of the appointment of the arbitrator or of the arbitration proceedings or was otherwise unable to present his case.

Article V(1)(b) addresses due process in arbitral proceedings, which include three elements – first, proper notice of the appointment of the arbitrators; second, proper notice of the arbitration proceedings; and third, more broadly, parties' opportunity to present their case.[64] It is suggested that Article V(1)(b) has some interaction and overlap with Article V(2)(b) as due process is closely connected to public policy.[65] Refusal of recognition and enforcement of an arbitral award under the ground of 'proper notice' has been difficult, because if parties or their representatives managed to present their case in the proceedings, it would often be considered as not insufficient notice.[66] An arbitral award may be refused only if there was evidence of insufficient notice, such as a lack of proof of delivery of notice, non-disclosure of arbitrators' names in the notice or parties' failing to present at the proceedings in absence of notice.[67] In ODR systems, a qualified electronic time stamp[68] may be used to prove the delivery of notice of appointment of arbitrators and of the arbitral proceedings.

---

63. Regulation (EU) No 910/2014 of the European Parliament and of the Council of 23 July 2014 on electronic identification and trust services for electronic transactions in the internal market and repealing Directive 1999/93/EC, OJ L 257, 28.8.2014, pp. 73–114. Article 3(25) provides that 'electronic seal' means data in electronic form, which is attached to or logically associated with other data in electronic form to ensure the latter's origin and integrity; and Article 3(26) 'advanced electronic seal' means an electronic seal, which meets the requirements set out in Article 36.

64. UNCITRAL Secretariat Guide on the Convention on the Recognition and Enforcement of Foreign Arbitral Awards (New York, 1958), 2016 Edition, p. 155.

65. UNCITRAL Secretariat Guide on the Convention on the Recognition and Enforcement of Foreign Arbitral Awards (New York, 1958), 2016 Edition, p. 156.

66. *OOO Sandora (Ukraine) v OOO Euro-Import Group (Russian Federation)*, Federal Arbitrazh Court, District of Moscow, Russian Federation, 12 November 2010, A40-51459/10-63-440; and *Union Générale de Cinéma SA (France) v XYZ Desarrollos, S.A. (Spain)*, Supreme Court, Spain, 11 April 2000, XXXII Y.B. Com. Arb. 525 (2007).

67. *Aiduoladuo (Mongolia) Co., Ltd. v Zhejiang Zhancheng Construction Group Co., Ltd.*, Supreme People's Court, China, 8 December 2009, Min Si Ta Zi No. 46; *Cosmos Marine Managements S.A. v Tianjin Kaiqiang Trading Ltd.*, Supreme People's Court, China, 10 January 2007, Min Si Ta Zi No. 34; and *Bayerisches Oberstes Landesgericht [BayObLG]*, Germany, 16 March 2000, 4 Z Sch 50/99. Non-disclosure of arbitrators' names in the notice, see *Danish Buyer v German (F.R.) Seller, Oberlandesgericht [OLG]*, Köln, Germany, 10 June 1976, IV Y.B. Com. Arb. 258 (1979).

68. Regulation (EU) No 910/2014 of the European Parliament and of the Council of 23 July 2014 on electronic identification and trust services for electronic transactions in the internal market and repealing Directive 1999/93/EC, OJ L 257, 28.8.2014, pp. 73–114. Article 3(33) provides that 'electronic time stamp' means data in electronic form which binds other data in electronic form to a

(c) third ground: The award deals with a difference not contemplated by or not falling within the terms of the submission to arbitration, or it contains decisions on matters beyond the scope of the submission to arbitration, provided that, if the decisions on matters submitted to arbitration can be separated from those not so submitted, that part of the award which contains decisions on matters submitted to arbitration may be recognized and enforced.

Article V(1)(c) addresses decisions of arbitral awards concerning matters 'beyond the scope of the submission to arbitration'. 'Submission to arbitration' refers to 'the scope of the arbitration agreement' that if arbitral awards deal with matters beyond parties' agreement to arbitrate, recognition and enforcement of such awards may be refused.[69] It is suggested that Article V(1)(a) and Article V(1)(c) are often considered together by courts regarding the challenge of the validity of an arbitration agreement, because the nature of both articles is similar in that they both concern whether an arbitral award has been rendered on the basis of a valid arbitration agreement.[70] In ODR systems, the usual determination of the validity of an electronic record of an arbitration agreement and its durability, authenticity and integrity shall apply.[71]

(d) fourth ground: The composition of the arbitral authority or the arbitral procedure was not in accordance with the agreement of the parties, or, failing such agreement, was not in accordance with the law of the country where the arbitration took place.

Article V(1)(d) addresses the parties' agreement concerning the composition of the tribunal and the arbitral procedure; and, in the absence of such agreement, the law of the country in the legal seat of arbitration shall apply to determine the appropriate composition of the arbitral tribunal and/or procedure. In an intelligent/ advanced ODR system, a system may be designed to generate a pre-decision suggestion supervising the composition of the arbitral tribunal or procedure such as the required numbers of arbitrators according to pre-defined procedural rules by parties. For example, in *Encyclopedia Universalis S.A. v Encyclopedia Britannica, Inc*, an arbitral award was rejected as one of the arbitrators failed to contact the other arbitrator for the appointment of a third arbitrator – a chairman in the event of failing a decision by the two arbitrators according to

---

particular time establishing evidence that the latter data existed at that time; and Article 3(34) provides that 'qualified electronic time stamp' means an electronic time stamp which meets the requirements laid down in Article 42.

69. *Parsons & Whittemore Overseas Co. v Société Générale de l'Industrie du Papier (RAKTA)*, Court of Appeals, Second Circuit, United States of America, 23 December 1974, 508 F.2d 969, 976, para. 11.

70. UNCITRAL Secretariat Guide on the Convention on the Recognition and Enforcement of Foreign Arbitral Awards (New York, 1958), 2016 Edition, p. 182. *Astro Nusantara International BV et al. v PT Ayunda Prima Mitra et al.*, Court of First Instance, High Court of the Hong Kong Special Administrative Region, Hong Kong, 21 March 2012, HCCT 45/2010, para. 19.

71. See Chapters 4 and 5 concerning the determination of a durable record and a valid electronic arbitration agreement.

parties' arbitration agreement.[72] An intelligent/advanced ODR system may be designed to provide an automated alert to prompt the two arbitrators to notify each other for the appointment of a third arbitrator when the system detects that no decision was yet made according to the pre-defined time frame. This will help ensuring the appropriate composition of the arbitral tribunal or procedure during the arbitral proceedings.

> (e) fifth ground: The award has not yet become binding on the parties, or has been set aside or suspended by a competent authority of the country in which, or under the law of which, that award was made.

Article V(1)(e) addresses that an arbitral award shall be 'binding' or not set aside in order to be enforced subject to the law of the country where the award was made. There is debate over the definition and determination of 'binding'. It was suggested that an award was binding when it was 'no longer open to an appeal on the merits'[73] or it was not subject to ordinary recourse any more.[74] In ODR systems, after the period of correction and review of an arbitral award ends, a final arbitral award shall be issued by the system on behalf of arbitrators or arbitral tribunals, indicating that it is binding. On that point, the system shall lock and close all functions of revising, updating and uploading any further materials.

Furthermore, Article V(2) of the New York Convention provides two additional grounds for refusal of recognition and enforcement of an arbitral award by courts' own motion on the basis of (a) incapability of settlement by arbitration for the subject matter of the dispute under the law of that country; or (b) contradiction to the public policy of that country. Article V(2)(a) coupled with Article II(1) addresses 'arbitrability' that whether a subject matter is 'capable of settlement by arbitration' or shall be resolved by courts instead. In the EU, the Court of Justice of the European Union (CJEU) also held on several occasions that, if a national court determined that a pre-dispute arbitration clause was unfair, that arbitral award would be annulled even though the consumer failed to raise the unfair nature of a term during the arbitration proceedings.[75] In *Elisa María Mostaza Claro v Centro Móvil Milenium SL*, the court ruled that

> a national court seized of an action for annulment of an arbitration award must determine whether the arbitration agreement is void and annul that award where that agreement contains an unfair term, even though the consumer has not pleaded

---

72. *Encyclopedia Universalis S.A. v Encyclopedia Britannica, Inc.*, Court of Appeals, Second Circuit, United States of America, 31 March 2005, 04-0288-CV.
73. *Société Nationale d'Opérations Pétrolières de la Côte d'Ivoire – Holding v Keen Lloyd Resources Limited*, High Court of the Hong Kong Special Administrative Region, Court of First Instance, Hong Kong, 20 December 2001, 55 of 2011, XXIX Y.B. Com. Arb. (2004).
74. *Diag Human Se v Czech Republic* [2014] EWHC 1639 (Comm) (22 May 2014), available at www.bailii.org/ew/cases/EWHC/Comm/2014/1639.html (last accessed 30 March 2017), para. 18.
75. Case C-168/05, *Elisa María Mostaza Claro v Centro Móvil Milenium SL*, Judgment of the Court (First Chamber) 26 October 2006; and C-40/08 *Asturcom Telecomunicaciones SL v Cristina Rodríguez Nogueira*, Judgment of the Court (First Chamber) of 6 October 2009.

that invalidity in the course of the arbitration proceedings, but only in that of the action for annulment.[76]

In *Asturcom Telecomunicaciones SL v Cristina Rodríguez Nogueira*, the court held that

> a national court or tribunal hearing an action for enforcement of an arbitration award which has become final and was made in the absence of the consumer is required, where it has availability to it the legal and factual elements necessary for that task, to assess of its own motion whether an arbitration clause in a contract concluded between a seller or supplier and a consumer is unfair, in so far as, under national rules of procedure, it can carry out such an assessment in similar actions of a domestic nature. If that is the case, it is for that court or tribunal to establish all the consequences thereby arising under national law, in order to ensure that the consumer is not bound by that clause.[77]

In intelligent/advanced ODR systems, arbitrability and public policy may be checked against by those systems crawling the databases subject to public policy of the country of the legal seat of arbitration, the pre-defined terms of the arbitration agreement and the subject matters of disputes before parties commit themselves to the arbitral process.

It was suggested that the recognition and enforcement of arbitral awards could be refused only on very limited grounds in Article V.[78] Courts may exercise discretion to refuse recognition and enforcement of arbitral awards in various circumstances. In some contracting states, courts have exercised this discretion by reference to the permissive language of the New York Convention that recognition and enforcement 'may' be refused if one of the grounds for refusal under Article V is present.[79] It is proposed that there are six hypotheses that may summarise the way in which national courts decide cases within the framework of Article V of the New York Convention,[80] so that if the award-debtor establishes one of the grounds of non-enforcement, the enforcing court shall refuse to order

---

76. Case C-168/05, *Elisa María Mostaza Claro v Centro Móvil Milenium SL*, Judgment of the Court (First Chamber) 26 October 2006, para. 40.

77. C-40/08 *Asturcom Telecomunicaciones SL v Cristina Rodríguez Nogueira*, Judgment of the Court (First Chamber) of 6 October 2009, para. 60.

78. Bonnin Reynes, V. (2013), Forum non conveniens: A Hidden Ground to Refuse Enforcement of Arbitral Awards in the United States, *Journal of International Arbitration*, Volume 30, Number 2, pp. 165–76, p. 165.

79. UNCITRAL Secretariat Guide on the Convention on the Recognition and Enforcement of Foreign Arbitral Awards (New York, 1958), 2016 Edition, p. 125; see also *China Agribusiness Development Corporation v Balli Trading*, High Court of Justice, England and Wales, 20 January 1997, XXIV Y.B. Com. Arb. 732 (1999); *Nigerian National Petroleum Corporation v IPCO (Nigeria) Ltd.*, Court of Appeal, England and Wales, 21 October 2008, [2008] EWCA Civ 1157; *Chromalloy Aeroservices v Arab Republic of Egypt*, District Court, District of Columbia, United States of America, 31 July 1996, 94–2339; and *China Nanhai Oil Joint Service Corporation Shenzhen Branch v Gee Tai Holdings Co. Ltd.*, High Court, Supreme Court of Hong Kong, Hong Kong, 13 July 1994, 1992 No. MP 2411.

80. Hill, J. (2016), The Exercise of Judicial Discretion in Relation to Applications to Enforce Arbitral Awards under the New York Convention 1958, *Oxford Journal of Legal Studies*, Volume 36 Issue 2, pp. 304–33, p. 308.

cross-border enforcement of the awards despite the use of the word 'may' in Article V of the Convention.[81] It is also suggested that forum non conveniens is often a hidden ground for refusal of recognition and enforcement of arbitral awards.[82] In the UK leading case of *Spiliada Maritime Corp v Cansulex Ltd*, the principle of forum non conveniens was interpreted so that 'a stay will only be granted where the court is satisfied that there is some other available forum in which the case may be tried more suitably for the interests of all the parties and the ends of justice'.[83] In forum non conveniens cases, burden of proof rests on the defendant.[84] In *Figueiredo Ferraz e Engenharia de Projeto Ltda. v Republic of Peru*, the Second Circuit held that enforcement of arbitral awards is subject to the US common law doctrine of forum non conveniens.[85] This opinion raises various criticisms.[86] The American Bar Association (ABA) affirms that

> the U.S. common law doctrine of forum non conveniens is not an appropriate basis for refusing to confirm or enforce arbitral awards that are subject to the provisions of the Convention on the Recognition and Enforcement of Foreign Arbitral Awards or the Inter-American Convention on International Commercial Arbitration.[87]

---

81. Hill, J. (2016), The Exercise of Judicial Discretion in Relation to Applications to Enforce Arbitral Awards under the New York Convention 1958, *Oxford Journal of Legal Studies*, Volume 36 Issue 2, pp. 304–33.

82. Bonnin Reynes, V. (2013), Forum non conveniens: A Hidden Ground to Refuse Enforcement of Arbitral Awards in the United States, *Journal of International Arbitration*, Volume 30, Number 2, pp. 165–76.

83. *Spiliada Maritime Corp v Cansulex Ltd* [1986] UKHL 10 (19 November 1986), available at www.bailii.org/uk/cases/UKHL/1986/10.html (last accessed 30 March 2017).

84. *Spiliada Maritime Corp v Cansulex Ltd* [1986] UKHL 10 (19 November 1986), available at www.bailii.org/uk/cases/UKHL/1986/10.html (last accessed 30 March 2017).

85. *Figueiredo Ferraz e Engenharia de Projeto Ltda. v Republic of Peru*, Nos. 09–3925-cv (L), 10–1612-cv (CON), 2011 U.S. App. LEXIS 24748 (2d Cir. 14 December 2011).

86. Adler, M.H. (2012), *Figueiredo v Peru*: A Step Backward for Arbitration Enforcement, *Northwestern Journal of International Law & Business*, Volume 32, Issue 4, 38A.

87. American Bar Association Section of International Law Report to the House of Delegates (107C), 2013, available at www.americanbar.org/content/dam/aba/uncategorized/international_law/2013_hod_annual_meeting_107C.authcheckdam.pdf (last accessed 30 March 2017).

Summary

The selection of the legal seat of arbitration is fundamentally important as the legal seat of arbitration is one of the most significant and close connecting factors for the determination of law applicable to the validity of arbitration agreements, and subsequently the recognition and enforcement of arbitral awards by national or international law. In the absence of particular national and international legislation concerning online arbitration agreements and online arbitral awards, legal and technological measures for forming arbitration agreements and arbitral awards via electronic communications or on ODR platforms shall be in line with the general requirements of durability, reliability, authenticity and security of an electronic record at the international standard. The building of ODR systems, in particular, intelligent/advanced ODR systems, should be designed to assist parties with compliance of the arbitration procedural rules that are pre-defined by parties or arbitral tribunals before the arbitral proceedings. Such machine assistance may include signalling each step to parties during the process, alerting parties to breach of pre-agreed procedures, prompting parties to take actions within a pre-defined timeframe and providing services such as qualified advanced electronic signatures, electronic seals, electronic authentication certificates and time stamps to ensure that the legal requirements of formation are met during the arbitral process.

PART IV

CONCLUSIONS AND AFTERTHOUGHTS

CHAPTER 7

The way forward: International harmonised best practices

7.1 Future legislative trends

The deployment of online arbitration for commercial and consumer disputes makes dispute resolutions relatively easier and faster compared with traditional arbitration. Online arbitration may be more cost effective than traditional arbitration. However, it challenges the scope and sufficiency of national and international traditional arbitration laws. There is no specific legislation concerning online arbitration for commercial disputes, though there are some relevant legislative movements in the EU and the United Nations Commission on International Trade Law (UNCITRAL). In 2013 the European Commission launched a general ODR regulation concerning online purchase/service consumer disputes only. The EU Regulation on Consumer ODR in conjunction with the EC Directive on Consumer ADR do not provide specific provisions on online arbitration. The greatest achievement of the EU Regulation on Consumer ODR is to boost consumers' confidence in the online marketplaces by providing a single entry EU-wide ODR platform. Once consumers file a case, consumers and traders can choose a competent ADR entity on the list of approved ADR entities on the EU ODR portal/platform. Competent authorities in member states have the responsibility to monitor the quality of services provided by ADR entities. Between 2010 and 2016, the UNCITRAL ODR Working Group had been working on the UNCITRAL Draft ODR Procedural Rules, which are applicable to international commercial and consumer disputes. Track I of the Rules has specific provisions on online arbitration. In 2016 the UNCITRAL ODR Working Group produced the outcome of the work on procedural rules as Technical Notes on Online Dispute Resolution (2016).[1] The Technical Notes are non-binding, which are intended to foster ODR development and provide assistance in the ODR process.[2] In 2014,

---

1. UNCITRAL Online dispute resolution for cross-border electronic commerce transactions, Note by the Secretariat, Draft outcome document reflecting elements and principles of an ODR process, 22 December 2015, A/CN.9/WG.III/WP.140, p. 3.
2. UNCITRAL Online dispute resolution for cross-border electronic commerce transactions, Note by the Secretariat, Draft outcome document reflecting elements and principles of an ODR process, 22 December 2015, A/CN.9/WG.III/WP.140, p. 3.

the China International Economic and Trade Arbitration Commission (CIETAC) updated its institutional online arbitration rules.

As there is no specific online arbitration law at national, regional and international level, there is need to seek further interpretation or explanation of existing concepts and laws relevant to online arbitration in judicial practices. Consistency of interpretation or explanation may be difficult to achieve due to the difference of laws and legal culture in different countries. It is sensible that future legislative strategy shall be tailored in response to the deployment of technology in judicial systems. Relevant legislative tasks, approaches and enhancement shall be considered as follows:

Firstly, the future trend of the *legislative tasks* on online dispute resolution in particular online arbitration by the international organisations, regional and national legislative councils shall be twofold: 1) continuing working on the modernisation and harmonisation of relevant existing and traditional legislation; and 2) carrying on drafting new subject-specific laws, when necessary taking into consideration technological development.

As discussed in this book, there is strong evidence showing that Internet-related disputes have their unique characteristics. The entire concept of online arbitration is the same as traditional arbitration, but the actual conduct of online arbitration may be different in particular in an intelligent/advanced ODR system where the system may automatically generate suggested agreements, arguments and decisions for parties' consideration and reference. Although it seems that online arbitration can follow traditional institutional arbitration procedures and national arbitration laws, traditional arbitration procedures and laws do not factor two additional elements involved during the online arbitration process: one is technology and the other is the providers of technology. Although the traditional ADR rules and laws can be partly adapted to ODR, new subject matters, such as the validity of electronic dispute-resolution agreements or clauses, the enforceability of electronic dispute-resolution decisions as well as the liability of ODR service providers, need to be fully regulated. Thus, amendment or modernisation of relevant existing arbitration institutional rules and national laws is much needed to increase legal certainty and facilitate the harmonisation of the conduct of online arbitration. It can be achieved by changing some wording or incorporating new provisions on online arbitration, taking into consideration general requirements of appropriate technological measures, online arbitrators and ODR service providers.

Meanwhile, new subject-specific laws may be required in certain areas of online dispute resolution due to the complexity of issues concerning international/cross-border commercial arbitration for high-value claims and cross-border consumer arbitration for high-volume claims. As discussed in this book, procedural irregularities and mistakes may be considered as valid grounds for setting aside an arbitral award for international commercial disputes under the New York Convention 1958. In cross-border consumer arbitration, the validity of pre-dispute arbitration clauses or agreements is also interpreted differently in different countries. Specialised international model laws, conventions and rules as well as national and regional laws on ODR with separate provisions or rules on online mediation and arbitration should be developed to promote the use of technology in resolving Internet-related disputes efficiently, cost-effectively and fairly and to remove legal barriers of the recognition and enforcement of cross-border commercial and consumer arbitral awards concluded via ODR platforms. International arbitration can be complicated mainly because it usually involves more than one system of law or of legal rules and is a network of a complex interaction of laws. It is expected that international online arbitration would be even more complicated simply due to the fact that the technological and legal measures for ODR systems and services are different in different countries without a harmonised standard of practices. While legislative processes may take a long time, international best practices of ODR in particular online mediation and arbitration shall be established based on the past successful experiences of ODR systems and services.

Secondly, the future trend of the *legislative approaches* to online dispute resolution, in particular online arbitration by international organisations, regional and national legislative councils, shall be threefold: 1) technique-neutral approach; 2) party autonomy approach; and 3) most close connection approach.

In the process of modernisation and harmonisation of existing and traditional arbitration rules and laws, adopting the appropriate approaches is essential as it affects the future success of the legislation. Due to the fast-growing use of the technology, employing a technique-neutral approach in online arbitration shall be of paramount importance for adapting to different technological developments in different countries, avoiding the risk of the legislation being out of date quickly and facilitating the cross-border recognition of IT-generated evidential documents.

The principle of party autonomy shall be implemented in online arbitration procedures to promote fairness, flexibility and independence of the arbitration process. Parties shall be free to agree on a wide variety of issues such as arbitration agreements, composition of arbitral tribunals, appointment of arbitrators, arbitration procedure and process, admission of evidence, expert witnesses and applicable laws to arbitration procedural rules and the substance of disputes. The party autonomy approach will increase the legal certainty of jurisdiction and applicable law and maximise the benefits of choosing arbitration as a way of resolving cross-border commercial and consumer Internet-related disputes.

Owing to the global and unlocalised nature of cyberspace, the place of business is difficult to determine through traditional physical links, such as offices and building etc. That is why the selection of the legal seat of arbitration is fundamentally important. It can be used as one of the most significant and close connecting factors for the determination of law applicable to the validity of arbitration agreements, and subsequently the recognition and enforcement of arbitral awards by national or international law. Thus, the most close connection approach shall be employed as the measure of determining jurisdiction and applicable law for arbitration issues in the information society through the parties' intention and the closest links between the seat of the arbitration and the law applicable to the arbitration clauses/agreements.

Thirdly, the future trend of the *legislative enhancement* of online dispute resolution, in particular online arbitration by international organisations, regional and national legislative councils, shall also be threefold: awareness/training/education, collaboration/strategic alliance and experiment/accreditation/trustmark schemes. As all users including disputing parties, neutrals, practitioners, arbitrators and ODR administrators require relevant knowledge of how to use ODR systems and services, ODR training courses and detailed users' guides shall be offered to all users by public organisations and private companies offering such services.

Different public organisations and private entities have different expertise, experience and resources concerning ODR systems and services. As discussed in this book, the collaboration and strategic alliance between different organisations and entities have mutual benefits of strengthening their expertise, authority and reputation. The collaboration and strategic alliances among online marketplaces, technology companies and legal/arbitral institutions are also the key to combine different areas of expertise for the building of a trusted ODR system, which subsequently boost users' confidence and attract potential users to choose ODR services to resolve their disputes.

Lastly, the process of the modernisation and harmonisation of the legislative framework for ODR in particular online arbitration shall be an ongoing experiment. It requires prompt and accurate insight to the newly arising legal issues and needs up-to-date interpretation and recommendation. It requires continued dialogue among lawmakers, judges, legal practitioners, IT experts and entrepreneurs to share information and experience. The quality of basic and intelligence/advanced ODR systems and services shall be continuously enhanced through comprehensive accreditation programmes and relevant trustmark schemes.

7.2 Solutions to obstacles in online arbitration

It is notable that there are various legal and technological obstacles in using and implementing international online arbitration to resolve cross-border commercial and consumer Internet-related disputes. The two dominant factors that could distinguish the legal consequences of online arbitration from traditional offline arbitration are: the determination of the legal seat of arbitration in the absence of parties' choice or agreement; and the determination of the validity of electronic arbitration agreements and arbitral awards. These two factors would lead to different outcomes in relation to applicable law and jurisdiction concerning arbitration as well as recognition and enforcement relating to arbitral awards. When arbitral procedures are conducted by robotic arbitrators in an intelligent/advanced ODR system, legal certainty would be further challenged, due to the main fact that robotic arbitrators may not be considered as a natural person. There are controversial debates over the capability of robotic arbitrators. Thus, appropriate legal and technological measures shall be sought to put in place in order to improve legal certainly without jeopardising technological innovation and market development in the field of ODR.

Solution 1: To produce a well-drafted arbitration agreement.

A well-drafted arbitration agreement is crucial for the success of arbitration. A well-drafted arbitration agreement shall include traditional elements such as the legal seat/place of arbitration and/or hearing; the language of arbitration; the number of arbitrators; the nationality of arbitrators; the method/procedure of selection/appointment of arbitrators; admission of evidence; and the applicable law of the contract; and the application law to the arbitral procedure or summary procedure. In ODR systems, a well-drafted arbitration agreement shall also include additional elements such as valid means of electronic communications for forming evidential documents and final arbitral awards during the arbitration process; and the method of the conduct of online hearings and the scope of the involvement of artificial intelligence in decision-making during the process.

Solution 2: To choose a reliable ODR service provider for online arbitration service.

There are five main types of ODR service providers: 1) specialised independent ODR private entities; 2) online marketplaces embedding internal ODR services; 3) ODR services offered by organisations such as arbitration institutions or a national private sector ombudsman scheme; 4) ODR services offered by government, for example, the European Commission offers a single entry EU-wide ODR portal for consumer online purchase/service disputes; and 5) ODR services offered by courts and judicial services. In order to have a positive experience of using ODR systems and services, it is important to choose a reliable ODR service provider. There are five possibilities that can be considered as indicated factors for a reliable ODR service provider, system or service: 1) a long-standing private ODR service with good market reputation; 2) newly established private ODR service providers accredited by competent authorities or qualified trustmarks; 3) ODR service providers partnered with well-reputed traditional dispute resolution bodies; 4) exclusive ODR services in collaboration with well-established online marketplaces; and 5) ODR service providers specialising in certain dispute resolution services with approval of public organisations or governments.

Solution 3: To deploy appropriate technical measures for ODR systems.

Nowadays, users' expectations of computer software are that it is highly reliable, secure and easy to use for non-experts. A company developing an ODR system may well offer it as a SaaS (software as a service) model, with access via a thin client. Core functionality shall include a secure, password-protected log-in with the system supporting messaging between parties, the ability to upload documents with fine-grained security, document version control and notifications to keep parties informed as to the state of the process. Video conferencing may be provided internally to the system, or externally via third-party software provided serious consideration is given to the technical reliability and storage of audio/video streams. Systems may also need to be flexible and customisable to cope with different legal requirements depending on the subject field and legal seat of arbitration.

Basic ODR systems have been described as moving ADR into an online environment, whereas intelligent ODR systems take a step further to automating the arbitration process using artificial intelligence to replace or supplement the arbitrator.

As the number of online B2B and B2C transactions increase, affordable ODR becomes increasingly desirable. Government agencies, private companies and academia have been attempting to automate the function of lawyers since at least the 1990s, with some success where the subject matter is highly constrained. The approaches have commonly centred on the field of expert systems, which are predominantly rule-based and involve development of a knowledge base where rules are stored and an inference engine to form lines of reasoning.

The key obstacles to automation of a complex human task such as arbitration include: a) the encoding of legal rules into unambiguous conditional statements; and b) the integration of previous cases to produce outcomes from previous arbitral decisions. Success in this area should be placed in the context of expectations of the system; it is unlikely that the entire job of an arbitrator could be replaced by an artificial intelligence system in the short term and perhaps medium term, but individual simple tasks can gradually be automated and suggestions given where the subject matter is constrained. By the time artificial intelligence has the answer to complex human issues, society will be a very different place than it is today.

Solution 4: To interpret main provisions of online arbitration procedural rules taking into consideration technological understanding.

The main provisions of online arbitration procedures that are most affected by the interplay of technology on ODR platforms are: formality of arbitration agreements; the selection and determination of the legal seat of online arbitration; selection of online arbitrators with special knowledge and IT skills; admission of electronic evidence, electronic records of online hearing; as well as format and issuance of online arbitration awards.

A well-built ODR system shall provide clause builder tools that enable parties to create custom ADR clauses, for example the American Arbitration Association (AAA) and the International Centre for Dispute Resolution (ICDR) offer a ClauseBuilder tool. A sophisticated ODR system may also be built to generate an automated clause for the legal seat/place of arbitration depending on various information that parties select or provide to the ODR intelligence system.

With regard to the appointment of online arbitrators, the ODR systems shall be designed to build in an automated ethical checking system to check against submitted disclosure information from parties and nominated arbitrators; and to adopt an online arbitrator rating system (or a credit rating system) that enables clients to review and rate the service of online arbitrators. The ODR systems shall also provide a list of recommended qualified online arbitrators through aggregated data according to the criteria of required arbitrators.

With regard to the admission of evidential materials, electronic evidence with a reliable electronic signature shall have the same admissibility and weight as evidence with a handwritten signature or affixed seal.[3] Accordingly, any evidential records including electronic expert witness documents shall be valid as long as they are authentic, reliable and durable. In the absence of specific regulations on legal and technological measures of producing and keeping electronic evidence, relevant rules and legislation concerning electronic communications for consumer and commercial transactions may be used to interpret format requirements of electronic evidence in arbitration, in which the principles include authenticity, reliability, appropriateness, convenience and economical cost.[4] If a recording of the video conference is required for hearings or expert witness evidence, it may be preferable to make the recording on a reliable central server hosting the video conferencing call (known as server-side recording).

In the absence of specific rules concerning the formality of online arbitration agreements and online arbitral awards, legal and technological measures of forming arbitration agreements and arbitral awards via electronic communications or on ODR platforms shall be in line with the general requirements of durability, reliability, authenticity and security of an electronic record at the international standard.

---

3. CIETAC Online Arbitration Rules 2015, Article 29.
4. CIETAC Online Arbitration Rules 2015, Article 29; and IBA Rules on the Taking of Evidence in International Arbitration (2010), Article 3(12).

Solution 5: To determine the validity of electronic arbitration agreements and arbitral awards as well as the recognition and enforcement of arbitral awards concluded by electronic communications.

The selection of the legal seat of arbitration is fundamentally important as the legal seat of arbitration is one of the most significant and close connecting factors for the determination of law applicable to the validity of arbitration agreements, and subsequently the recognition and enforcement of arbitral awards by national or international law. The building of ODR systems, in particular intelligent/advanced ODR systems, should be designed to assist parties with compliance of the arbitration procedural rules that are pre-defined by parties or arbitral tribunals before the arbitral proceedings. Such machine assistance may include signalling each step to parties during the process, alerting parties to breach of pre-agreed procedures, and prompting parties to take actions within a pre-defined time frame.

In order to minimise the possibility of procedural irregularities or mistakes that may lead to refusal of recognition and enforcement of arbitral awards under the New York Convention 1958 or national arbitration laws, ODR systems shall provide quality services such as qualified advanced electronic signatures, electronic seals, electronic authentication certificates and time stamps to ensure that legal requirements of formation are met during the arbitral process. For example, during the arbitral proceedings, once all materials are available for the arbitrator to make a decision, ODR systems shall prevent further uploads unless invited and use timestamps to determine acceptable documents that are submitted within a timeframe. In addition, the awareness test for the incorporation of terms shall apply to the determination of parties' awareness of pre-dispute arbitration clauses, in particular concerning consumer arbitration.

In ODR systems, there are five main technological measures that may be used to tackle legal obstacles of recognising and enforcing electronic arbitral awards: 1) parties shall sign an arbitration agreement, for which the ODR system shall generate a time stamp, electronic seal and authentication certificate once submitted;[5] 2) a qualified electronic time stamp[6] shall be used to prove the delivery of notice of appointment

---

5. Regulation (EU) No 910/2014 of the European Parliament and of the Council of 23 July 2014 on electronic identification and trust services for electronic transactions in the internal market and repealing Directive 1999/93/EC, OJ L 257, 28.8.2014, pp. 73–114. Article 3(25) provides that 'electronic seal' means data in electronic form, which is attached to or logically associated with other data in electronic form to ensure the latter's origin and integrity; and Article 3(26) 'advanced electronic seal' means an electronic seal, which meets the requirements set out in Article 36.

6. Regulation (EU) No 910/2014 of the European Parliament and of the Council of 23 July 2014 on electronic identification and trust services for electronic transactions in the internal market and repealing Directive 1999/93/EC, OJ L 257, 28.8.2014, pp. 73–114. Article 3(33) provides that 'electronic time stamp' means data in electronic form which binds other data in electronic form to a particular time establishing evidence that the latter data existed at that time; and Article 3(34) provides that

of arbitrators and of the arbitral proceedings; 3) the usual determination of the validity of an electronic record and its durability, authenticity and integrity shall apply[7] to determine whether electronic arbitration agreements and arbitral awards are valid. There is a consistent requirement in case law and relevant regulations that an electronic record shall be kept in a durable medium; 4) both basic and intelligent/advanced ODR systems shall be designed to provide an automated alert to prompt further necessary actions to relevant people when the system detects that no decision/action was taken according to the pre-defined timeframe; and 5) arbitrability and public policy may be checked against by intelligent/advanced ODR systems crawling their own databases subject to the public policy of the country of the legal seat of arbitration, the pre-defined terms of the arbitration agreement and the subject matters of disputes before parties commit themselves to the arbitral process.

* * *

By and large, the purpose of this book is to provide analysis and evaluation of up-to-date online arbitration practice and legislative development; and to seek for improvement of the legal certainty of the use of online arbitration to resolve cross-border commercial and consumer disputes. This book works towards facilitating the process of harmonisation and modernisation of legal and technological measures for the deployment of ODR systems at the international level, or at least to serve as the interpretation of new concepts in the existing laws and a framework for the design of both basic and intelligent/advanced ODR systems.

'qualified electronic time stamp' means an electronic time stamp which meets the requirements laid down in Article 42.

7. See Chapters 4 and 5 concerning the determination of a durable record and a valid electronic arbitration agreement.

APPENDIX I

Regulation (EU) No 524/2013 of the European Parliament and of the Council of 21 May 2013

On online dispute resolution for consumer disputes and amending Regulation (EC) No 2006/2004 and Directive 2009/22/EC (Regulation on consumer ODR)

THE EUROPEAN PARLIAMENT AND THE COUNCIL OF THE EUROPEAN UNION,
Having regard to the Treaty on the Functioning of the European Union, and in particular Article 114 thereof,
Having regard to the proposal from the European Commission,
After transmission of the draft legislative act to the national parliaments,
Having regard to the opinion of the European Economic and Social Committee ([1]),
Acting in accordance with the ordinary legislative procedure ([2]),
Whereas:

(1) Article 169(1) and point (a) of Article 169(2) of the Treaty on the Functioning of the European Union (TFEU) provide that the Union is to contribute to the attainment of a high level of consumer protection through measures adopted pursuant to Article 114 TFEU. Article 38 of the Charter of Fundamental Rights of the European Union provides that Union policies are to ensure a high level of consumer protection.

(2) In accordance with Article 26(2) TFEU, the internal market is to comprise an area without internal frontiers in which the free movement of goods and services is ensured. In order for consumers to have confidence in and benefit from the digital dimension of the internal market, it is necessary that they have access to simple, efficient, fast and low-cost ways of resolving disputes which arise from the sale of goods or the supply of services online. This is particularly important when consumers shop cross-border.

(3) In its Communication of 13 April 2011 entitled 'Single Market Act – Twelve levers to boost growth and strengthen confidence – "Working together to create new growth" ', the Commission identified legislation on alternative dispute resolution (ADR) which includes an electronic commerce dimension as one of the twelve levers to boost growth and strengthen confidence in the Single Market.

---

1. OJ C 181, 21.6.2012, p. 99.
2. Position of the European Parliament of 12 March 2013 (not yet published in the Official Journal) and Decision of the Council of 22 April 2013.

(4) Fragmentation of the internal market impedes efforts to boost competitiveness and growth. Furthermore, the uneven availability, quality and awareness of simple, efficient, fast and low-cost means of resolving disputes arising from the sale of goods or provision of services across the Union constitutes a barrier within the internal market which undermines consumers' and traders' confidence in shopping and selling across borders.

(5) In its conclusions of 24–25 March and 23 October 2011, the European Council invited the European Parliament and the Council to adopt, by the end of 2012, a first set of priority measures to bring a new impetus to the Single Market.

(6) The internal market is a reality for consumers in their daily lives, when they travel, make purchases and make payments. Consumers are key players in the internal market and should therefore be at its heart. The digital dimension of the internal market is becoming vital for both consumers and traders. Consumers increasingly make purchases online and an increasing number of traders sell online. Consumers and traders should feel confident in carrying out transactions online so it is essential to dismantle existing barriers and to boost consumer confidence. The availability of reliable and efficient online dispute resolution (ODR) could greatly help achieve this goal.

(7) Being able to seek easy and low-cost dispute resolution can boost consumers' and traders' confidence in the digital Single Market. Consumers and traders, however, still face barriers to finding out-of-court solutions in particular to their disputes arising from cross-border online transactions. Thus, such disputes currently are often left unresolved.

(8) ODR offers a simple, efficient, fast and low-cost out-of-court solution to disputes arising from online transactions. However, there is currently a lack of mechanisms which allow consumers and traders to resolve such disputes through electronic means; this leads to consumer detriment, acts as a barrier, in particular, to cross-border online transactions, and creates an uneven playing field for traders, and thus hampers the overall development of online commerce.

(9) This Regulation should apply to the out-of-court resolution of disputes initiated by consumers resident in the Union against traders established in the Union which are covered by Directive 2013/11/EU of the European Parliament and of the Council of 21 May 2013 on alternative dispute resolution for consumer disputes (Directive on consumer ADR) ([3]).

(10) In order to ensure that the ODR platform can also be used for ADR procedures which allow traders to submit complaints against consumers, this Regulation should also apply to the out-of-court resolution of disputes initiated by traders against consumers where the relevant ADR procedures are offered by ADR entities listed in accordance with Article 20(2) of Directive 2013/11/EU. The application of this Regulation to such disputes should not impose any obligation on Member States to ensure that the ADR entities offer such procedures.

(11) Although in particular consumers and traders carrying out cross-border online transactions will benefit from the ODR platform, this Regulation should also apply to domestic online transactions in order to allow for a true level playing field in the area of online commerce.

---

3. See page 63 of this Official Journal.

APPENDIX I

(12) This Regulation should be without prejudice to Directive 2008/52/EC of the European Parliament and of the Council of 21 May 2008 on certain aspects of mediation in civil and commercial matters ([4]).

(13) The definition of 'consumer' should cover natural persons who are acting outside their trade, business, craft or profession. However, if the contract is concluded for purposes partly within and partly outside the person's trade (dual purpose contracts) and the trade purpose is so limited as not to be predominant in the overall context of the supply, that person should also be considered as a consumer.

(14) The definition of 'online sales or service contract' should cover a sales or service contract where the trader, or the trader's intermediary, has offered goods or services through a website or by other electronic means and the consumer has ordered those goods or services on that website or by other electronic means. This should also cover cases where the consumer has accessed the website or other information society service through a mobile electronic device such as a mobile telephone.

(15) This Regulation should not apply to disputes between consumers and traders that arise from sales or service contracts concluded offline and to disputes between traders.

(16) This Regulation should be considered in conjunction with Directive 2013/11/EU which requires Member States to ensure that all disputes between consumers resident and traders established in the Union which arise from the sale of goods or provisions of services can be submitted to an ADR entity.

(17) Before submitting their complaint to an ADR entity through the ODR platform, consumers should be encouraged by Member States to contact the trader by any appropriate means, with the aim of resolving the dispute amicably.

(18) This Regulation aims to create an ODR platform at Union level. The ODR platform should take the form of an interactive website offering a single point of entry to consumers and traders seeking to resolve disputes out-of-court which have arisen from online transactions. The ODR platform should provide general information regarding the out-of-court resolution of contractual disputes between traders and consumers arising from online sales and service contracts. It should allow consumers and traders to submit complaints by filling in an electronic complaint form available in all the official languages of the institutions of the Union and to attach relevant documents. It should transmit complaints to an ADR entity competent to deal with the dispute concerned. The ODR platform should offer, free of charge, an electronic case management tool which enables ADR entities to conduct the dispute resolution procedure with the parties through the ODR platform. ADR entities should not be obliged to use the case management tool.

(19) The Commission should be responsible for the development, operation and maintenance of the ODR platform and provide all technical facilities necessary for the functioning of the platform. The ODR platform should offer an electronic translation function which enables the parties and the ADR entity to have the information which is exchanged through the ODR platform and is necessary for the resolution of the dispute translated, where appropriate. That function should be capable of

---

4. OJ L 136, 24.5.2008, p. 3.

dealing with all necessary translations and should be supported by human intervention, if necessary. The Commission should also provide, on the ODR platform, information for complainants about the possibility of requesting assistance from the ODR contact points.

(20) The ODR platform should enable the secure interchange of data with ADR entities and respect the underlying principles of the European Interoperability Framework adopted pursuant to Decision 2004/387/EC of the European Parliament and of the Council of 21 April 2004 on interoperable delivery of pan-European eGovernment services to public administrations, businesses and citizens (IDABC) ([5]).

(21) The ODR platform should be made accessible, in particular, through the 'Your Europe portal' established in accordance with Annex II to Decision 2004/387/EC, which provides access to pan-European, multilingual online information and interactive services to businesses and citizens in the Union. The ODR platform should be given prominence on the 'Your Europe portal'.

(22) An ODR platform at Union level should build on existing ADR entities in the Member States and respect the legal traditions of the Member States. ADR entities to which a complaint has been transmitted through the ODR platform should therefore apply their own procedural rules, including rules on cost. However, this Regulation intends to establish some common rules applicable to those procedures that will safeguard their effectiveness. This should include rules ensuring that such dispute resolution does not require the physical presence of the parties or their representatives before the ADR entity, unless its procedural rules provide for that possibility and the parties agree.

(23) Ensuring that all ADR entities listed in accordance with Article 20(2) of Directive 2013/11/EU are registered with the ODR platform should allow for full coverage in online out-of-court resolution for disputes arising from online sales or service contracts.

(24) This Regulation should not prevent the functioning of any existing dispute resolution entity operating online or of any ODR mechanism within the Union. It should not prevent dispute resolution entities or mechanisms from dealing with online disputes which have been submitted directly to them.

(25) ODR contact points hosting at least two ODR advisors should be designated in each Member State. The ODR contact points should support the parties involved in a dispute submitted through the ODR platform without being obliged to translate documents relating to that dispute. Member States should have the possibility to confer the responsibility for the ODR contact points on their centres of the European Consumer Centres Network. Member States should make use of that possibility in order to allow ODR contact points to fully benefit from the experience of the centres of the European Consumer Centres Network in facilitating the settlement of disputes between consumers and traders. The Commission should establish a network of ODR contact points to facilitate their cooperation and work and provide, in cooperation with Member States, appropriate training for ODR contact points.

(26) The right to an effective remedy and the right to a fair trial are fundamental rights laid down in Article 47 of the Charter of Fundamental Rights of the European

---

5. OJ L 144, 30.4.2004, p. 62.

Union. ODR is not intended to and cannot be designed to replace court procedures, nor should it deprive consumers or traders of their rights to seek redress before the courts. This Regulation should not, therefore, prevent parties from exercising their right of access to the judicial system.

(27) The processing of information under this Regulation should be subject to strict guarantees of confidentiality and should comply with the rules on the protection of personal data laid down in Directive 95/46/EC of the European Parliament and of the Council of 24 October 1995 on the protection of individuals with regard to the processing of personal data and on the free movement of such data ([6]) and in Regulation (EC) No 45/2001 of the European Parliament and of the Council of 18 December 2000 on the protection of individuals with regard to the processing of personal data by the Community institutions and bodies and on the free movement of such data ([7]). Those rules should apply to the processing of personal data carried out under this Regulation by the various actors of the ODR platform, whether they act alone or jointly with other such actors.

(28) Data subjects should be informed about, and give their consent to, the processing of their personal data in the ODR platform, and should be informed about their rights with regard to that processing, by means of a comprehensive privacy notice to be made publicly available by the Commission and explaining, in clear and simple language, the processing operations performed under the responsibility of the various actors of the platform, in accordance with Articles 11 and 12 of Regulation (EC) No 45/2001 and with national legislation adopted pursuant to Articles 10 and 11 of Directive 95/46/EC.

(29) This Regulation should be without prejudice to provisions on confidentiality in national legislation relating to ADR.

(30) In order to ensure broad consumer awareness of the existence of the ODR platform, traders established within the Union engaging in online sales or service contracts should provide, on their websites, an electronic link to the ODR platform. Traders should also provide their email address so that consumers have a first point of contact. A significant proportion of online sales and service contracts are concluded using online marketplaces, which bring together or facilitate online transactions between consumers and traders. Online marketplaces are online platforms which allow traders to make their products and services available to consumers. Such online marketplaces should therefore have the same obligation to provide an electronic link to the ODR platform. This obligation should be without prejudice to Article 13 of Directive 2013/11/EU concerning the requirement that traders inform consumers about the ADR procedures by which those traders are covered and about whether or not they commit to use ADR procedures to resolve disputes with consumers. Furthermore, that obligation should be without prejudice to point (t) of Article 6(1) and to Article 8 of Directive 2011/83/EU of the European Parliament and of the Council of 25 October 2011 on consumer rights ([8]). Point (t) of Article 6(1) of Directive 2011/83/EU stipulates for consumer contracts concluded at a distance or off premises, that the trader is to inform the consumer

---

6. OJ L 281, 23.11.1995, p. 31.
7. OJ L 8, 12.1.2001, p. 1.
8. OJ L 304, 22.11.2011, p. 64.

about the possibility of having recourse to an out-of-court complaint and redress mechanism to which the trader is subject, and the methods for having access to it, before the consumer is bound by the contract. For the same consumer awareness reasons, Member States should encourage consumer associations and business associations to provide an electronic link to the website of the ODR platform.

(31) In order to take into account the criteria by which the ADR entities define their respective scopes of application the power to adopt acts in accordance with Article 290 TFEU should be delegated to the Commission to adapt the information which a complainant is to provide in the electronic complaint form made available on the ODR platform. It is of particular importance that the Commission carry out appropriate consultations during its preparatory work, including at expert level. The Commission, when preparing and drawing up delegated acts, should ensure a simultaneous, timely and appropriate transmission of relevant documents to the European Parliament and to the Council.

(32) In order to ensure uniform conditions for the implementation of this Regulation implementing powers should be conferred on the Commission in respect of the functioning of the ODR platform, the modalities for the submission of a complaint and cooperation within the network of ODR contact points. Those powers should be exercised in accordance with Regulation (EU) No 182/2011 of the European Parliament and of the Council of 16 February 2011 laying down the rules and general principles concerning mechanisms for control by Member States of the Commission's exercise of implementing powers ([9]). The advisory procedure should be used for the adoption of implementing acts relating to the electronic complaint form given its purely technical nature. The examination procedure should be used for the adoption of the rules concerning the modalities of cooperation between the ODR advisors of the network of ODR contact points.

(33) In the application of this Regulation, the Commission should consult, where appropriate, the European Data Protection Supervisor.

(34) Since the objective of this Regulation, namely to set up a European ODR platform for online disputes governed by common rules, cannot be sufficiently achieved by the Member States and can therefore, by reason of its scale and effects, be better achieved at Union level, the Union may adopt measures in accordance with the principle of subsidiarity as set out in Article 5 of the Treaty on European Union. In accordance with the principle of proportionality, as set out in that Article, this Regulation does not go beyond what is necessary in order to achieve that objective.

(35) This Regulation respects fundamental rights and observes the principles recognised in particular by the Charter of Fundamental Rights of the European Union and specifically Articles 7, 8, 38 and 47 thereof.

---

9. OJ L 55, 28.2.2011, p. 13.

(36) The European Data Protection Supervisor was consulted in accordance with Article 28(2) of Regulation (EC) No 45/2001 and delivered an opinion on 12 January 2012 ([10]),

HAVE ADOPTED THIS REGULATION:

Chapter 1

General provisions

Article 1

Subject matter

The purpose of this Regulation is, through the achievement of a high level of consumer protection, to contribute to the proper functioning of the internal market, and in particular of its digital dimension by providing a European ODR platform ('ODR platform') facilitating the independent, impartial, transparent, effective, fast and fair out-of-court resolution of disputes between consumers and traders online.

Article 2

Scope

1. This Regulation shall apply to the out-of-court resolution of disputes concerning contractual obligations stemming from online sales or service contracts between a consumer resident in the Union and a trader established in the Union through the intervention of an ADR entity listed in accordance with Article 20(2) of Directive 2013/11/EU and which involves the use of the ODR platform.
2. This Regulation shall apply to the out-of-court resolution of disputes referred to in paragraph 1, which are initiated by a trader against a consumer, in so far as the legislation of the Member State where the consumer is habitually resident allows for such disputes to be resolved through the intervention of an ADR entity.
3. Member States shall inform the Commission about whether or not their legislation allows for disputes referred to in paragraph 1, which are initiated by a trader against a consumer, to be resolved through the intervention of an ADR entity. Competent authorities shall, when they notify the list referred to in Article 20(2) of Directive 2013/11/EU, inform the Commission about which ADR entities deal with such disputes.
4. The application of this Regulation to disputes referred to in paragraph 1, which are initiated by a trader against a consumer, shall not impose any obligation on Member States to ensure that ADR entities offer procedures for the out-of-court resolution of such disputes.

---

10. OJ C 136, 11.5.2012, p. 1.

Article 3

Relationship with other union legal acts
This Regulation shall be without prejudice to Directive 2008/52/EC.

Article 4

Definitions
1. For the purposes of this Regulation:
   (a) 'consumer' means a consumer as defined in point (a) of Article 4(1) of Directive 2013/11/EU;
   (b) 'trader' means a trader as defined in point (b) of Article 4(1) of Directive 2013/11/EU;
   (c) 'sales contract' means a sales contract as defined in point (c) of Article 4(1) of Directive 2013/11/EU;
   (d) 'service contract' means a service contract as defined in point (d) of Article 4(1) of Directive 2013/11/EU;
   (e) 'online sales or service contract' means a sales or service contract where the trader, or the trader's intermediary, has offered goods or services on a website or by other electronic means and the consumer has ordered such goods or services on that website or by other electronic means;
   (f) 'online marketplace' means a service provider, as defined in point (b) of Article 2 of Directive 2000/31/EC of the European Parliament and of the Council of 8 June 2000 on certain legal aspects of information society services, in particular electronic commerce, in the Internal Market ('Directive on electronic commerce') ([11]), which allows consumers and traders to conclude online sales and service contracts on the online marketplace's website;
   (g) 'electronic means' means electronic equipment for the processing (including digital compression) and storage of data which is entirely transmitted, conveyed and received by wire, by radio, by optical means or by other electromagnetic means;
   (h) 'alternative dispute resolution procedure' ('ADR procedure') means a procedure for the out-of-court resolution of disputes as referred to in Article 2 of this Regulation;
   (i) 'alternative dispute resolution entity' ('ADR entity') means an ADR entity as defined in point (h) of Article 4(1) of Directive 2013/11/EU;
   (j) 'complainant party' means the consumer who or the trader that has submitted a complaint through the ODR platform;
   (k) 'respondent party' means the consumer against whom or the trader against whom a complaint has been submitted through the ODR platform;
   (l) 'competent authority' means a public authority as defined in point (i) of Article 4(1) of Directive 2013/11/EU;
   (m) 'personal data' means any information relating to an identified or identifiable natural person ('data subject'); an identifiable person is one who can be identified, directly or indirectly, in particular by reference to an identification number or to one or more factors specific to that person's physical, physiological, mental, economic, cultural or social identity.

---

11. OJ L 178, 17.7.2000, p. 1.

2. The place of establishment of the trader and of the ADR entity shall be determined in accordance with Article 4(2) and (3) of Directive 2013/11/EU, respectively.

Chapter II

ODR platform

Article 5

Establishment of the ODR platform

1. The Commission shall develop the ODR platform (and be responsible for its operation, including all the translation functions necessary for the purpose of this Regulation, its maintenance, funding and data security. The ODR platform shall be user-friendly. The development, operation and maintenance of the ODR platform shall ensure that the privacy of its users is respected from the design stage ('privacy by design') and that the ODR platform is accessible and usable by all, including vulnerable users ('design for all'), as far as possible.
2. The ODR platform shall be a single point of entry for consumers and traders seeking the out-of-court resolution of disputes covered by this Regulation. It shall be an interactive website which can be accessed electronically and free of charge in all the official languages of the institutions of the Union.
3. The Commission shall make the ODR platform accessible, as appropriate, through its websites which provide information to citizens and businesses in the Union and, in particular, through the 'Your Europe portal' established in accordance with Decision 2004/387/EC.
4. The ODR platform shall have the following functions:
   (a) to provide an electronic complaint form which can be filled in by the complainant party in accordance with Article 8;
   (b) to inform the respondent party about the complaint;
   (c) to identify the competent ADR entity or entities and transmit the complaint to the ADR entity, which the parties have agreed to use, in accordance with Article 9;
   (d) to offer an electronic case management tool free of charge, which enables the parties and the ADR entity to conduct the dispute resolution procedure online through the ODR platform;
   (e) to provide the parties and ADR entity with the translation of information which is necessary for the resolution of the dispute and is exchanged through the ODR platform;
   (f) to provide an electronic form by means of which ADR entities shall transmit the information referred to in point (c) of Article 10;
   (g) to provide a feedback system which allows the parties to express their views on the functioning of the ODR platform and on the ADR entity which has handled their dispute;
   (h) to make publicly available the following:
      (i) general information on ADR as a means of out-of-court dispute resolution;
      (ii) information on ADR entities listed in accordance with Article 20(2) of Directive 2013/11/EU which are competent to deal with disputes

covered by this Regulation;
- (iii) an online guide about how to submit complaints through the ODR platform;
- (iv) information, including contact details, on ODR contact points designated by the Member States in accordance with Article 7(1) of this Regulation;
- (v) statistical data on the outcome of the disputes which were transmitted to ADR entities through the ODR platform.

5. The Commission shall ensure that the information referred to in point (h) of paragraph 4 is accurate, up to date and provided in a clear, understandable and easily accessible way.
6. ADR entities listed in accordance with Article 20(2) of Directive 2013/11/EU which are competent to deal with disputes covered by this Regulation shall be registered electronically with the ODR platform.
7. The Commission shall adopt measures concerning the modalities for the exercise of the functions provided for in paragraph 4 of this Article through implementing acts. Those implementing acts shall be adopted in accordance with the examination procedure referred to in Article 16(3) of this Regulation.

Article 6

Testing of the ODR platform

1. The Commission shall, by 9 January 2015 test the technical functionality and user-friendliness of the ODR platform and of the complaint form, including with regard to translation. The testing shall be carried out and evaluated in cooperation with experts in ODR from the Member States and consumer and trader representatives. The Commission shall submit a report to the European Parliament and the Council of the result of the testing and take the appropriate measures to address potential problems in order to ensure the effective functioning of the ODR platform.
2. In the report referred to in paragraph 1 of this Article, the Commission shall also describe the technical and organisational measures it intends to take to ensure that the ODR platform meets the privacy requirements set out in Regulation (EC) No 45/2001.

Article 7

Network of ODR contact points

1. Each Member State shall designate one ODR contact point and communicate its name and contact details to the Commission. The Member States may confer responsibility for the ODR contact points on their centres of the European Consumer Centres Network, on consumer associations or on any other body. Each ODR contact point shall host at least two ODR advisors.
2. The ODR contact points shall provide support to the resolution of disputes relating to complaints submitted through the ODR platform by fulfilling the following functions:
   - (a) if requested, facilitating communication between the parties and the competent ADR entity, which may include, in particular:
     - (i) assisting with the submission of the complaint and, where appropriate,

relevant documentation;
- (ii) providing the parties and ADR entities with general information on consumer rights in relation to sales and service contracts which apply in the Member State of the ODR contact point which hosts the ODR advisor concerned;
- (iii) providing information on the functioning of the ODR platform;
- (iv) providing the parties with explanations on the procedural rules applied by the ADR entities identified;
- (v) informing the complainant party of other means of redress when a dispute cannot be resolved through the ODR platform;
- (b) submitting, based on the practical experience gained from the performance of their functions, every two years an activity report to the Commission and to the Member States.

3. The ODR contact point shall not be obliged to perform the functions listed in paragraph 2 in the case of disputes where the parties are habitually resident in the same Member State.

4. Notwithstanding paragraph 3, the Member States may decide, taking into account national circumstances, that the ODR contact point performs one or more functions listed in paragraph 2 in the case of disputes where the parties are habitually resident in the same Member State.

5. The Commission shall establish a network of contact points ('ODR contact points network') which shall enable cooperation between contact points and contribute to the performance of the functions listed in paragraph 2.

6. The Commission shall at least twice a year convene a meeting of members of the ODR contact points network in order to permit an exchange of best practice, and a discussion of any recurring problems encountered in the operation of the ODR platform.

7. The Commission shall adopt the rules concerning the modalities of the cooperation between the ODR contact points through implementing acts. Those implementing acts shall be adopted in accordance with the examination procedure referred to in Article 16(3).

Article 8

Submission of a complaint

1. In order to submit a complaint to the ODR platform the complainant party shall fill in the electronic complaint form. The complaint form shall be user-friendly and easily accessible on the ODR platform.

2. The information to be submitted by the complainant party shall be sufficient to determine the competent ADR entity. That information is listed in the Annex to this Regulation. The complainant party may attach documents in support of the complaint.

3. In order to take into account the criteria by which the ADR entities, that are listed in accordance with Article 20(2) of Directive 2013/11/EU and that deal with disputes covered by this Regulation, define their respective scopes of application, the Commission shall be empowered to adopt delegated acts in accordance with Article 17 of this Regulation to adapt the information listed in the Annex to this Regulation.

4. The Commission shall lay down the rules concerning the modalities for the electronic complaint form by means of implementing acts. Those implementing acts

shall be adopted in accordance with the advisory procedure referred to in Article 16(2).
5. Only data which are accurate, relevant and not excessive in relation to the purposes for which they are collected shall be processed through the electronic complaint form and its attachments.

Article 9

Processing and transmission of a complaint

1. A complaint submitted to the ODR platform shall be processed if all the necessary sections of the electronic complaint form have been completed.
2. If the complaint form has not been fully completed, the complainant party shall be informed that the complaint cannot be processed further, unless the missing information is provided.
3. Upon receipt of a fully completed complaint form, the ODR platform shall, in an easily understandable way and without delay, transmit to the respondent party, in one of the official languages of the institutions of the Union chosen by that party, the complaint together with the following data:
    (a) information that the parties have to agree on an ADR entity in order for the complaint to be transmitted to it, and that, if no agreement is reached by the parties or no competent ADR entity is identified, the complaint will not be processed further;
    (b) information about the ADR entity or entities which are competent to deal with the complaint, if any are referred to in the electronic complaint form or are identified by the ODR platform on the basis of the information provided in that form;
    (c) in the event that the respondent party is a trader, an invitation to state within 10 calendar days:
    • whether the trader commits to, or is obliged to use, a specific ADR entity to resolve disputes with consumers, and
    • unless the trader is obliged to use a specific ADR entity, whether the trader is willing to use any ADR entity or entities from those referred to in point (b);
    (d) in the event that the respondent party is a consumer and the trader is obliged to use a specific ADR entity, an invitation to agree within 10 calendar days on that ADR entity or, in the event that the trader is not obliged to use a specific ADR entity, an invitation to select one or more ADR entities from those referred to in point (b);
    (e) the name and contact details of the ODR contact point in the Member State where the respondent party is established or resident, as well as a brief description of the functions referred to in point (a) of Article 7(2).
4. Upon receipt from the respondent party of the information referred to in point (c) or point (d) of paragraph 3, the ODR platform shall in an easily understandable way and without delay communicate to the complainant party, in one of the official languages of the institutions of the Union chosen by that party, the following information:
    (a) the information referred to in point (a) of paragraph 3;
    (b) in the event that the complainant party is a consumer, the information about the ADR entity or entities stated by the trader in accordance with point (c) of

APPENDIX I

paragraph 3 and an invitation to agree within 10 calendar days on an ADR entity;
- (c) in the event that the complainant party is a trader and the trader is not obliged to use a specific ADR entity, the information about the ADR entity or entities stated by the consumer in accordance with point (d) of paragraph 3 and an invitation to agree within 10 calendar days on an ADR entity;
- (d) the name and contact details of the ODR contact point in the Member State where the complainant party is established or resident, as well as a brief description of the functions referred to in point (a) of Article 7(2).

5. The information referred to in point (b) of paragraph 3 and in points (b) and (c) of paragraph 4 shall include a description of the following characteristics of each ADR entity:
   - (a) the name, contact details and website address of the ADR entity;
   - (b) the fees for the ADR procedure, if applicable;
   - (c) the language or languages in which the ADR procedure can be conducted;
   - (d) the average length of the ADR procedure;
   - (e) the binding or non-binding nature of the outcome of the ADR procedure;
   - (f) the grounds on which the ADR entity may refuse to deal with a given dispute in accordance with Article 5(4) of Directive 2013/11/EU.
6. The ODR platform shall automatically and without delay transmit the complaint to the ADR entity that the parties have agreed to use in accordance with paragraphs 3 and 4.
7. The ADR entity to which the complaint has been transmitted shall without delay inform the parties about whether it agrees or refuses to deal with the dispute in accordance with Article 5(4) of Directive 2013/11/EU. The ADR entity which has agreed to deal with the dispute shall also inform the parties of its procedural rules and, if applicable, of the costs of the dispute resolution procedure concerned.
8. Where the parties fail to agree within 30 calendar days after submission of the complaint form on an ADR entity, or the ADR entity refuses to deal with the dispute, the complaint shall not be processed further. The complainant party shall be informed of the possibility of contacting an ODR advisor for general information on other means of redress.

Article 10

Resolution of the dispute

An ADR entity which has agreed to deal with a dispute in accordance with Article 9 of this Regulation shall:

- (a) conclude the ADR procedure within the deadline referred to in point (e) of Article 8 of Directive 2013/11/EU;
- (b) not require the physical presence of the parties or their representatives, unless its procedural rules provide for that possibility and the parties agree;
- (c) without delay transmit the following information to the ODR platform:
  - (i) the date of receipt of the complaint file;
  - (ii) the subject-matter of the dispute;
  - (iii) the date of conclusion of the ADR procedure;
  - (iv) the result of the ADR procedure;
- (d) not be required to conduct the ADR procedure through the ODR platform.

Article 11

Database

The Commission shall take the necessary measures to establish and maintain an electronic database Sin which it shall store the information processed in accordance with Article 5(4) and point (c) of Article 10 taking due account of Article 13(2).

Article 12

Processing of personal data
1. Access to information, including personal data, related to a dispute and stored in the database referred to in Article 11 shall be granted, for the purposes referred to in Article 10, only to the ADR entity to which the dispute was transmitted in accordance with Article 9. Access to the same information shall be granted also to ODR contact points, in so far as it is necessary, for the purposes referred to in Article 7(2) and (4).
2. The Commission shall have access to information processed in accordance with Article 10 for the purposes of monitoring the use and functioning of the ODR platform and drawing up the reports referred to in Article 21. It shall process personal data of the users of the ODR platform in so far as it is necessary for the operation and maintenance of the ODR platform, including for the purposes of monitoring the use of the ODR platform by ADR entities and ODR contact points.
3. Personal data related to a dispute shall be kept in the database referred to in paragraph 1 of this Article only for the time necessary to achieve the purposes for which they were collected and to ensure that data subjects are able to access their personal data in order to exercise their rights, and shall be automatically deleted, at the latest, six months after the date of conclusion of the dispute which has been transmitted to the ODR platform in accordance with point (iii) of point (c) of Article 10. That retention period shall also apply to personal data kept in national files by the ADR entity or the ODR contact point which dealt with the dispute concerned, except if the procedural rules applied by the ADR entity or any specific provisions of national law provide for a longer retention period.
4. Each ODR advisor shall be regarded as a controller with respect to its data processing activities under this Regulation, in accordance with point (d) of Article 2 of Directive 95/46/EC, and shall ensure that those activities comply with national legislation adopted pursuant to Directive 95/46/EC in the Member State of the ODR contact point hosting the ODR advisor.
5. Each ADR entity shall be regarded as a controller with respect to its data processing activities under this Regulation, in accordance with point (d) of Article 2 of Directive 95/46/EC, and shall ensure that those activities comply with national legislation adopted pursuant to Directive 95/46/EC in the Member State where the ADR entity is established.

6. In relation to its responsibilities under this Regulation and the processing of personal data involved therein, the Commission shall be regarded as a controller in accordance with point (d) of Article 2 of Regulation (EC) No 45/2001.

Article 13

Data confidentiality and security
1. ODR contact points shall be subject to rules of professional secrecy or other equivalent duties of confidentiality laid down in the legislation of the Member State concerned.
2. The Commission shall take the appropriate technical and organisational measures to ensure the security of information processed under this Regulation, including appropriate data access control, a security plan and a security incident management, in accordance with Article 22 of Regulation (EC) No 45/2001.

Article 14

Consumer information
1. Traders established within the Union engaging in online sales or service contracts, and online marketplaces established within the Union, shall provide on their websites an electronic link to the ODR platform. That link shall be easily accessible for consumers. Traders established within the Union engaging in online sales or service contracts shall also state their e-mail addresses.
2. Traders established within the Union engaging in online sales or service contracts, which are committed or obliged to use one or more ADR entities to resolve disputes with consumers, shall inform consumers about the existence of the ODR platform and the possibility of using the ODR platform for resolving their disputes. They shall provide an electronic link to the ODR platform on their websites and, if the offer is made by e-mail, in that e-mail. The information shall also be provided, where applicable, in the general terms and conditions applicable to online sales and service contracts.
3. Paragraphs 1 and 2 of this Article shall be without prejudice to Article 13 of Directive 2013/11/EU and the provisions on consumer information on out-of-court redress procedures contained in other Union legal acts, which shall apply in addition to this Article.
4. The list of ADR entities referred to in Article 20(4) of Directive 2013/11/EU and its updates shall be published in the ODR platform.
5. Member States shall ensure that ADR entities, the centres of the European Consumer Centres Network, the competent authorities defined in Article 18(1) of Directive 2013/11/EU, and, where appropriate, the bodies designated in accordance with Article 14(2) of Directive 2013/11/EU provide an electronic link to the ODR platform.
6. Member States shall encourage consumer associations and business associations to provide an electronic link to the ODR platform.

7. When traders are obliged to provide information in accordance with paragraphs 1 and 2 and with the provisions referred to in paragraph 3, they shall, where possible, provide that information together.

Article 15

Role of the competent authorities
The competent authority of each Member State shall assess whether the ADR entities established in that Member State comply with the obligations set out in this Regulation.

CHAPTER III

FINAL PROVISIONS

Article 16

Committee procedure
1. The Commission shall be assisted by a committee. That committee shall be a committee within the meaning of Regulation (EU) No 182/2011.
2. Where reference is made to this paragraph, Article 4 of Regulation (EU) No 182/2011 shall apply.
3. Where reference is made to this paragraph, Article 5 of Regulation (EU) No 182/2011 shall apply.
4. Where the opinion of the committee under paragraphs 2 and 3 is to be obtained by written procedure, that procedure shall be terminated without result when, within the time-limit for delivery of the opinion, the chair of the committee so decides or a simple majority of committee members so request.

Article 17

Exercise of the delegation
1. The power to adopt delegated acts is conferred on the Commission subject to the conditions laid down in this Article.
2. The power to adopt delegated acts referred to in Article 8(3) shall be conferred for an indeterminate period of time from 8 July 2013.
3. The delegation of power referred to in Article 8(3) may be revoked at any time by the European Parliament or by the Council. A decision to revoke shall put an end to the delegation of the power specified in that decision. It shall take effect the day following the publication of the decision in the *Official Journal of the European Union* or at a later date specified therein. It shall not affect the validity of any delegated acts already in force.
4. As soon as it adopts a delegated act, the Commission shall notify it simultaneously to the European Parliament and to the Council.
5. A delegated act adopted pursuant to Article 8(3) shall enter into force only if no objection has been expressed either by the European Parliament or the Council within a period of two months of notification of that act to the European

Parliament and the Council or if, before the expiry of that period, the European Parliament and the Council have both informed the Commission that they will not object. That period shall be extended by two months at the initiative of the European Parliament or of the Council.

Article 18

Penalties

Member States shall lay down the rules on penalties applicable to infringements of this Regulation and shall take all measures necessary to ensure that they are implemented. The penalties provided for must be effective, proportionate and dissuasive.

Article 19

Amendment to regulation (EC) No 2006/2004

In the Annex to Regulation (EC) No 2006/2004 of the European Parliament and of the Council ([12]) *the following point is added:*

> *'21. Regulation (EU) No 524/2013 of the European Parliament and of the Council of 21 May 2013 on online dispute resolution for consumer disputes (Regulation on consumer ODR) (OJ L 165, 18.6.2013, p. 1): Article 14.'*

Article 20

Amendment to Directive 2009/22/EC

Directive 2009/22/EC of the European Parliament and of the Council ([13]) *is amended as follows:*

(1) in Article 1(1) and (2) and point (b) of Article 6(2), the words 'Directives listed in Annex I' are replaced with the words 'Union acts listed in Annex I';

(2) in the heading of Annex I, the words 'LIST OF DIRECTIVES' are replaced by the words 'LIST OF UNION ACTS';

(3) in Annex I, the following point is added:
> '15. Regulation (EU) No 524/2013 of the European Parliament and of the Council of 21 May 2013 on online dispute resolution for consumer disputes (Regulation on consumer ODR) (OJ L 165, 18.6.2013, p. 1): Article 14.'

Article 21

Reports

1. The Commission shall report to the European Parliament and the Council on the functioning of the ODR platform on a yearly basis and for the first time one year after the ODR platform has become operational.

---

12. OJ L 364, 9.12.2004, p. 1.
13. OJ L 110, 1.5.2009, p. 30.

2. By 9 July 2018 and every three years thereafter the Commission shall submit to the European Parliament and the Council a report on the application of this Regulation, including in particular on the user-friendliness of the complaint form and the possible need for adaptation of the information listed in the Annex to this Regulation. That report shall be accompanied, if necessary, by proposals for adaptations to this Regulation.
3. Where the reports referred to in paragraphs 1 and 2 are to be submitted in the same year, only one joint report shall be submitted.

Article 22

Entry into force

1. This Regulation shall enter into force on the twentieth day following that of its publication in the *Official Journal of the European Union*.
2. This Regulation shall apply from 9 January 2016, except for the following provisions:
    - Article 2(3) and Article 7(1) and (5), which shall apply from 9 July 2015,
    - Article 5(1) and (7), Article 6, Article 7(7), Article 8(3) and (4) and Articles 11, 16 and 17, which shall apply from 8 July 2013.

This Regulation shall be binding in its entirety and directly applicable in all Member States.
Done at Strasbourg, 21 May 2013.

M. SCHULZ
For the European Parliament
The President
L. CREIGHTON
For the Council
The President

Annex

Information to be provided when submitting a complaint

(1) Whether the complainant party is a consumer or a trader;
(2) The name and e-mail and geographical address of the consumer;
(3) The name and e-mail, website and geographical address of the trader;
(4) The name and email and geographical address of the complainant party's representative, if applicable;
(5) The language(s) of the complainant party or representative, if applicable;
(6) The language of the respondent party, if known;
(7) The type of good or service to which the complaint relates;
(8) Whether the good or service was offered by the trader and ordered by the consumer on a website or by other electronic means;
(9) The price of the good or service purchased;
(10) The date on which the consumer purchased the good or service;
(11) Whether the consumer has made direct contact with the trader;
(12) Whether the dispute is being or has previously been considered by an ADR entity or by a court;
(13) The type of complaint;
(14) The description of the complaint;
(15) If the complainant party is a consumer, the ADR entities the trader is obliged to or has committed to use in accordance with Article 13(1) of Directive 2013/11/EU, if known;
(16) If the complainant party is a trader, which ADR entity or entities the trader commits to or is obliged to use.

APPENDIX II

China International Economic and Trade Arbitration Commission (CIETAC) Online Arbitration Rules

(Adopted by the China Council for the Promotion of International Trade/China Chamber of International Commerce in 2008 and updated on November 4, 2014. Effective as from January 1, 2015)

Chapter 1

General provisions

Article 1

These Rules are formulated in order to independently, impartially, efficiently and economically resolve, by means of online arbitration, disputes arising from economic and trade transactions of a contractual or non-contractual nature.

These Rules shall apply to the resolution of electronic commerce disputes and may also be applied to the resolution of other economic and trade disputes upon the agreement of the parties.

Article 2

Key terms in these Rules are defined as follows:

1. "CIETAC" refers to the China International Economic and Trade Arbitration Commission (also known as the Arbitration Institute of the China Chamber of International Commerce);
2. "CIETAC Arbitration Rules" refers to the current China International Economic and Trade Arbitration Commission Arbitration Rules;
3. "CIETAC Panel of Arbitrators" refers to the current China International Economic and Trade Arbitration Commission Panel of Arbitrators;
4. "CIETAC Online Dispute Resolution Center" refers to a specialized online dispute resolution service provider established by CIETAC to resolve Internet domain name and electronic commerce disputes;
5. "CIETAC Online Dispute Resolution Center Website" refers to a specialized website developed by the CIETAC Online Dispute Resolution Center to resolve online disputes. The current website address of the CIETAC Online Dispute Resolution Center iswww.cietacodr.org;
6. "Written Form" refers to information-carrying forms, such as contracts, correspondence and data messages (including telegrams, telexes, faxes, electronic data

interchange and emails), which can tangibly exhibit their contents and may be accessed at any time for subsequent reference.
7. "Electronic Evidence" refers to data messages that are generated, sent, received or stored by electronic, optical, magnetic, or other similar methods;
8. "Electronic Signature" refers to data in electronic form, in or attached to a data message, used to identify a signer and to express his acknowledgment of the content of the data message;
9. "Online Oral Hearing" refers to an oral hearing conducted on the Internet through video conferencing and other electronic or computer communication forms;
10. "Online Mediation" refers to mediation conducted on the Internet through video conferencing and other electronic or computer communication forms.

Article 3

These Rules shall govern any disputes accepted by CIETAC for arbitration where the parties have agreed to their application. In the absence of such an agreement, the CIETAC Arbitration Rules or other rules agreed by the parties shall apply.

Article 4

Where the parties have agreed upon any modification of these Rules, the parties' agreement shall prevail, except where such an agreement is inoperative or in conflict with a mandatory provision of the law of the place of arbitration.

Article 5

Where the parties agree to refer their dispute to arbitration under these Rules without providing the name of an arbitration institution, they shall be deemed to have agreed to refer the dispute for arbitration by CIETAC.

Article 6

An "Arbitration Agreement" is either an arbitration clause incorporated in a contract agreed by and between the parties or any other form of a written agreement between the parties providing for the settlement of disputes by arbitration.

The arbitration agreement shall be in writing. An arbitration agreement is in writing if it is contained in a tangible form of a document, such as a contract, letter, telegram, telex, facsimile, electronic data interchange (EDI), or email.

Article 7

CIETAC shall have the power to determine the existence and validity of an arbitration agreement and its jurisdiction over an arbitration case. CIETAC may, if necessary, delegate such power to the arbitral tribunal.

The arbitration shall proceed regardless of an objection by either party to the validity of the arbitration agreement and/or jurisdiction over the arbitration case.

Article 8

Where the parties have agreed on the place of arbitration, their agreement shall prevail. In the absence of such an agreement, the place of arbitration shall be the location of CIETAC.

The arbitral award shall be deemed as being made at the place of arbitration.

Article 9

Unless otherwise agreed by the parties or determined by the arbitral tribunal, information submitted or transmitted by email, EDI or facsimile, whose record of submission or transmission can be provided, shall be deemed to satisfy the requirements in these Rules that notices, pleadings, documentation or any other communications shall be in writing.

CHAPTER 2

COMMUNICATIONS

Article 10

All documents, notices and written materials related to the arbitration shall be sent by the Arbitration Court of CIETAC to the parties and/or their authorized representatives by email, EDI, facsimile or any other similar means. Based on the procedure particulars of a case, the Arbitration Court of CIETAC or the arbitral tribunal may also decide to send the documents to the parties, primarily or secondarily, by regular mail, express mail or any other appropriate means.

Parties shall submit their requests for arbitration, statements of defense, written statements, evidence and other documents and materials related to the arbitration by email, EDI or facsimile, etc. Based on the specific circumstances of the case, the Arbitration Court of CIETAC or the arbitral tribunal may request, at its sole discretion, that the parties submit their documents through, either primarily or secondarily, regular mail, express mail or any other means. The parties may also submit their documents in this manner with the consent of the Arbitration Court of CIETAC or the arbitral tribunal.

Article 11

Any document submitted or transmitted under these Rules shall conform to the following requirements:

(a) Any document sent by the Arbitration Court of CIETAC may be copied to the other party at the same time;
(b) Neither party or anyone acting on its behalf may have any unilateral communication with any member of the arbitral tribunal. All communications between a party and the arbitral tribunal shall be conducted through the Arbitration Court of CIETAC;
(c) It shall be the responsibility of the sender of a document to retain records of the fact and circumstances of the sending, which shall be made available for inspection by the related parties and for reporting purposes;
(d) In the event that a party sending a document is notified of the non-delivery of the document or believes it has not delivered the document successfully, the party shall promptly notify the Arbitration Court of CIETAC of the circumstances of the

notification. Further proceedings concerning the communication and any response shall be directed by the Arbitration Court of CIETAC;

(e) Any party that changes its specified means of communications, addresses or any other contact details shall promptly notify the Arbitration Court of CIETAC.

Article 12

Any written communication to the Claimant or to the Respondent under these Rules shall be made in the way specified by the concerned party. Where the Claimant or Respondent has not made such specification, the Arbitration Court of CIETAC may select one or several of the methods of transmission listed below based on the specific circumstances of the case:

(a) Electronically via the Internet, provided a record of transmission is available;
(b) By facsimile, with a confirmation of transmission;
(c) By postal or courier service with available tracer;
(d) By other effective methods.

Article 13

Unless otherwise agreed by the parties or decided by the arbitral tribunal, all communications under these Rules shall be deemed to have been received by the receiver under the following circumstances:

(a) If via the Internet: at the time that the data message entered the specific system designated by the receiver or at the first time that the data message entered any system of the receiver when there is no such specification
(b) If by facsimile: on the date shown on the confirmation of transmission
(c) If by postal or courier service: on the date marked on the tracer
(d) If by other effective methods: on the date the message was actually received or should have been received by the receiver according to the method

Article 14

Except as otherwise provided in these Rules, the time periods stipulated in these Rules shall begin to run on the earliest date that the communication is deemed to have been received as defined in the previous article.

Article 15

CIETAC shall make reasonable efforts to ensure secure online transmission of case data among the parties, the arbitral tribunal and CIETAC, and to store case information through data encryption.

Article 16

CIETAC shall not be liable for loss where data transmitted online is acquired by persons other than the intended receiver due to Internet system failure during the arbitral proceedings.

APPENDIX II

Chapter 3

ARBITRAL PROCEEDINGS

Section 1 Request for arbitration, defense and counterclaim

Article 17

The arbitral proceedings shall commence on the date on which the Arbitration Court of the CIETAC receives a Request for Arbitration.

Article 18

A party applying for arbitration shall meet the following requirements:
1. Submit a written Request for Arbitration signed by and/or affixed with the seal of the Claimant and/or his authorized representative(s) according to the requirements of the "Arbitration Application Format" and the "Arbitration Application Filing Guide" set up by CIETAC and released on the CIETAC Online Dispute Solution Center website, which shall include:
   (a) The names, addresses and methods of communication of the Claimant and the Respondent, including their zip codes, telephone numbers, fax numbers, email addresses and any other means of electronic communication;
   (b) The designated method of communication of the Claimant;
   (c) A reference to the arbitration agreement invoked;
   (d) The claim;
   (e) A statement of the facts of the case and the main issues in dispute;
   (f) The facts and grounds on which the claim is based.
2. Attach to the Request for Arbitration the relevant evidence supporting the facts on which the Claimant's claim is based.
3. Make payment of the arbitration fee in advance to CIETAC according to its "Arbitration Fee Schedule of Online Arbitration Cases" (See Attachment 2).

Article 19

Where the Arbitration Court of CIETAC finds that a Request for Arbitration satisfies the requirements for arbitration, it shall notify the parties in writing of its acceptance of the Request within five (5) days from the date of receipt of the Request. Should the Arbitration Court of CIETAC find that the Request for Arbitration does not satisfy the requirements for arbitration, it shall notify the parties in writing of its rejection of the Request with reasons stated.

Article 20

When the Arbitration Court of CIETAC sends to the Claimant the Notice of Arbitration indicating its acceptance of the Request for Arbitration, it shall also provide the Claimant with the Internet address of the websites where the Claimant can consult these Rules, the CIETAC Arbitration Rules and the CIETAC Panel of Arbitrators. According to the specific circumstances of each case, the Arbitration Court of CIETAC may also attach copies of the above documents to the Notice of Arbitration.

When the Arbitration Court of CIETAC sends to the Respondent the Notice of Arbitration indicating its acceptance of the Request for Arbitration, it shall also provide the Respondent with the Internet address of the websites where the Respondent can consult the Claimant's Request for Arbitration, these Rules, the CIETAC Arbitration Rules and the CIETAC Panel of Arbitrators. According to the specific circumstances of each case, the Arbitration Court of CIETAC may also attach copies of the above documents to the Notice of Arbitration.

Article 21

Unless otherwise agreed by the parties, the Respondent shall submit its written Statement of Defense and the relevant evidence to the Arbitration Court of CIETAC within thirty (30) days from the date of receipt of the Notice of Arbitration, according to the requirements of the "Arbitration Defense Format" and the "Arbitration Defense Filing Guide" set up by CIETAC and released on the CIETAC Online Dispute Resolution Center website. The Statement of Defense shall be signed by and/or affixed with the seal of the Respondent and/or his authorized representative(s), and shall include:

(a) The names, addresses and methods of communication of the Respondent, including the zip code, telephone numbers, fax numbers, email addresses or any other means of electronic communication;
(b) The designated methods of communication of the Respondent;
(c) The defense to the Request for Arbitration setting forth the facts and grounds on which the defense is based; and
(d) The relevant evidence supporting the defense.

Unless otherwise agreed by the parties, if the Respondent wishes to file a Counterclaim, it must do so in writing within the above mentioned time period according to the "Arbitration Counterclaim Format" set up by CIETAC and released on the CIETAC Online Dispute Resolution Center website.

Article 22

Unless otherwise agreed by the parties, the Claimant shall submit its written Statement of Defense to the Respondent's Counterclaim with the Arbitration Court of CIETAC within twenty (20) days from the date of receipt of the Respondent's Statement of Counterclaim, according to the "Defense of Counterclaim Format" set up by CIETAC and released on the CIETAC Online Dispute Resolution Center website.

Article 23

The time periods specified in Articles 21 and 22 may be extended if the arbitral tribunal believes that there exist justifiable reasons.

Section 2 The arbitral tribunal

Article 24

The arbitral tribunal shall be composed of either one or three arbitrators.

Unless otherwise agreed by the parties or stipulated by these Rules, the arbitral tribunal shall be composed of three arbitrators.

Article 25

The parties shall appoint arbitrators from the Panel of Arbitrators provided by CIETAC.

Where the parties have agreed to appoint an arbitrator from outside of CIETAC Panel of Arbitrators, the arbitrator so appointed by the parties or nominated according to the agreement of the parties may act as arbitrator after the appointment has been confirmed by the Chairman of CIETAC in accordance with the law. CIETAC is not required to make explanation on the confirmation or rejection of an arbitrator appointed or nominated in such a manner.

Where the appointment of an arbitrator is to be made by the Chairman of CIETAC, unless the parties agree otherwise, the Chairman shall appoint an arbitrator from the CIETAC Panel of Arbitrators.

Article 26

An arbitrator appointed by the parties or by the Chairman of CIETAC shall sign a Declaration disclosing to CIETAC any circumstances likely to give rise to justifiable doubts as to his or her impartiality or independence.

Article 27

Unless otherwise agreed by the parties, where the arbitral tribunal is composed of one arbitrator, the Claimant and the Respondent shall, within six (6) days from the date of receipt of the Notice of Arbitration by the party who last receives it, jointly appoint a sole arbitrator or entrust the Chairman of CIETAC to make such an appointment.

Unless otherwise agreed by the parties, where the arbitral tribunal is composed of three arbitrators, the Claimant and the Respondent shall, within six (6) days from the date of receipt of the Notice of Arbitration, each appoint an arbitrator or entrust the Chairman of CIETAC to make such an appointment, and within six (6) days from the date of receipt of the Notice of Arbitration by the party who last receives it, jointly appoint a third arbitrator, or alternatively, jointly entrust the Chairman of CIETAC to make such an appointment. The third arbitrator shall be the presiding arbitrator.

Where there are two or more Claimants and/or Respondents in an arbitration case, the Claimant's side and the Respondent's side shall each, through consultation, jointly appoint an arbitrator, or alternatively, jointly entrust the Chairman of CIETAC to make such an appointment within the time limit stated above.

Unless otherwise agreed by the parties, where a party fails to appoint an arbitrator or fails to entrust the Chairman of CIETAC to make such an appointment within the specified time period, the arbitrator shall be appointed by the Chairman of CIETAC.

With the consent of the President of the Arbitration Court of CIETAC, the time period specified in this article may be extended.

Section 3 Hearing

Article 28

Unless otherwise agreed by the parties, and on the condition that it abides by these Rules, the arbitral tribunal may conduct the arbitration in any way that it deems appropriate. Under any circumstances, the arbitral tribunal shall treat the parties equally and afford each party reasonable opportunity to present its case.

According to the specific circumstances of each case, the arbitral tribunal may adopt approaches including issuing procedural orders and lists of questions and producing terms of reference, among other measures, in order to increase the speed and efficiency of arbitration proceedings.

The arbitral tribunal shall determine the admissibility, relevance, materiality and weight of evidence.

Article 29

The evidence submitted by the parties may be electronic evidence that is generated, sent, received or stored by electronic, optical, magnetic or other similar means.

The following factors shall be taken into consideration when the authenticity of electronic evidence is examined:

(a) The reliability of the methods used to generate, store or transmit the data message;
(b) The reliability of the methods used to maintain the integrity of the contents of the data message;
(c) The reliability of the methods used to identify the sender of the data message;
(d) Other relevant factors.

Electronic evidence with a reliable electronic signature shall have the same admissibility and weight as evidence with a handwritten signature or affixed seal.

Article 30

Where a time period for producing evidence has been agreed upon by the parties or has been set by the arbitral tribunal, the parties shall submit their evidence to the arbitral tribunal within the specified time period.

Unless otherwise agreed by the parties or decided by the arbitral tribunal, the arbitral tribunal may refuse to admit any written statement or evidence submitted by any party after the expiration of the time period for producing evidence. The arbitral tribunal may, at its sole discretion, request that the parties submit additional statements or documents related to the case.

Article 31

The arbitral tribunal may, if necessary, investigate facts and collect evidence related to the case from e-commerce service providers, logistics distribution companies and payment banks, etc. The arbitral tribunal may make requests of the parties at its sole discretion, and the parties are obligated to cooperate actively and positively with the tribunal.

The arbitral tribunal shall, through the Arbitration Court of CIETAC, transmit the evidence collected by itself to the parties and afford them an opportunity to comment.

Article 32

Unless the parties agree to hold oral hearings, or the arbitral tribunal decides it is necessary to do so, the arbitral tribunal shall hear the case on a documents-only basis in accordance with the written materials and evidence submitted by the parties.

Article 33

Where an oral hearing is to be held, it shall be conducted by means of online oral hearings such as video conferencing or other electronic or computer communication forms. The arbitral tribunal may also decide to hold traditional oral hearings in person based on the specific circumstances of each case.

Article 34

Where an oral hearing is to be held, the arbitral tribunal shall fix the date, time, place (if applicable) and manner of the hearing. The Arbitration Court of CIETAC shall serve a Notice of Oral Hearing on each party at least twelve (12) days in advance of the date of the oral hearing. A party with justifiable reasons may request a postponement of the oral hearing. However, such a request must be communicated to the arbitral tribunal in writing at least five (5) days in advance of the date of the oral hearing. The arbitral tribunal shall decide whether to postpone the oral hearing or not.

A Notice of Oral Hearing subsequent to the first oral hearing and a Notice of a Postponed Oral Hearing are not subject to the twelve (12)-day time limit provided for in the previous paragraph.

Article 35

Where an oral hearing is to be held, the evidence shall be exhibited at the hearing and examined by the parties. With regard to the evidence that has already been exchanged between the parties and no objections have been raised before the oral hearing, the arbitral tribunal may simplify the examination proceedings if the parties so agree. Such a decision shall be recorded duly in the case file.

In the event that evidence is submitted after the oral hearing, and the arbitral tribunal decides to admit the evidence without holding further oral hearings, the arbitral tribunal may require the parties to provide written examination opinions on the submitted evidence within a specified time period.

Article 36

Where an oral hearing is to be held, the witnesses may testify by online video conferencing, by regular oral hearing in person or by any other appropriate manner as decided by the arbitral tribunal.

Article 37

The arbitral tribunal may conduct online mediation by means of video conferencing or other electronic or computer communication methods during the course of the arbitration proceedings upon the agreement or request of the parties.

The arbitral tribunal may also decide to conduct mediation in person according to the specific circumstances of the case.

Mediation may be conducted separately or may be combined with the oral hearings.

Section 4 Arbitral award

Article 38

Unless otherwise agreed by the parties, the arbitral tribunal shall render an arbitral award within four (4) months from the date on which the arbitral tribunal is formed.

Upon the request of the arbitral tribunal, the Chairman of CIETAC may extend the above time period if he or she considers it truly necessary and the reasons for the extension truly justified.

Article 39

The award shall be made in written form, shall state the date on which the award is made as well as the place where the award is made, and shall be signed by the arbitrators, with the official seal of CIETAC affixed to it.

Article 40

The arbitral tribunal shall submit a draft award to CIETAC for its scrutiny before signing the award. CIETAC may bring an issue or issues in the award to the tribunal's attention on the condition that the arbitral tribunal's independence in rendering the award remains unaffected.

CHAPTER 4

SUMMARY PROCEDURES

Article 41

Unless otherwise agreed by the parties, the Summary Procedures shall apply to any case where the amount in dispute exceeds RMB100, 000 but does not exceed RMB1,000,000, or to any case where the amount in dispute exceeds RMB1,000,000, but one party applies for arbitration under the Summary Procedures and the other party agrees in writing.

Where no monetary claim is specified or the amount in dispute is not clear, CIETAC shall determine whether or not to apply the Summary Procedures after full consideration of factors such as the complexity of the case and the interests involved as well as other relevant elements.

Article 42

An arbitral tribunal composed of a sole arbitrator shall be formed in accordance with Article 27 of these Rules to hear the case under the Summary Procedures.

Article 43

Within fifteen (15) days from the date of receipt of the Notice of Arbitration, the Respondent shall submit its Statement of Defense and the relevant evidence to the Arbitration Court of CIETAC; Counterclaims, if any, shall also be filed with supporting evidence within this time period.

Within ten (10) days from the date of receipt of the Counterclaim and its attachments, the Claimant shall file with the Arbitration Court of CIETAC its Statement of Defense to the Respondent's Counterclaim.

The arbitral tribunal may extend this time period if it believes that there exist justifiable reasons.

Article 44

The arbitral tribunal shall render an arbitral award within two (2) months from the date on which the arbitral tribunal is formed.

Upon the request of the arbitral tribunal, the Chairman of CIETAC may extend this time period if he or she considers it truly necessary and the reasons for the extension truly justified.

Article 45

The application of the Summary Procedures shall not be affected by any amendment to the claim or by the filing of a counterclaim. Where the amount in dispute of the amended claim or that of the counterclaim exceeds RMB1,000,000, the Summary Procedures shall continue to apply to the case, unless the parties have agreed or the arbitral tribunal considers it necessary to change the Summary Procedures to the General Procedures.

Article 46

As to matters not covered in this Chapter, the relevant provisions in the other Chapters of these Rules shall apply.

CHAPTER 5

EXPEDITED PROCEDURES

Article 47

Unless otherwise agreed by the parties, the Expedited Procedures shall apply to any case where the disputed amount does not exceed RMB100,000, or to any case where the disputed amount exceeds RMB100,000, but one party applies for arbitration under the Expedited Procedures and the other party agrees in writing.

Where no monetary claim is specified or the amount in dispute is not clear, CIETAC shall determine whether or not to apply the Expedited Procedures after a full consideration of factors such as the complexity of the case and the interests involved as well as other relevant elements.

Article 48

An arbitral tribunal composed of a sole arbitrator shall be formed in accordance with Article 27 of these Rules to hear a case under the Expedited Procedures.

Article 49

Within ten (10) days from the date of receipt of the Notice of Arbitration, the Respondent shall submit its Statement of Defense and the relevant evidence to the Arbitration Court of CIETAC. Counterclaims, if any, shall also be filed with supporting evidence within this time period.

Within five (5) days from the date of receipt of the Counterclaim and its attachments, the Claimant shall file its Statement of Defense to the Respondent's Counterclaim.

The arbitral tribunal may extend this time period if it believes that there exist justifiable reasons.

Article 50

The arbitral tribunal shall render an award within fifteen (15) days from the date on which the arbitral tribunal is formed.

Upon the request of the arbitral tribunal, the President of the Arbitration Court of CIETAC may extend this time period if he or she considers it truly necessary and the reasons for the extension truly justified.

Article 51

The application of the Expedited Procedures shall not be affected by any amendment to the claim or by the filing of a counterclaim. Where the amount in dispute of the amended claim or that of the counterclaim exceeds RMB100,000, the Expedited Procedures shall continue to apply to the case, unless the parties have agreed or the arbitral tribunal considers it necessary to change the Expedited Procedures to the Summary Procedures or the General Procedures.

Article 52

As for matters not covered in this Chapter, the relevant provisions in the other Chapters of these Rules shall apply.

CHAPTER 6

MISCELLANEOUS

Article 53

The CIETAC Online Dispute Resolution Center is authorized by CIETAC to accept cases submitted for arbitration according to these Rules.

Article 54

In the event of any inconsistency between these Rules and the CIETAC Arbitration Rules, these Rules shall prevail.

For matters not covered in these Rules, the CIETAC Arbitration Rules shall apply.
CIETAC shall make decision where the application of these Rules conflicts with the CIETAC Arbitration Rules and other Arbitration Rules implemented by CIETAC.

Article 55

CIETAC is responsible for interpreting these Rules.

INDEX

AAA 1.2–3.3, 2.1.2
AAA–Cybersettle Strategic Alliance 4.2; advance case filing and management systems 4.2; experience 4.2; merits 4.2; professional regulation 4.2; reputation 4.2
AAA WebFile 3.2
ABA 1.2–3–3
accessibility 2.1.8.3
accessibility of online arbitration platforms 4.6
accountability 2.1.8.2
accreditation 2.1.8.4
advanced technologies 4.1
alternative dispute resolution: popularity of 1.1.2
Amazon: notice and takedown procedures 4.2
applicable law 6.2; foreign awards 6.2; instructions of parties 6.2; international arbitration 6.2; location of party 6.2; New York Convention 6.2; pre–agreement 6.2; UK Arbitration Act 1996 6.2
appointment of online arbitrators 4.3; harmonised best practice 4.3; neutrals' ethics 4.3; personal data 4.3; specific knowledge or expertise 4.3; UNCITRAL Draft Procedural Rules 4.3
arbitral awards 1.1.2, 1.1.3, 1.2.3.2, 1.2.3.4, 2.1.8.1, 2.1.8.6, 3.4, 3.8, 4.3, 4.7, 5.1.1, 6.1, 6.2, 6.3, 6.4, 7.1, 7.2
arbitration agreements 3.6; China 5.1.2; dispute resolution clause 3.6; electronic contracts, as 5.1.1; EU Directives 5.1.2; format 3.6; generating 3.6; incorporation via electronic means 5.1.2; meaning 5.1.1; online, validity of 5.1; reasonableness and fairness test 5.1.2; recognised in writing 5.1.1; recognised methods of incorporation 5.1.2; recognition of forming 5.1.1; separability 5.1.2; submitting 3.6; technological measures of agreeing 5.1.2; UK legislation 5.1.2; unconscionableness test 5.1.2; US legislation 5.1.2
Arbitrator Intelligence 4.3
artificial intelligence 4.6
artificial intelligence technologies 4.1
authority 4.2
automated alert 6.4, 7.2
automated clause 4.7, 7.2
automated computing 3.1, 4.1, 4.6
automated decision 4.2, 4.8
automated ethnical checking system 3.4

basic ODR 4.6
best practice 2.1–2.2; core principles 2.1.8; developing 2.1; growth of 2.1.7
big data 1.2.1, 1.2.2, 1.2.3.4, 3.1, 4.1

case–based reasoning 4.6
challenge of awards 6.3; errors 6.3; grounds 6.3; purpose 6.3; UNCITRAL Model Law 6.3
Chinese approach 1.2.3.4; Arbitration Law 1.2.3.4; eCourt systems 1.2.3.4; mediation 1.2.3.4; Online Arbitration Rules 1.2.3.4
choice of procedure rules 3.3
choice of service provider 3.2
CIETAC 2.1.4, 2.1.7
CIETAC Online Arbitration Rules 3.1, 3.2
cloud computing 3.1, 3.2
commencement of arbitration proceedings 3.7
commercial arbitration agreements 5.3; applicable law 5.3; categories for

INDEX

determination of validity 5.3; contracts of adhesion 5.3; reasonable notification 5.3
confidentiality 2.1.8.2
consent awards 6.1
consumer arbitration agreements 5.2; confirmation in durable medium 5.2.1; display on website 5.2.1; emergence of new technologies, and 5.2.1; enforceability 5.2.1; hyperlink 5.2.1; pre–dispute 5.2.1; private 5.2; reasonableness and fairness 5.2.1; UK Consumer Agreements Act 1988 5.2.1; US 5.2.1
contracts of adhesion 5.3
cooperation agreements 4.2
credibility 2.1.8.4
Cybersettle 2.1.2

dispute resolution: traditional means 1.1.1
disputing parties 4.1
domain names: online arbitration 1.2.1
due process 6.4
durable medium 4.4

eBay 2.1.1
efficiency 2.1.8.1
electronic evidence 3.5, 4.4; admission 4.4; authenticity 4.4; CIETAC, and 4.4; discretion as to 4.4; durable medium 4.4; harmonisation, need for 4.4; record 4.4; reliability 4.4; UN Convention 4.4; UNCITRAL Draft Procedural Rules 4.4
electronic mediation agreement 2.1.8.6
electronic records 1.2.1, 2.1.8.1, 2.1.8.5, 2.1.8.6, 4.4, 7.2
electronic seal 4.4
electronic signature 4.4
enforceability 2.1.8.6
enforcement of online arbitral awards 6.1–6.4
eQuibbly 3.2
ethics of online arbitrators 3.4
EU framework 1.2.3.2; consumers' confidence 1.2.3.2; description of ODR platform 1.2.3.2; Directive on Electronic Commerce 1.2.3.2; encouragement of ADR 1.2.3.2; mediation 1.2.3.2; recognition of benefit of ODR 1.2.3.2; Regulation on Consumer ODR 2013 1.2.3.2
EU ODR Regulation 3.1

EU single ODR portal 3.1
European Small Claims Procedure 3.1
evidence, format of 3.5
evidentiary hearing 3.5
expansion of general ODR systems 4.1
expert determination 3.5
expert systems 4.6
expert witnesses 3.5
expertise 4.2

future legislative trends 7.1; appropriate approaches 7.1; legislative enhancement 7.1; party autonomy 7.1; place of business 7.1; subject–specific laws 7.1

general regulations: further development 3.1

hearings 3.7
HKIAC 2.1.4

ICANN 2.1.3
impartiality of arbitrators 3.4
institutional arbitration rules 3.3
integrity of online arbitration platforms 4.6
intelligent/ advanced ODR 4.6
international harmonisation 1.2.3.4
international harmonised best practices 7.1, 7.2
international procedural rules 3.3
international regulatory development 1.2.3.1
internet–related disputes: unique characteristics 7.1
internet–related issues: online arbitration, and 1.2.1

jurisdiction 6.2; foreign awards 6.2; international arbitration 6.2; location of party 6.2; New York Convention 6.2; UK Arbitration Act 1996 6.2

legal framework for online arbitral awards 6.1; consent awards 6.1; hard copy originals 6.1; level of reasoning 6.1; UNCITRAL Draft ODR Procedural Rules 6.1; writing requirement 6.1
legal seat of arbitration 6.2, 6.3, 6.4, 7.1, 7.2
legislative measures 1.2.3

machine learning 4.6
mediation: Chinese approach 1.2.3.4; EU framework 1.2.3.2

mediation agreements 2.1.8.6, 3.6, 4.7
mediation settlement agreements 2.1.8.6
Modria 2.1.6
MSODR 2.1.6

negotiation 1.1.2, 1.2.3.1, 1.2.3.3, 2.1.2, 2.1.5, 2.1.8.6, 3.1, 3.2, 4.1, 4.2, 4.6
New York Convention 1.2.3.4, 2.1
notice and takedown procedures 4.2

online arbitral awards 3.8; contents 3.8; design of ODR platform 3.8; format 3.8; issuance 3.8; time limits 3.8
online arbitration: digital products 1.2.1; domain names 1.2.1; internet–related issues 1.2.1; obstacles to use 1.2; suitability of types of cases 1.2.1
online arbitration rules: text Appendix II
Online Dispute Resolution (ODR); advent of 1.1.3; concepts of 1.1; definition 1.1.3; enforceability, principle of 2.1.7; harmonisation 1.1.3; *in rem* jurisdiction 1.2.1; international element 1.2.3.1; international regulatory development 1.2.3.1; legal issues 1.2.3.1; legislative development 1.1.3; legislative measures 1.2.3; recent development of services 2.1.6; technological advancement and constraints 1.2–2; Technological Notes 1.2.3.1; technologically neutral definition 1.2.3.1; UN Working Group 1.2.3.1; underlying technical principles 1.1.3
online negotiation 1.1.3, 1.2.3.4, 2.1.1, 2.1.2, 2.1.6, 2.1.8.4, 3.1, 4.2
Oregon eCourt 4.1

party-appointed experts 3.5
personal IT equipment: use of 3.2
pre-agreed procedures 6.4, 7.2
pre-dispute arbitration agreement 5.2.1
pre-dispute arbitration clause 5.1.1, 5.2.1, 6.4, 7.1, 7.2
preliminary hearing 3.7
private companies 3.2
procedures 3.1–3.8
process of hearing 3.7
public/ statutory small claims arbitration 5.2.2; EU 5.2.2; US 5.2.2

Rechtwijzer 2.0 2.1.5
recognition and enforcement of awards 6.4; binding, meaning 6.4; composition of tribunal 6.4; due process 6.4; grounds for refusal 6.4; incapacity of parties 6.4; limited grounds for refusal 6.4; matters beyond scope of submission to arbitration 6.4; New York Convention 6.4; validity of agreement 6.4
recognition of forming arbitration agreements via electronic communications 5.1.1
Regulation (EU) No 524/2013; text Appendix I
reputation 4.2
robotic arbitrators 4.8, 7.2
robotisation of lawyers 4.6
Russian Online Arbitration Regulation 2.1.7

seat of online arbitration 4.7 *see also* applicable law; jurisdiction; failure to agree on 4.6; importance of 4.7; machine intelligence, and 4.6; national law 4.6; selection of 4.7; UNCITRAL Arbitration Rules 4.6; UNCITRAL Model Law 4.6; UNCTRIAL Notes on Organizing Arbitral Proceedings 4.6
security 2.1.8.5
security of online arbitration platforms 4.6
selection of online arbitrators 3.4; changing 3.4; China Arbitration Law 3.4; impartiality 3.4; multiple parties 3.4; technical issues 3.4
self–regulated rules 3.3
service-oriented computing 1.1.3, 4.1, 4.6, 4.8, 5.1.2
smart ODR systems 4.1
solutions to obstacles in online arbitration 7.2; appropriate technical measures 7.2; determination of validity of agreements and awards 7.2; interpretation of procedural rules 7.2; reliable service provider 7.2; well–drafted agreement 7.2
SquareTrade 2.1.1
strategic alliance 4.2
systemic legal development 4.1–4.8
systemic technological development 4.1–4.8

Technological Notes 1.2.3.1
time stamp 2.1.8.4, 3.2, 3.4, 6.4, 7.2
training for users 4.8
transparency 2.1.8.2

trust 4.2
trust service 3.2
trustwork schemes 3.2

UK Bar Council guidelines 3.2
UNCITRAL Draft ODR Procedural Rules 3.1
US trend 1.2.3.3; AAA 1.2.3.3; courts providing eFiling services 1.2.3.3; self–regulation 1.2.3.3
users' awareness 4.8
users' protection 4.8

validity of online arbitration agreements 5.1
VeRO 4.2

WIPO Arbitration and Mediation Centre 3.2
WIPO ECAF 3.2
WIPO–UDRP 2.1.3
witnesses 4.5; attendance 4.5; testimony 4.5

Youstice 2.1.6